KU-603-976

ublic education is the "growth industry" of the nat
Jext to defense, education is the single largest enterp
conomy and, unlike even defense, it is the one Ame.
ome way or at some time directly involves every single citizen.

f public education is quantitatively important, then the training of
eachers is one of the most qualitatively important undertakings of the
ntire educational enterprise. Indeed, the training of teachers is already
he single largest undertaking of American higher education, since more
ollege graduates enter the profession of teaching than any other vocation,
nd it may well be the most important undertaking of our colleges and
niversities.

ven so, despite the size of the American educational establishment,
 is remarkable how little is understood of the educative process,
specially of the intellectual bases of education that support all pedagogy;
nd of all those who have—in the language of defense rather than
ducation—a "need to know," the prospective teacher has the greatest
eed.

rospective teachers need to understand education through the historical
erspective of Western culture—and so the series includes a volume in
he history of education, a volume that may fairly be called an intellectual
istory of education, rather than a mere chronology of educationally
mportant dates or historically important pedagogues.

rospective teachers need to understand that the school, and the children
nd teachers in it, are social organisms inevitably influenced by the
ature of the society in which they exist—and so the series includes
 volume in the sociology of education, a volume showing how the public
chool reflects, for better or worse, the reality rather than the image of
ontemporary American society.

rospective teachers need to understand the psychological nature of
hildren and how it limits, if not determines, what schools should or
hould not do (Is it reasonable to expect, as many teachers do, a six- or
even-year-old to sit quietly and attentively for a major portion of his
vaking day?)—and so the series includes a volume in the psychology
f education, a volume that pays particular attention to the ways in
vhich children grow, develop, mature, learn, and change their behavior.

rospective teachers need to understand the close functional relationship
etween philosophy and practice in education and, at the same time, to

FOUNDATIONS OF EDUCATION SERIES

see that many of the practical problems they will face as teachers (e.g How shall I grade? Shall I use drill? Should children be segregated on such bases as talent, color, or religion?) are solvable only in terms of prior philosophic inquiry—and so the series includes a volume in philosophy of education, a volume that views philosophy as dressed in the working clothes of a practical discipline rather than in the formal attire of impractical abstractions.

Prospective teachers need perspective to see the historical, philosophical, social, and psychological foundations of education in a context both different and larger than any one locality, region, or nation affords—and so the series includes a volume in comparative education, a volume designed to help the teacher compare and contrast his experience and educational system with the experiences and systems of other teachers in other nations and cultures.

These things the prospective teacher needs to know; he needs to be well grounded in the foundations of education, for they represent the intellectual tools that can give him scholarly leverage in his profession. But, given the thinness of time and the immensity of need in teacher education curriculums, how is this to be done?

The authors of this series believe that no single volume, be it a large, well-edited book of readings or a long treatise by one scholar, can meet the challenge of offering prospective teachers what they need to know as well as can a series of smaller volumes, each written by a specialist in one particular aspect of the foundations of education. Each volume in this series, by design, can stand alone as an introduction to an intellectual discipline; but when taken together the volumes unite these independent yet related disciplines into a series that offers prospective teachers a fuller, more unified introduction to the subject matters that underlie the profession of teaching.

We are convinced that prospective teachers who study these volumes in the foundations of education, and who discuss the concepts and issues presented with their instructors, will take to their future classrooms a firmer understanding not only of how to do the teaching job at hand but, more significant, of why their teaching job is so surpassingly important.

Hobert W. Burns

For various reasons, international and comparative education have in recent years gained accelerated momentum. The threat of foreign competition, the increasing importance attached to the new nations of Africa, Asia, and the Near East, and America's overseas commitments have highlighted the need for a searching examination of our own educational system and for an understanding of the educational systems of other nations. In addition, there is a wider recognition than ever before, that in spite of differences in economic development and in political ideologies, certain problems (population and educational expansion, efficient allocation of manpower resources, dropout rates, etc.) are shared by most countries of the world.

The renewed impetus in the examination of our own and other systems of education has had varied results. It has at one level created a great deal of popular commotion which, although potentially a healthy sign, very often has turned into popular confusion. At another, more sophisticated, level, this interest has resulted in voluminous criticisms or apologies concerning our pedagogical beliefs, practices, and values. Here, again, a potentially healthy climate of controversy has resulted in professional confusion.

Finally, interest in education abroad has expanded the study of comparative and international education as an academic area in institutions of higher learning, especially in those preoccupied with the training of teachers and administrators. Inevitably at this level, a major concern has been to define the subject matter of the field and to clarify its methodology.

This volume seeks to shed light on some substantive issues and problems in education and on the nature and scope of comparative education. It does not intentionally seek to vindicate the superiority of one system over another; rather, it attempts, as dispassionately as possible, to examine education in a variety of cultures and to point to an interdisciplinary approach to the study of comparative education.

We do not presume that this is the only or the best approach, nor do we make any claims to comprehensiveness. Our main intention was to introduce the reader to other systems of education and to provide a method for analyzing them.

Small parts of this volume have originally appeared in the *Comparative Education Review*, the *International Review of Education*, the Indiana University School of Education *Bulletin*, and in *Foundations of Education*, edited by G. F. Kneller (John Wiley & Sons, Inc., 1963). The authors are grateful to the publishers of these sources, as well as to The University of Chicago Press, for granting permission to use copyrighted material.

Andreas M. Kazamias
Byron G. Massialas

PREFACE

CONTENTS

PART ONE THE NATURE AND SCOPE OF COMPARATIVE EDUCATION

There is currently a great deal of controversy surrounding the nature and scope of comparative education. Divergence of opinion exists among writers and scholars on several issues pertaining to this field: whether comparative education is or should be thought of as a scholarly discipline in its own right, with distinctive method and content; on what areas of education it should focus and in what context; whether it should be anchored to one or more of the established disciplines in the social sciences and in the arts; and to what extent it should be approached from the theoretical or the applied standpoint. Although in the present study we do not intend to engage in a detailed examination of such and related issues, we feel that it is necessary to dwell on some relevant methodological questions in order to provide a framework for our study. Our main contention is that comparative education, as a field of study, can be pursued in a systematic and scholarly manner and that this can be done by drawing from other disciplines, depending on the types of problems that are investigated. For our particular concerns, we have relied mostly on the concepts and methods of history, political science, and sociology.

THE COURSE OF COMPARATIVE EDUCATION

The starting point of comparative education as a field of study is often associated with the appearance in 1817 of Marc Antoine Jullien's

1

COMPARATIVE EDUCATION AS A FIELD OF STUDY

1

Esquisse et vues preliminaires d'un ouvrage sur l'éducation comparé
(Plan and Preliminary Views for a Work on Comparative Education)
In reading Jullien's plan, one is impressed with his foresight and his con
cern for a systematic approach to a comparative examination of educa
tional institutions and practices. Deeply perturbed by the social and politi
cal conditions of the time, he envisaged education as a means of socia
and moral improvement. At the same time, he viewed education as a
positive science that could be refined and perfected through comparative
analysis. Hence, he called for "collections of facts and observations, ar
ranged in analytic charts, which permit them to be related and compared
[in order] to deduct from them certain principles, [and] determined rules."
The types of questions Jullien included in his plan were designed, for the
most part, to gather information on the structural aspects of education
and on matters of contemporary significance—such as the prevalence o
smallpox in schools, nourishment of children, and so on. As he himself
put it, he considered the science of comparative education to be analogous
to comparative anatomy. Hence, he only touched upon questions that per
tained to any interrelationships between education and other social institu
tions. Of course, not having conducted a study based on his plan, we do not
know the extent to which he would have considered this other aspect of
education.

Jullien's proposed method of investigation was not followed by sub
sequent nineteenth century writers. What actually appeared was a series
of reports written, for the most part, by administrators and social reformers
who gathered information on foreign systems of education without any
clearly defined approach and without any concern for what Jullien called
principles and rules. Such writers as John Griscom, Calvin Stowe, Henry
Barnard, and Horace Mann in America; Victor Cousin in France; and
Matthew Arnold, Joseph Kay, Robert Morant, and Michael Sadler in
England belonged to this category. They sought to gather information
and data on problems of immediate concern to them in their roles as
administrators in their respective countries. Their overriding consideration
was to use such information in order to press for educational reforms at
home. Moreover, they looked at education more as an autonomous entity
and less as one related to other institutions or other elements in the society.

In general, the nineteenth century writings in comparative education
may be characterized as follows: (1) they were mostly descriptive; (2)
they were eulogistic in the sense that they extolled uncritically certain
features of other systems of education (for example, American writers
looked with admiration at the Prussian system as a model to be emulated);
(3) they were governed by a utilitarian purpose, that is, they were mostly
concerned with the value of comparative education in national "development"; and (4) they were melioristic in that they were based on certain
a priori values concerning the improvement of education.

Of the nineteenth century pioneers, Michael Sadler stands out as the
forerunner of the methodological approach that characterized comparative
studies in the twentieth century. Although his actual studies of the European national systems were essentially governed by the same principles
as those of Arnold, Mann, and the others, his statements about what the

---

[1] Stewart Fraser, ed., *Jullien's Plan for Comparative Education 1816-1817* (New
York: Bureau of Publications, Teachers College, Columbia University, 1964),
p. 40.

investigator should look for in studying foreign systems of education have become classic expressions in the field. Foremost among these was his famous dictum that "the things outside the schools matter even more than the things inside the schools." Thus, he pointed to the inadequacies of approaches that treated education autonomously. Equally important, insofar as Sadler's influence upon subsequent studies is concerned, was his emphasis on the concept of national character as a methodological tool to explain educational ideas and practices. Finally, his reemphasis upon improvement of one's system became an integral part of twentieth century comparative studies. The Sadlerian principles have become the cornerstones of the theoretical orientation of twentieth century comparative education. This is most clearly evident in the work of the most representative and best known contemporary comparative educator, namely, I. L. Kandel.

Kandel's methodology is governed by at least three major purposes; the first may be called the "reportorial-descriptive" purpose. The reader is furnished with certain facts or, to use his own words, "information about" the school systems of various nations. In classifying these facts, Kandel employs mainly "common-sense" categories, such as organization and administration of education, elementary and secondary education, and preparation of elementary and secondary teachers. Kandel, quite rightly, regards the mere reporting of the facts as inadequate and limited but as an essential first step in the process of comparative study. All comparative educators have followed this basic principle of Kandel's method.

The second, and in his opinion, identifying feature of comparative education, may be called the "historical-functional" purpose. Though necessary, it is not sufficient to report on mere facts. The comparative educator, according to Kandel, must look into "the causes" that have produced certain problems, and he must appreciate Sadler's "intangible, spiritual, and cultural forces that underlie an educational system." [2] Education, Kandel points out, cannot be viewed as an autonomous enterprise. It must be viewed in relation to national background and the social, economic, political, and intellectual environment. This important view has also become an integral part of comparative analysis.

The third element in Kandel's approach may be termed the "melioristic" purpose. In both his 1933 and 1955 works, Kandel exhibits great concern for the improvement of education in the world. He hoped that by studying other systems as well as his own, the student of comparative education would develop a more desirable philosophical approach, which would ultimately result in improvement of his own system and in fostering the spirit of internationalism. This purpose has led Kandel to assume a certain body of values, e.g., democratic systems of education are better, centralization is bad, education should aim at the total development of man and at beliefs such as progress, individual responsibility, and so on.

In seeking to incorporate the element of interpretation or explanation into the comparative approach and in seeking further to illuminate educational phenomena by looking at the general culture of a nation, Kandel fulfilled the expectations of previous writers on the subject—for example, the already mentioned Michael Sadler—and he set the stage for a more "scientific" examination of educational forms and practices.

In one form or another, these Kandelian elements have been followed

3

[2] I. L. Kandel, *Comparative Education* (Boston: Houghton Mifflin Company, 1933), p. xix.

by many subsequent and current writers. One could classify this approach, which also underlay the works of other well-known comparative educators like Nicholas Hans and Robert Ulich, as essentially historical. Indeed, in a more recent statement, Kandel explicitly stated that "comparative education may be considered a continuation of the study of the history of education into the present." [3]

Recently, however, another group of writers have turned more to the social sciences (sociology, anthropology, and to some degree political science and economics) than to history for the development of appropriate methodological tools and concepts. To these writers, history may be of help; however, they argue that in so far as it deals with essentially unique phenomena having an ineradicable temporal and spatial locus, its value to the comparative educator is at best limited. For the comparative educator must make generalizations and must abstract elements that can be taken out of the unique cultural context and applied in a nontemporal or nonspatial framework. Since comparisons cannot be made of unique events or phenomena, the comparative educator's task differs from that of the historian and becomes identical to that of the social scientist, who searches for repetitive patterns and regularities in social relationships.[4] We shall refer to this as the social-science approach to comparative education.

There are at least two other nascent approaches to the study of comparative education, which overlap to a degree with the foregoing but which may, nevertheless, be identified as possessing their own distinguishing features. These are the philosophical approach, best represented by Joseph Lauwerys and the problem approach, represented by G. Z. F. Bereday and Brian Holmes.

It is possible, according to Lauwerys, to establish "national styles" in philosophy or "different styles of arguing": e.g., British empiricism, French nationalism, Cartesianism, and perhaps existentialism; German idealism and romanticism; and American pragmatism. Assuming this to be the case, the comparative educator could then seek to establish and interpret the relations between "modes of philosophical argumentation" and educational practices and systems. As an example, Lauwerys briefly delineates five different approaches to the notion of "General Education" (Liberal Education in England, *Culture Générale* in France, *Allgemeinbildung* in Germany, General Education in the United States, and Polytechnization in Russia). The different conceptions and practices concerning general education presuppose a complex of philosophical arguments. The job of the comparative educator would be to examine why X outlook was accepted in Y country and rejected in Z, a pursuit that would involve an analysis of philosophical, historical, sociological, psychological, administrative, and pedagogical factors. This would not only be a "fruitful" pursuit, it would also contribute to the acquisition of a deeper insight into "what is likely to happen in any given society"; hence, it would lead to predictions.[5]

The problem-approach, according to Bereday, may be used in the in-

[3] Kandel, "The Methodology of Comparative Education," *International Review of Education*, V, No. 3 (1959), 273.

[4] See, for example, C. Arnold Anderson, "Methodology of Comparative Education," *International Review of Education*, VII, No. 1 (1961), 6.

[5] Joseph A. Lauwerys, "The Philosophical Approach to Comparative Education," *International Review of Education*, V, No. 3 (1959), 285-87.

vestigation of problems on a large scale, when all relevant data are brought to bear on the issue in question or in the analysis of more restricted topics. In the former category belong the types of problems included in the various issues of the *Yearbook of Education*, e.g., "The Gifted Child" or "Higher Education"—and in the latter, such topics as "Reform in France and Turkey" or "Indoctrination in Poland." [6] Because comparative education was traditionally considered an offshoot of the discipline of history and because the social-scientific approach (mostly the sociological-functional approach) seems to be gaining momentum, it would be appropriate to comment on these two disciplines in more detail.

HISTORY AND COMPARATIVE EDUCATION

By the historical method of studying educational systems, such writers as Kandel, Hans, and Ulich meant not only writing about past events but also identifying antecedent factors and forces that have influenced educational forms, policies, and practices, and that have "determined" the development and present status of educational systems. There are some variations in the historical approach of these three writers; in addition, their studies were governed by philosophical and melioristic considerations or they involved the use of the concept of national character.

In *The Education of Nations: A Comparison in Historical Perspective*, Ulich illustrates the historical approach. He presents us with a certain common historical background upon which the educational systems of several European nations and of the United States are based. Then he proceeds with historical analysis of these systems as examples of how, in its evolution, education followed different paths as a result of different national factors and characteristics. At the end, the author formulates certain generalizations about current problems of education in the new nations. He asserts that the "older" nations have at some time or other been confronted with such problems, and he exhorts those responsible for their solution to learn from the past in order to avoid repeating the same mistakes.

There are at least two significant elements in this approach. First, there is a reconstruction of the past that the author seeks to make both intelligent and intelligible—in the sense that he not only narrates events, but he also interprets them in terms of the antecedent forces or factors that shaped them. In addition, the author abstracts certain problems or generalizations from the current situation that, he avers, are to be seen in the past.

The question that must be posed here is whether such a historical treatment of comparative education is adequate or sufficient. Insofar as it is limited to the first of the two elements mentioned in the preceding paragraph, the answer is open to question. According to some historians, the reconstruction of the past in and of itself does not necessarily entail comparisons of two or more events. According to others, however, the historian—explicitly or implicitly—is engaged in comparisons. Moreover, if in reconstructing the past the researcher employs conceptual models in

5

[6] For a more detailed exposition of this approach, see George Z. F. Bereday, *Comparative Method in Education* (New York: Holt, Rinehart & Winston, Inc., 1964).

order to show similarities and/or variations, he engages much more directly in comparative analysis. Clearly, this has not been the case in Ulich's study, for the different national systems are treated separately.

The second element, namely, the abstraction of problems or the making of generalizations, raises questions of a different order. Herbert Butterfield criticizes the historian who tries to see the present in the past without realizing that "he is in a world of different connotations altogether" and that "he has merely tumbled upon what could be shown to be a misleading analogy." [7] It may be true that if one is exclusively preoccupied with current connotations, one may be led to insufficient historical descriptions and interpretations. But the historian, even if he examines the past as the past with its own world of connotations without reference to the present, *does* abstract and generalize and *does*—tacitly or explicitly—assume or use certain general principles of human behavior and the functioning of social institutions. Moreover, there are some writers who contend that "historians borrow ready-made generalizations whether they know it or not." [8] It might be further noted here that "uniqueness" in history is a matter of the historians' interest, not an inherent quality of historical events.

If one subscribes to this latter view of history, as we do, then there are at least four ways in which history may be useful for the comparative study of education: (1) it might furnish insights or suggest hypotheses that might be tested in other contexts—past and/or present—thus, stimulating further inquiry as well as adding to our understanding and knowledge of education; (2) the testing or confirmation of such hypotheses may be carried out through the methods and concepts of the social and behavioral sciences; (3) conversely, the experience of man in the past may furnish additional evidence to test hypotheses formulated in the present; and (4) knowledge of the past or of the historical background of a nation helps the comparative educator to supplement firsthand observations and interpretations.

In the existing studies in comparative education that we have characterized as historical, there is a conspicuous absence of considerations of the kind just mentioned; that is, such studies are based for the most part on the more traditional views of history. They exhibit hardly any attempts to utilize the insights, concepts, and findings of the social sciences. They show a lack of conceptual schemes and hypotheses, and they contain a melange of the philosophical, the historical, the sociological, and the melioristic. Moreover, some of them have attempted to show that each system is historically determined and different from any other. However, if systems of education are really unique and totally different, how is comparative education possible?

In order to illustrate one of the ways history may be used in comparative education, let us take one rather gross generalization that Ulich implies in the study mentioned previously. In discussing the relationship between the state and the individual, Ulich implies that political revolutions tend to create centralized systems of education. He found this to be the case in certain of the new nations that have recently had revolutions. We might reconstruct Ulich's implied reasoning as follows:

[7] H. Butterfield, *The Whig Interpretation of History* (New York: Charles Scribner's Sons, 1951), p. 12.
[8] See, for example, Louis Gottschalk, ed., *Generalization in the Writing of History* (Chicago: University of Chicago Press, 1963), p. 209.

1. Every revolution is apt to create its counterrevolution.
2. Counterrevolutions threaten the stability of the governments created by revolutions.
3. Therefore, governments created by revolutions tend to assume more power in order to maintain their stability and crush the opposition.
4. Centralized education is an important instrument in the preservation of the power assumed by such governments.
5. Therefore, nations that undergo a revolution incline towards centralized systems of education.[9]

The comparative educator may use this model or conceptual framework to examine other revolutions and their relationships to the educational systems that emerged. And this might be done with contemporary revolutions as well as with past revolutions.

To illustrate a total neglect of the findings and insights of the social sciences, one could cite the following inadequacies in Kandel's writings. In his attempts to show interrelationships, Kandel assigned to the State— by which he meant the government—a pre-eminent causal role in the operations of society. He felt that the State is the really important agent of change or stability. He seemed to accept as a basic principle the idea that "every State (government) has the type of education that it wills." [10] But such a statism, as extensive research in the social sciences and psychology has revealed, is not so self-evident. The education of children is a far more complex phenomenon. Similar functional inadequacies in the writings of Kandel and others are to be found in their attempts to explain education in terms of the evasive and highly complex concept, "national character."

Finally, comparative research in other disciplines has shown that very often similar functions are performed by different institutions. And conversely, institutions that *prima facie* appear similar may perform different functions. For example, recent studies in comparative government have shown that the political function called "interest articulation" is performed by different groups in various societies. And, more significantly, this function is performed in primitive societies through agents such as chiefs, without the appearance of anything like an organized pressure group. In spite of such findings, many comparative educators persist in criticizing one system—for example, the French *lycée*—for not doing the same things as another—for example, the American high school; and they ignore the fact that some of the functions of the latter may be performed in France by agencies other than the school.

In theorizing about society, many of these "classic" comparative educators have employed the concept of "national character" without defining it or elaborating on it with rigor and precision. Stated rather simply, national character is an abstraction used when people describe certain habits or traits of thinking and behaving shared by individuals who belong to a certain group or nation. The practice of describing different groups of people in terms of certain common characteristics is as old as man's ability to theorize about other men. Until very recently, such a practice was prevalent among travellers and, in the academic world, among historians. In 1940, Hamilton Fyfe indignantly rejected national character

7

[9] Robert Ulich, *The Education of Nations* (Cambridge: Harvard University Press, 1961), p. 292.
[10] Kandel, *op. cit.*, p. 82.

by saying that there were not now, and never had been, any typical English, Americans, French, or Germans. Since then, historians have been rather timid in discussing the concept, although they continue to use it. Meanwhile, the concept of national character has been revived and systematically examined by another group of social analysts, the behavioral scientists—namely, anthropologists, psychologists, and sociologists. In a brilliant essay on the subject, the American historian David M. Potter criticized the inadequacies of its treatment by historians as follows:

> . . . many of them have written freely about "national character" . . . without ever determining for themselves or indicating for the reader what they conceive the nature of "national character" to be, what components in a people's personality and behavior they regard as constituting "character"; what relationship they suppose to exist between a specific trait and the character as a totality; how they would define or delimit the "nation" as the unit to which the character is attributed; how they would distinguish the "national" characteristics from class characteristics, religious characteristics, or other group characteristics in a given aggregation of people; and, finally, how they would determine the relative importance of national character in comparison with other forms of group character as keys for the interpretation of society.[11]

Potter charged historians with "imprecision, looseness, and vagueness." He praised the work of the behavioral scientists who, through their systematic analyses of culture and personality, have shed considerable light on the nature of the concept. Rather than ignore national character, Potter called upon the historians to join hands with the behavioral scientists for "the rounded development of the subject." For although the methods and skills of the behavioral scientists have clarified the nature of national character by imbedding it in the culture of a group, it is in establishing the determinants of such a culture that the contribution of the historian may lie.[12]

The reason for this seeming digression from our frame of reference here will be apparent when we look at how national character has fared in the hands of comparative educators. Two studies are particularly relevant in this connection: Kandel's *Comparative Education* of 1933 and Vernon Mallinson's *An Introduction to the Study of Comparative Education*, which appeared in 1957.

Kandel cautions the reader against the dangers in the indiscriminate use of national character. He rejects the use of absolute and universal attributes as being present in all members of a national group. Instead, he claims that his generalizations about group characteristics would be used in the sense that groups behave differently from other groups in accordance with their historical traditions and ideals, their environment, and their outlook on life. Thus, in examining the English national character, he describes the Englishman as one who "dislikes to think or to formulate plans of action," as an empiricist who relies on his ability to compromise and to rely on common sense rather than on logic, as one who mistrusts national planning, as an amateur in government and social affairs, as an individualist, yet as one who possesses "an instinct for cooperation," and so on. On the

[11] David M. Potter, *People of Plenty: Economic Abundance and the American Character* (Chicago: University of Chicago Press, 1954), p. 20. Copyright 1954 by The University of Chicago Press.
[12] *Ibid.*, p. 62.

other hand, the Frenchman, according to Kandel, is a man of ideas who enjoys to think for the sheer pleasure of thinking. He is an individualist, but his individualism is regulated by reason; and he possesses such attributes as orderliness, logic, the ability to plan, and so on. Finally, according to Kandel, the outstanding feature of American life is its emphasis upon liberty and self-determination; and the most striking attributes of American character are "egalitarianism, resourcefulness, cooperation of social groups," etc.[13]

There are several questions that arise from such a description of national characteristics. The most obvious one is whether these generalizations are valid or empirically true. To take the characterization of the Englishman: Is it really true that he dislikes to think, or to formulate plans of action? The historical evidence that may be adduced to refute this is legion. Specifically, in education, one might cite the Balfour Act of 1902, the Fisher Act of 1918, and the Education Act of 1944 as examples of plans of action into which entered considerable thought. Indeed, the very words "compromise" and "compromisers," which Kandel and others have used to describe the English, far from excluding "thought" or "formulation of plans," imply essential elements of thinking such as deliberation and evaluation of a course of action.

The second question that may be raised is how national traits are established. Specifically, in Kandel's study, we are not given enough evidence concerning the sources of these character traits or the conditions that have contributed to making a national of England an Englishman, as distinguished from a national of France or of the United States. We are thus forced to conclude that many such statements are subjective, impressionistic generalizations, which are not empirically or historically validated.

Kandel further employs the concept of national character as a tool for the interpretation of certain educational practices in England. Thus, he causally explains the lack of system in the English educational organization partly in terms of the English character trait of a dislike for planning. Such an explanation presents some difficulties. In the first place, it does not clarify the important distinction drawn by Potter between traits as absolute and unchanging qualities that are common to all members of a nation and traits as relative qualities or dispositions to behave in certain ways, liable to gradual alteration in response to changing conditions and manifesting themselves as tendencies in the majority of members of the national group. Kandel hinted at this distinction; however, he did not elaborate on it, nor did he apply it in his character sketches. One might question whether the quality of disliking planning has always been present in all Englishmen at all times. Historically, this is clearly not quite true, as might easily be proved by an examination of the policies of the Fabians, the Political parties, and other organizations. If not universally applied to all Englishmen, is it a tendency manifested in the majority of the Englishmen? Here, again, the Education Act of 1944 and several other post World War II social and economic measures would be instances of a rejection of this attribute.

In the second place, the explanation offered by Kandel stems from his failure to take into account another important distinction drawn from Potter, namely, the distinction between national characteristics and other group characteristics—class, religious, and so on. To what extent are we

9

[13] Kandel, *Comparative Education,* op. cit., pp. 24-42.

to attribute the lack of system in English education, assuming for a moment this to be the case, to a trait characteristically "English" and to what extent are we to attribute it to traits—fortuitously displayed in England—characteristic of class-conscious, aristocratic, voluntaristic societies.[14]

In fairness to those writers who have used the concept of national character, it should be said that most analyses involving the examination of systems of education and, indeed, other social institutions inescapably imply some notions of how people think and behave as members of a national community. Furthermore, while we have raised some questions about the use of this concept as a methodological device, we by no means reject it as such. What we wish to emphasize, however, is the need for a more systematic and clear delineation of it.

As we have previously mentioned, most of the nineteenth and twentieth century writings in comparative education have been characterized by the element of meliorism, by which is meant: (1) the belief in certain values concerning how men should live and how they should educate their children; (2) the view that the study of comparative education should be governed by a reforming zeal, (3) the view that education, in the sense of formal schooling, can indeed improve society and guide man's destiny, and (4) the idea that by studying the education of other countries, a broader and a more desirable philosophical outlook can be developed for the improvement of education in one's own country.

While it may be true to say that the scholarly and the melioristic aims would remain undistinguished and unseparated in the mind of the social investigator, their blending would render any objective analysis quite difficult. If *ab initio* we assume what education *ought* to be, then it would be quite difficult to examine with any degree of objectivity what education *is*. The two can logically be distinguished, and the methods by which we arrive at the *ought* and the *is* are different. The researcher and the reformer may, indeed, be one and the same person; however, unless the reformer's preconceptions are somehow held as constant as possible, the researcher's findings will suffer. Furthermore, the researcher and the reformer need not necessarily be one and the same person. This does not mean that the study of education should be pursued for its own sake—even if this were possible —or that the findings of the researcher should not be used for purposes of improvement or, indeed, that inquiries on what ought to be done are without value. It merely means that for purposes of analysis, the reformer's aims, zeal, preconceptions, and philosophical inquiries must be delineated from his sociological or historical inquiries. One might further add here that each single instance of the reformer's job involves not only *knowledge* of underlying principles, but also judgment in *applying* appropriate principles. Also, the meliorist's belief in the role of education to improve society and guide man's destiny does not seem to be self-evident or clearly borne out by the findings of social analysts.

SOCIAL SCIENCE AND COMPARATIVE EDUCATION

It might be appropriate at the outset to delineate some of the most important features of social science in general and of the scientific method. The ultimate purpose of any science is prediction and control. In pursuing

---

[14] The same criticisms would apply to the use of the concept in Vernon Mallinson, *An Introduction to the Study of Comparative Education* (London: William Heinemann Limited, 1957).

these purposes, scientists in the main formulate explicit hypotheses, test them in laboratories or other situations, and seek to establish generalizations or universal laws. While natural scientists seek to establish universal laws concerning physical phenomena, social scientists attempt to do so with respect to social phenomena. At this stage of their development, however, the generalizations of the social sciences have not approached the same level of prediction and systematization as those of the natural sciences. Another feature of science in general is that the findings are subject to replication for purposes of refutation or confirmation. Furthermore, the instruments and techniques (questionnaires, interviews, etc.) used are similarly subject to replication. Finally, one of the essential concerns of the social scientist is explanation; that is, in addition to describing social phenomena, he is also interested in explaining why such phenomena are the way they are.

One of the best descriptions of the comparative method as used in the social sciences is given by S. F. Nadel, who defined it as the method of "co-variations." According to Nadel, variations of social phenomena are first observed, and then general uniformities or regularities are arrived at. Such correlations or co-variations are not causal connections; they are of the type: "X varies as Y does" or "when A occurs, B also occurs." This type of comparative method, according to Nadel, may be applied in any one of the following three situations:

1. One could examine the variations or relationships in a single society at a given time. For example, one could consider variations in modes of action or in education in contemporary United States between the South and the North.
2. One could examine two or more societies that have basic cultural similarities but are different in certain modes of action or relationships. For example, one could consider variations in modes of action or in education in contemporary Arabic Islamic countries of the Near East.
3. One could compare either many societies that are different in nature but share some common features or different historical periods in the life of one single society. In the former category, one could compare Turkey and Japan; in the latter, England in 1850 and England in 1960.[15]

One of the more recent approaches to comparative education, which is also related to Nadel's, has been the functional approach, based largely on the work of certain sociologists.

Educational institutions, according to the "functionalist" view, do not only have structure, they also perform certain functions. Indeed, although the structure may be the same, the functions may be different. For example, the primary schools in Turkey and the United States, although in the main similar in structure, perform different functions. In the former case, they are terminal institutions for the majority of the students; but in the latter, they are a stage that invariably leads to secondary education. Consequently, if comparisons are made of purely structural aspects of education, one might find that one is engaged in superficial comparisons and possibly in comparisons of incomparables. Functional analysis would be a more reliable method of finding out how institutions work and how they

[15] S. F. Nadel, *The Foundations of Social Anthropology* (London: Cohen and West Ltd., 1951), pp. 222-26.

are interrelated with other aspects of the society—social stratification, occupational structure, the status system, the economy, etc.—or with other aspects of the educational system.

Functional analysis, as a sociological method, has been the subject of controversy among sociologists; and the terms "function," "functional," and "dysfunctional" have connoted different meanings among those who have used them. This controversy prompted at least one sociologist to suggest the complete abandonment of the·term as not really signifying an approach distinct from that usually taken by sociologists.[16] On the other hand, the advocates of the concept "function" have maintained that it is a useful methodological device to examine how institutions in a society work. Our purpose here is not to discuss the validity of such claims and counterclaims in sociology, but to assess the value of the use of functional analysis in comparative education.

Clearly, finding out what the schools as social institutions do in various societies—finding out what their functions are—is or should be an essential task of any person engaged in the comparative analysis of education. Despite the variations in functional approaches among sociologists, those who have advocated the application of functionalism to comparative education have stressed the value of isolating manageable variables in the institutional structure of education, finding out what functions they perform, and establishing functional correlations between these variables and others within and without the educational-institutional complex. One could investigate, for example, the functional relationships between income distribution and school attendance, between urbanization and the literacy rate, between the social structure and the degree of equality of educational opportunity, between formal education and the formation of political elites, and so on. In such enterprises, generalizations may take the forms: "X is correlated with Y" or "as X varies, Y does", or "the function of X is to maintain Y". Such generalizations are arrived at through observations of a number of particular correlations in specific societies. The object of this type of analysis would presumably be similar to the object of all scientific analysis, namely, to establish generalizations and hypotheses about the relationships between variables that could be tested in other situations in order to be confirmed, refuted, or modified.

This description of the functional method has several merits if applied to the analysis of education in one or several societies. In the first place, by emphasizing both function and structure, it opens the way for more reliable comparisons. Second, by attempting to isolate variables, it lends itself to the analysis of more manageable levels of reality. Third, it formulates generalizations that can be empirically tested. Fourth, the findings can be made useful for the social planner. Functional correlations would help the person concerned with change in that they may point to the ways changes in one institution will affect changes in another.

The functional approach, however, can give us only some of the answers to inquiries involving systems of education for the following reasons:

1. As we stated previously, types of explanations of educational phenomena based on the functional approach may not necessarily give a com-

---

[16] Kingsley Davis, "The Myth of Functional Analysis as a Special Method in Sociology and Anthropology," in *Sociology: The Progress of a Decade*, eds., S. M. Lipset and N. J. Smelser (Englewood Cliffs, N.J.: Prentice-Hall, Inc., 1961), pp. 46-63.

plete picture of why certain relationships have been found to be true. Let us take an example of how functional analysis may be invoked in order to explain an educational phenomenon. Suppose one observed that enrollments in academic secondary schools increase at a relatively higher rate than enrollments in technical or vocational schools, and this in spite of attempts to strengthen institutions of the latter type. How can this phenomenon be explained? A functionalist's explanation would involve an examination of the functions these various schools perform. He would probably find that academic secondary schools train people for positions with higher income and prestige than do technical or vocational schools. The explanation would probably run as follows, "Enrollments in academic secondary schools increase at a higher rate than enrollments in other schools because parents tell their children that graduation from an academic secondary school will mean more prestige and more income."

In this instance, the explanation does not go beyond the present situation. The data would probably be established through such techniques as questionnaires, interviews, analyses of available statistical information on income distribution, and so on. In answer to questions such as: "Why do enrollments increase at a higher rate in X schools than in Y schools?" or "Why do parents prefer certain types of institutions to others and urge their children to go to them?" or "Why does society reward people differentially?" we could supplement the kind of functional explanation previously given with historical-evolutionary kinds of explanations, which would trace the origins and growth of certain events or institutions and the way certain patterns of behavior were themselves institutionalized.

2. The isolation of specific elements in the educational system without a concomitant examination of the society as a whole might result in the analysis of variables that are not relevant. In order to isolate the relevant elements in the institutional complex of a society and in order to trace their relationships with other institutional elements, it seems that one must possess a good understanding of the whole society—not only in its contemporary state, but also in its temporal dimension.

3. Social scientists applying the functional approach to the study of social institutions have used such concepts as "eufunctional" and "dysfunctional," to refer to whether certain conditions increase or maintain (eufunctional) or lessen (dysfunctional) adaptation or adjustment to the setting of the institution or unit. In using such concepts, especially in education, it is necessary to define as clearly as possible the criteria of adjustment or adaptation. Otherwise, as Carl G. Hempel has pointed out, there is the danger of making tautological and not particularly illuminating statements. For example, we know that the first *lycée* in Turkey was an institution borrowed from France. In the traditional setting of the Ottoman Empire, it was clearly different from the other educational institutions; therefore, it created conflicts. In one sense, this school was dysfunctional in that it did not reinforce the solidarity of the traditional structure; in another sense, however, it was eufunctional in that it strengthened the movement toward westernization and modernization. Hence, merely calling an educational institution functional or dysfunctional without reference to the particular cultural context may be misleading.[17]

13

17 For a good example of the application of these concepts in connection with institutional transfer, see David E. Apter, *The Gold Coast in Transition* (Princeton: Princeton University Press, 1955).

From the methodological standpoint, the study that follows is based on the following major assumptions. (1) The subject matter of comparative education is coterminous with the subject matter of education itself. Reduced to its most basic components education and, a fortiori, comparative education is concerned with the interaction between three units—a teacher, a pupil, and a curriculum, within both a formal and an informal setting. This interaction is carried out in what might be called secondary units, i.e., in schools, in youth organizations, in the family, in tribal ceremonies, and so on. Moreover, in most societies there is a structure within which this process takes place. (2) The differentiating characteristics of comparative education vis-à-vis education is that the former goes beyond the confines of education in one nation, society, or group, and it uses cross-national or cross-cultural methods and techniques. (3) Certain processes, e.g., socialization and differentiation, have been basic in all systems of education. (4) While systems of education exhibit variations in their structure and the interaction of their constituent units, they also exhibit fundamental similarities, which render them amenable to comparison. (5) Comparisons are possible with societies which are temporally and/or spatially separated. (6) Although the study of comparative education might contribute to application and planning, it need not be governed by such considerations. (7) While selection and examination of certain countries or societies, topics, and problems is unavoidable, one may apply objective criteria in one's selection.

In this book we have been mainly concerned with formal education and its relationships with other institutional processes and patterns. Several themes and problems are examined here, but if we are to subsume them under a broader topic, this is "tradition and change in education." Throughout the volume we have sought to describe and illuminate the interplay of the forces of tradition and the forces of innovation and change. There are several manifestations of this process, such as the interaction between aristocratic and egalitarian movements, religious and secular elements, and old and modern practices and outlooks on life. Educational change and the movement toward modernity have been and continue to be major concerns of most countries of the world and a subject of current interest among scholars in the field.

In the main, we have approached this topic from two interrelated dimensions: from that of selected societies, and from that of topics or problems that cut across cultures temporally and/or spatially. Thus, we have looked at the Japanese system of education separately, and the relationship between education and political elites in Japan, England, Turkey, and the United States. In our treatment of separate systems of education, we have included the following categories: administration and control, organization of schools, and curriculum. In addition, we have presented a brief historical introduction, and we have discussed recent plans at educational reform. The selection of countries was guided by three considerations. They were representative of major cultural areas with variations in traditions and in the stages of economic, political, and educational development. Data on them were readily available. They were countries with which we were familiar and in which we felt we had scholarly interest and competence.

The second dimension entailed the examination of certain themes, problems, and issues which we considered to be significant for these reasons. (1) They related to some aspects of education which are characteristic of all societies; (2) they were germane to the general theme of continuity and change in education; and (3) while in some countries they were bound up with the emergence of a modern state, in others they persisted as integral elements of the ongoing process of development. We have accordingly selected the following. (1) Recruitment, selection, and the related concept of equality of opportunity in education. Here we looked into various patterns typified by primitive, ancient, medieval, and modern societies. (2) Political socialization, expansion of educational provision, systems of examination, structural reorganization of schools, and the formation of political elites—all of which bear upon the central theme of education and political development.

On the basis of our analysis of both separate systems and issues we have drawn certain conclusions and formulated certain tentative generalizations. These generalizations could serve as working hypotheses for the examination of similar questions in other settings.

As we stated earlier, we have used concepts and methods primarily drawn from education, history, political science, and sociology. Thus, for example, we looked into recruitment and selection over a temporal span, but at the same time we examined it largely through a sociological framework. In issues relating to political development we have employed such concepts as political socialization and political elites, which more appropriately belong to the discipline of political science.

PRIMITIVE SOCIETIES

Formal education is often thought to be a characteristic of "civilized" or advanced societies and to take place only in organized institutions known as schools. Yet education, both formal and informal, is as old and as universal a phenomenon as man. The "scholiocentric" approach of educators and their interpretation of education solely in terms of intellectual written tradition have limited their perspective by ignoring the variety of educational practice associated with "primitive" societies and brought to our attention by the research of anthropologists. In many primitive cultures, formal education is, in part, carried out in the form of initiation ceremonies by special classes of people: the elders, priests, wizards, or shamans. Every individual in the specific tribe is required to pass through such ceremonies before he becomes a member of that tribe. In their social functions, initiation ceremonies in primitive cultures are as formal and important as educational institutions in advanced cultures.[1]

[1] See, for example, Ruth Benedict, *Patterns of Culture* (New York: Mentor Books, 1953), p. 54. Also see Thomas Woody, *Life and Education in Early Societies* (New York: The Macmillan Company, 1949), pp. 16-19.

16

PRIMITIVE AND ANCIENT SOCIETIES

2

Through the initiation ceremonies, which in some cases are virtual tests of endurance, the youth are inducted into the culture of the society. They are also trained in the appropriate skills necessary to reproduce the mode of life of that society. Such training may include not only practical skills necessary for survival (hunting, fishing, warring) and moral instruction, but also specialized job training. Allocation of different tasks to men and women and "industrial specialization" are not uncommon among primitive tribes. The primitive child learns the various tasks allotted to him mostly by imitating adults. As one anthropologist puts it: "Primitive people do not lay stress on telling. In many languages the word for 'teach' is the same as the word for 'show,' and the synonymity is literal." [2]

Another characteristic of some primitive societies is their system of rank differentiation. Chiefs, priests, shamans, war leaders, or the elders of the tribe stand at the highest levels of the prestige hierarchy. High rank of this kind more often than not is attained through meritorious distinction in some enterprise, rather than through birth or wealth. Where there is a looser form of social organization, as in the Manus of New Guinea, there are, according to Margaret Mead, "faint echoes of rank in the privileges claimed by certain families who are called *lapan* in contradistinction to other families who are called *lau*." [3]

In primitive societies which are relatively homogeneous, where there is little division of labor and a simple system of social stratification, education is largely a process by which the individual is inducted into his cultural inheritance. Yet even in such societies there is specialization and differentiation, and a period of training for the performance of certain specialized roles. Take, for example, the education of the Samoan children. By the time they are six or seven years old, they have not only learned a series of avoidances, but also a number of simple techniques, e.g., simple weaving, making pinwheels of palm leaves, climbing cocoanut trees, playing a number of games, bringing water from the sea, and baby tending. Gradually, as they grow older, children learn more complicated tasks in weaving, fishing, and so on. During adolescence there is a differentiation in the types of tasks performed by boys and girls. Among girls there is little specialization except in the case of those who will be trained in medicine and midwifery. On the other hand, boys at 17 or 18, after they have learned basic techniques in fishing, planting, meat cutting, and canoe sailing, enter the *Aumaga*, a society of young men and untitled older men, where they are trained to be efficient through competition, precept, and example.

Samoan youth aspire to membership in the *Fono*, the assembly of headmen, for which they must demonstrate proficiency in some technique (housebuilding, fishing, oratory, or woodcarving). Membership in the Fono will give them a right to drink *Kava* with chiefs, to work with chiefs rather than with young men, and to sit inside the house.[4]

Primitive societies afford some interesting comparisons with modern edu-

---

[2] This is especially true of tribes in Oceania. See Franz Boas, ed., *General Anthropology* (Boston: D. C. Heath & Company, 1938), pp. 371, 471.

[3] See, for example, G. P. Murdock, *Our Primitive Contemporaries* (New York: The Macmillan Company, 1933), p. 76 and Margaret Mead, *Growing Up in New Guinea* (New York: Mentor Books, 1961), p. 176.

[4] For a more detailed analysis, see Margaret Mead, *Coming of Age in Samoa* (New York: Mentor Books, 1961), pp. 21-31.

cational systems concerning two aspects of the recruitment problem: the concept of leadership and the idea of equality of opportunity.

In primitive societies, distinctions between the ruler and the ruled may not be clearly demarcated. For example, in the Manus villages the privileged groups do not have power of control over the rest of the tribe. The village unit is a social group organized democratically in terms of paternal exogamous clans, which are loosely tied together through marriage and economic obligations. On the other hand, in the Zuni theocracy high-ranking priests constitute the council, which is a ruling body.

In some primitive societies a leader may be a priest who has mastered the secret cults, or he may be a person who has demonstrated proficiency in some craft. Leadership status, however, is achieved rather than ascribed. There are no special classes from which leaders are recruited, and no assumed innate distinctive traits among people from different households or clans. Although those who become leaders have to go through certain educational experiences, such experiences are not the sole prerogative of a special group. Educational activities are common to every member of the society; they are not purposely used to select the fit from the unfit. Although the young man may aspire to become a member of the priesthood or the assembly of headmen, his aspirations are tempered by the cultural checks placed upon virtuosity, precocity, and hunger for power. In other words, the Samoan youth must be proficient in some technique to become a leader, but he should not be too efficient, too outstanding, or too precocious, lest he incur the hatred or disapproval of his peers and his elders. The Zuni man who aspires to be a leader among men and wield personal authority is censured and will very probably be persecuted for sorcery. In such societies youth may wish to excel, but competition to select the most capable and to invest them with power over others, does not seem to be present. Among the Zunis the ideal man is one of dignity and affability, but not one who has tried to lead; he avoids greatness or office which, to use Malvolio's words but not his conceit, he may have "thrust upon him." Among the Manus youth groups, leadership is rather spontaneous and informal and has not developed any rigorous devices to coerce the unwilling. There seems to be respect for the uniqueness of the individual that leaves no room for measuring the worth of one against the other. There is no educational concept that places a higher premium on the gifted, rewards and differentiates him from the dullard, and goads the latter to perform faster than he is able.

In such societies concepts of equality and equal opportunity have no substantive meaning. The principle of equality in the Western tradition dates back to the origins of democratic institutions in ancient Greece and in the modern times it has emerged as a basic principle of democracy. In both ancient and modern times equality has signified the possession of certain rights, mostly legal and political, by every member of the body politic. It was introduced as a means to eliminate or lessen existing inequalities, whereby certain individuals or groups were treated differentially, possessed more advantages, or exercised undue authority over others. Equality has also been justified on the grounds that it is necessary to attain the goal of the worth of the individual.[5] Equality of opportunity, educational or otherwise, has been applied similarly to situations in which certain people, by virtue

[5] See Dorothy Lee, *Freedom and Culture* (Englewood Cliffs, N.J.: Prentice-Hall, Inc., 1959), p. 39.

of their wealth or birth, have more chances to acquire certain things than their fellow men or are treated specially.

In many primitive societies, however, the conditions that would necessitate the application of such principles are absent. There are no classes or groups which receive preferential treatment by virtue of birth or wealth; there are no special strata from which people are recruited to high positions; and rights are not distributed according to ascriptive criteria. Any existing inequalities become, as Lee points out, "irrelevant to evaluation, being viewed as another kind of difference, to be recognized and accepted as valid." [6] They do not become yardsticks for comparison. Hence, the need to introduce the external element of equality, to *create* conditions for people to get what others may have, to actualize the worth of the individual, does not seem to arise. In sum, what actually differentiates these primitive cultures from Western cultures is that in the former the worth of the individual as an individual supersedes his specific social status.

ANCIENT SOCIETIES: THREE HELLENIC PATTERNS

There are several reasons why the study of education in ancient Greece has meaning and relevance for the modern educator. In many respects the Greeks are the intellectual ancestors of Western civilization. They were responsible for education as we know it in Europe and the United States and, one might say, for some of the problems that have plagued us. Moreover, Greek educational development from the archaic to the classical period provides the oldest example of transition from a warrior, semiprimitive and semifeudal aristocratic culture to a highly developed, mature, and in many respects democratic culture.

THE ARISTOCRATIC PATTERN

Homer supplies us with the documentary evidence to reconstruct the origins of Greece education in the image of the hero, the aristocrat-warrior, the leader among men with mythical, godlike stature. Homer's archaic society was aristocratic, not dissimilar in structure from the medieval, knightly cultures of the West. At the top of the social pyramid was the king, who was surrounded by an inner council, so to speak, of the greatest warriors and of old men venerated for their experience and wisdom. Below them there were the young warriors or nobles (*Kouroi*) similar to the medieval knights. Then came the serfs (*thetes*) comprising the lower classes of the society (*dēmos*).

There was little room for the commoner in this culture; occasionally, a roaming vagabond might attain the status of a *Kouros*. Our information about education thus applies to the aristocracy of warriors. Education was largely in the form of an apprenticeship, to equip the young courtier with the skills and attitudes necessary to participate in knightly culture; it was carried out at home or in the court under the tutorship of such pedagogues as Chiron and Phoenix, Achilles' mentors.

In addition to explicit and semiformal training, the everyday activities of the youthful aristocrat were themselves educative. Sports, music, participation in religious festivals, and a style of courtly living and savoir

[6] *Ibid.*, p. 41.

faire, combined with training in the arts of war and speech, constituted the educative experiences and ideals of the Homeric hero.

The heroic pattern contrasts sharply with the primitive patterns discussed earlier. To be a hero or leader in the Homeric sense meant to be essentially unique. The youthful recruit into the society of heroes was imbued with the ideal that he must strive to be "always the best" and to "surpass all others." There was no room for the sluggish, the weak, the timid or the foolhardy. Military valor, excellence in oratory, perfect courtesy, a high sense of responsibility, magnanimity even towards the vanquished, and a high sense of duty toward oneself were the attributes of a leader. He was feared, respected, and to a degree even hated by his fellowmen.

The aristocratic ideal was very influential in shaping subsequent Greek educational thought and, we might say, Western European thought. Although Pindar in the sixth century was the last spokesman of this idea in its Homeric purity, elements of it survived down to the period of Athenian democracy in the fourth century and even later. The aristocratic emphasis on military valor and glory was woven into a philosophy of life and into a social system by Sparta—the first rigid monolithic state.

In a further analysis of the ancient origins of a rational approach to education, it will be helpful to examine more closely the two contrasting classical patterns that in some respects have modern parallels: the intellectually robust and democratic Athenian culture, and the intellectually bankrupt and monolithic Spartan culture.

THE SPARTAN PATTERN

Spartan society was very clearly and rigidly stratified. At the top were the *Spartiates*, numbering perhaps not more than 45,000 and constituting the privileged or elite citizen group; below them were the *perioikoi*, a class of free people without political rights; and at the bottom were the *helots* or serfs, who were severely kept down, tilled the soil, and contributed half of the produce to the citizens to whom they were bound. The *Spartiates'* overriding educational ideal was not the knightly hero in the full Homeric sense, but the devoted soldier. The Homeric ideal was a profoundly personal one, whereas the Spartan ideal was collective.

From their early years, the Spartan youth were brought up under a severe discipline in order to win their place among the group of citizen soldiers. The strong, who survived the tests of endurance, simple diet, exposure to the cold waters of the Evrotas and to the ruggedness of the mountains of Taygetos, pugilistic exercises, and the *pankration* and other contests, were inducted into the society of heroes; the weak and dull were disgraced and eliminated.

Spartan *agōgē*, one of the most exacting forms of education ever invented by man, was a lifelong process administered not only by special pedagogues (*paidonomoi*), but by all the adult citizens. Although there were no formal schools, the military training of the Spartan youth in the skills of war was done in the most systematic manner through the *paidonomoi*, through the youth organizations under the charge of the pluckiest boys, in the public messes, through games, and generally through a special mode of living. Spartan education is the classical model of a system in which individuality and freedom were subjected to the interests of the city-state (*polis*).

Like the Homeric aristocratic pattern, Spartan *agōgē* was the privilege of those who were citizens, generally by birth. There were rare occasions when citizenship rights were extended to certain *helots*. The Spartan citizen class was closed and self-perpetuating—characteristics that may account for its gradual diminution in numbers.

Within the citizen group, however, the special training not only inducted the youth into the values and mores of the society; it also acted as a selective agency for recruitment of leaders. In addition, every citizen was in large measure equal, and he could rise to leadership positions depending on his demonstrated proficiency in the most valued skills and attributes, namely, the military ones.

In the case of Athens, the archaic aristocratic traditions developed into a form different from that in Sparta. Athens passed from a warrior culture to what has been called a scribe culture. If Spartan education is epitomized in the word *agōgē*, Athenian education is epitomized in the word *paideia*. To a large degree Sparta carried out its *agōgē* through its youth organizations; Athens exercised its *paideia* through the first schools of Greece. Both systems retained elements of the aristocratic tradition. Even during the Golden Age of Athenian history, among the citizens (already a privileged group), the landed proprietors had more opportunities than the average Athenian. In spite of the common Hellenic heritage and many other similarities, the ideas, the content, and the form of Athenian education were quite different from the Spartan.

By the time of Pericles in the mid-fifth century, all Athenian citizens constituted the Assembly, which was the sole and final legislative body and which selected rulers by lot.

The Athenian constitution of the Periclean age accorded equality before the law and political rights, e.g., voting and speaking in the Assembly, to all Athenian citizens.[7] Appointment of state officials by lot lessened the possibility of attaining office through personal connections and financed electioneering. The highest officers of the state (the generals or admirals) were elected annually. This made it quite possible for an Athenian to be a general in one campaign and a private in another. Theoretically, every freeborn Athenian might receive the experience of every civic office. Political careers were open to everybody. Differences between the rich and the poor were not so great as to create groups which derived their power exclusively from economic status. In his funeral oration, as reported by Thucydides, Pericles was not painting an unrealistic picture of Athens when he called its government a democracy. In a well-known statement Pericles identified the salient features of Athenian democracy.

21

> It is true that we are called a democracy. For the administration is in the hands of the many and not of the few. But while the law secures equal justice to all alike in their private disputes, the claim of excellence is also recognized; and when a citizen is in any way distinguished, he is preferred to the public service, not as a matter of privilege, but as the reward of merit. . . .[8]

[7] Of course, as in Sparta, the citizen group in Athens was itself a sort of elite; below them in prestige and rights were the *metics*, freedmen, and slaves.
[8] Thucydides, "The Peloponnesian War" tr. Benjamin Jowett, in *The Greek Historians*, ed. F. R. B. Godolphin (New York: Random House, 1942), I, 648.

It was in the sixth and the fifth centuries that Athenian education reached its maturity, as conscious efforts were made to bring it in line with the development of Greek civilization. In the older period, education, though systematic, was carried out at home or, in special cases, under the *paidagogos* (leader of youth, teacher), who was usually a slave. In the sixth century at least two types of schools emerged: the *palaistra*, where young boys were engaged in physical exercises and the *didaskaleion* where music and the essentials for literacy were taught. The education that an Athenian citizen's son received had more symbolic than functional value in that positions in the society were not determined by the type of education one had.

But by the fifth century there were changes not only in the content of the citizen's education, but also in the role education performed in the society. Of major importance was the emergence of a group of teachers, called the Sophists, who assumed the task of training young Athenian aristocrats to become capable statesmen. The emergence of the Sophists on the Greek educational scene coincided with the breakdown of the old aristocracy eulogized by Homer, Pindar, and Theognis, and the emergence of a "bourgeois" city-state and a new citizen ideal. This necessitated a transformation of the old aristocratic concept of *aretē*, with its emphasis on heredity and warlike valor, into political *aretē*. Thus, in the fifth century, an intellectual component of education emerged which has dominated Greek and Western educational thought ever since. The Sophists claimed that political *aretē*, the sine qua non of political leadership, should be founded on knowledge. They professed, as all good teachers do, that they were capable of teaching such knowledge. The developments in the fifth century did not mean that Athens discarded all the vestiges of its aristocratic tradition, or that the system of the Sophists opened all the doors for the emergence of a new class of democratic politicians. The leaders continued for the most part to be recruited from the older or the wealthier families. Educational opportunities, even among the citizen group, varied depending on the socio-economic background of the parent.

Yet, in spite of these differentiations, education had acquired a new significance not only among the leaders, but also among the rest of the citizen group. For the latter, education was necessary in order to participate in the affairs of the polis; for the former, it was necessary in order to rise to political leadership, which was regarded as the noblest and the most highly coveted activity. But, although leadership may still have had a narrow recruiting base, the public affairs of the Athenian state were no longer considered to be the prerogative of a few families. Leadership was perhaps the more important of the two, and the Sophistic system of education aimed at precisely that. The Sophists always addressed themselves to a select audience. Their aim was the training of orators with skills in persuasion and political discourse.

The two problems that confronted Greek education of the fifth century, namely, education for citizenship and education for leadership, are universal problems of the modern state; they are not as conspicuous or pressing in primitive societies where there is no concern for the development of the intellectual powers of the individual. Before examining these problems in their modern context, we shall examine the Platonic model of education, which posits some provocative ideas regarding education for leadership. This model has also furnished some of the theoretical justifications of many European systems.

Much has been written and said about the *Republic,* the oldest and most systematic treatise on education. It has been eulogized, criticized, admired, and feared. Some have seen in it the archetype of the closed society and of indoctrination; others, the beginning of an open society and of a liberal education. For our purpose, the *Republic* will be examined as a model or an ideal type of a system of education.

The ideal expounded in the *Republic* and the purpose of the *Academy* centered in the education of an elite group destined to be the leaders of society, the guardians, and more importantly, the philosopher-kings. Yet it must not be forgotten that the Platonic elite was not a hereditary one based on ascriptive criteria of birth and wealth;[9] the crucial criteria for elite status were a certain type of knowledge and character, which could only be attained through a vigorous and selective system of education. Hence, in the Platonic framework education acquires a functional value: it alone determines the degree to which a person will be a craftsman, an auxiliary, or a philosopher-king. Furthermore, the education of the prospective rulers must be of a specific kind, and it must go beyond the level considered sufficient for the majority of citizens. At the highest level it included mathematics and dialectic. Excellence, in the Platonic scheme, was a composite of physical, moral, and intellectual excellence which very few people in the society had the ability and motivation to attain. Science, wisdom, and philosophy, the desiderata for leadership, can not be taught to the masses, since they lack the capacity or the desire to profit by them. Their capacities lay elsewhere; they could be used most profitably in the productive sectors of the society (craftsmen), and in the executive and defense sectors (auxiliaries). But the initiation and deliberation of policy must rest with the superelite group, the philosopher-kings. They alone are capable to direct the affairs of the state, because they alone know what is best for society. The philosopher-kings can never make a mistake.

The perfect and just society, therefore, according to Plato, is that which recognizes certain fundamental differences in human nature and potential, and assigns people to perform those functions for which they are best suited. This was based on the psychological principle that there are three elements in human nature, the appetitive, the spirited, and the philosophic or rational, each of which corresponds to three social subdivisions: the craftsmen, merchants, and farmers; the auxiliaries; and the philosopher-kings. Thus, for example, those who possess the appetitive element may best satisfy it through productive activities aiming at wealth and gain; those with the spirited nature are characterized by courage, a desire for competition, and warlike activities; and those with the philosophic element possess all the necessary moral and intellectual qualities for leadership functions.

In this pyramidal three-tiered social structure, tasks are assigned on the basis of demonstrated competence and achievement. Since every individual performs the role for which he is best suited, he will have no claims or

---

[9] It is true, of course, that in the ideal state, Plato envisaged a society where rulers would breed rulers; hence, there would be little, if any, admixture of the various social classes and little mobility. However, he also stated quite explicitly that it is possible for an individual to be born into the lowest social stratum and climb the ladder to leadership status, and conversely, for a highborn individual to go down the social ladder.

aspirations to any other position. Doing what he is capable and desirous of doing will also ensure his own happiness and *pari passu* the happiness of his fellowmen and the society as a whole. Ideally this felicitous state need not be changed since any change of the perfect and harmonious will result in imperfection and disharmony. Such questions as equality of opportunity and individual freedom have no substantive meaning, because equality presupposes the existence of inequality, and freedom presupposes a state of affairs which constrains the individual. To be sure, in the Platonic scheme the rulers initiate and direct policy. They are at the helm of the state craft, and they are not accountable to anybody. Unlike the Athenian democratic ideal eulogized by Pericles, they are both the originators and the sound judges of policy.

To some, this social philosophy is essentially totalitarian in the sense that the individual is subjected to the will of the state and that the decisions of the rulers do not depend on public will. Furthermore, the individual has no rights in the modern meaning of the term, except in the functions or services he performs. Karl Popper, one of Plato's severest modern critics, heaps upon the ancient philosopher all that is associated with totalitarianism (statism, holism, militarism, racism, anti-individualism, etc.). According to Popper, Plato's social system is a caste system; the intermingling of classes is forbidden, the breeding and the education of the rulers are nothing else but a class symbol and prerogative, and an indispensable instrument to ensure the stability of an elite system. Popper further maintains that Plato relegated a most burdensome task to educational institutions by assuming that their function should be the selection of future leaders and their training for leadership.[10]

A more careful analysis of the Platonic system suggests that it resembles a class system more than a caste system. As in most class systems, there is a social hierarchy with the rulers (philosopher-kings) at the top, the auxiliaries in the middle, and the farmers and merchants at the bottom. Each of these classes has different responsibilities, different powers, and common values. Of the three classes the superelite group is also the most important for the proper functioning of the state. However, it should also be borne in mind that Plato allowed for both upward and downward social mobility, at least in the early stages of the development of the state. Furthermore, unlike caste systems, one of the ruler's responsibilities is to descend, so to speak, or to return to the cave, as Plato puts it, in order to enlighten the people and break the chains of their ignorance. Finally, and this is perhaps most important, the rulers were not recruited and selected because of their noble blood or their race, but because of demonstrated superior ability and educational attainment. Thus, education in the Platonic system, unlike caste-systems, is an agency of intellectual and *ipso facto* social selection—a function, it should be noted, which is becoming more and more characteristic of many modern societies. Plato, in short, provides us with the earliest example of the perfect meritocracy.

The exceedingly heavy educational demands made upon the individual, and the highly idealistic nature of the scheme proposed by Plato, were questioned by his contemporaries, and notably by the great classical teacher Isocrates. To those bred in the Periclean age, an educational system which was *exclusively* concerned with the selection and training of a

---

[10] K. R. Popper, *The Open Society and Its Enemies* (London: Routledge & Kegan Paul, Ltd., third ed., 1957), I, 47-51, 86-119, 121-27.

small group of expert statesmen, although a challenge, was quite impractical. It is true that the Periclean system of government was based on the notion that even in a democracy there will always be the few who will originate policy; but it was also founded on the further idea that policy should be *judged* by every citizen, hence education should be both for the leaders and for the citizens. In a sense the Periclean concept of democracy has its parallel in the American political philosophy, namely, that each citizen is capable of full participation in the body politic. Plato's scheme was a dialectical reaction to the Periclean one. For Plato, Periclean democracy was nothing more than rule by the mob, what he called *ochlocracy*. But he also had no illusions about the utopian nature of his ideal state. Plato realized this himself, and in the end he turned to a "personalist type of wisdom." The original ideal of a perfect state was thus transformed to a personal ideal of inner perfection.[11]

SUMMARY

In primitive cultures and in the Hellenic societies of antiquity, education was found to be largely a process of socialization and imitation. The young were inducted into the values of the society and trained in certain skills by parents, elders, or—as in the case of the Homeric world—by special tutors. In some respects, all those cultures were found to be highly personal, and centering in the individual family unit. Yet, even in such societies, certain educational activities were found to be highly formal and aimed at the training of the young for specific social roles.

The review of the Hellenic cultures revealed that, unlike many primitive societies, the early stages of what we normally refer to as civilized existence placed heavy emphasis upon the education and training of leaders who would be clearly differentiated from the rest of the people. Thus, in the Western tradition, formal education for leadership emerged as a distinct cultural characteristic in classical Greece. The aristocratic, personal tradition portrayed by Homer was followed by the growth of communal existence within cities and the growth of different social classes. On the one hand, there was Sparta with its monolithic militaristic social order and its emphasis upon warlike valor, obedience, and austerity; and on the other, there was Athens, which by the middle of the fifth century had developed into a "bourgeois" type of democracy, with a constitution that accorded equal rights to the citizens but not to the slaves metics, with a scribe rather than a military culture, and with schools and inquiring minds.

The reason for these differences in the development of the two cities must be sought in such factors as the growth of the Athenian mercantile economy and the rise of a middle class, as well as the appearance of the sophists who were well versed in the skills of persuasion and public debate. The wealthy middle classes of Athens were influential in breaking down the old hereditary aristocracy, and they jolted traditional beliefs and values; the Sophists presented a new ideal of leadership and questioned older views of man and society. It is interesting to observe that the political participation by a group of people who are trained in the art of persuasion, e.g.,

[11] See H. I. Marrou, *A History of Education in Antiquity*, tr. George Lamb (New York: Sheed and Ward, 1956), p. 78.

lawyers and some types of intellectuals, has been found to be associated with the growth of political democracy. Conversely, such a group has been found to be relatively absent in nondemocratic countries, e.g., Sparta and the Soviet Union.

In both Athenian and Spartan societies education performed a selective social function in that positions were allocated or achieved in terms of the established educational criteria. In addition, however, there was a status hierarchy associated with the different social positions. Thus, education was an important factor in the status role of the individual as well. It should be emphasized, however, that selection did not apply to the noncitizen groups (slaves, *perioikoi, metics*). This *de jure* discrimination concerning educational opportunities between the citizens and the noncitizens has in varying degrees and forms modern parallels, e.g., the Union of South Africa with its policy of *apartheid*. In the United States, discrimination against the Negroes took different forms: from 1896 to 1954 the prevalent doctrine of "separate but equal" made it legal for schools to differentiate between white and Negro; in 1954 this practice was declared unconstitutional. Yet, even today there is ample evidence to show that in some states the idea of "separate but equal" persists, while in others there is *de facto* segregation.

Moreover, although in both Athens and Sparta there was what may be called legal and political equality, there were differences in educational opportunities even among the citizen group; some individuals had, by virtue of wealth or birth, more educational advantages. This, as will be shown later, again has its modern parallels. Plato's theoretical system of education is also selective, and has been interpreted in at least two different ways: as a caste system with sole emphasis upon ascriptive criteria of selection; and as a class system with emphasis upon talent, interest, and achievement. It would appear that in Plato's ideal *Republic* the concept of equality of educational opportunity would have no substantive meaning, since ultimately recruitment into the various strata would be conditioned and self-perpetuating. People would not have the capacity, motivation, or interest to attain more than what they are actually doing.

In the primitive cultures, we found that educational activities induce the individual into the common values of the culture and train him to perform certain specialized roles. Although the members of such societies are differentiated according to certain types of activity and position, nevertheless there is a relative absence of evaluative criteria according to which people are placed within a status hierarchy. As Dorothy Lee has observed, the idea of equality of opportunity becomes irrelevant.

We have seen that the ancient Athenian society was differentiated into social groups with the citizens possessing certain privileges and rights. Within the citizen group itself there were social classes with corresponding educational opportunities for each class. However, because of the size of the citizen group and its relative economic equality, the educational inequalities were not very pronounced. We have also seen that the Greeks raised some significant questions about education. On the one hand, the Sophists, although concerned with the training of the political elite, maintained that all individuals are educable in the affairs of citizenship. In the same vein, Pericles implied that everybody is capable of judging policy. On the other hand, Plato distrusted the masses and their ability to be sound judges, and he vested all authority in the hands of a selected few. European education was deeply rooted in the Greek intellectual tradition. In particular, the Platonic scheme remained a blueprint of many systems of education. Although the content of the ideal ruler underwent transformations, the concern for the education of the leaders rather than the masses has

THE MEDIEVAL BACKGROUND AND THE EMERGENCE OF NATIONAL SYSTEMS

3

characterized European education right up to the last couple of centuries, and in some instances pervades educational thinking and practice today.

FEUDAL EUROPEAN SOCIETIES

In the medieval European feudal period societies were demarcated into distinct social classes. Feudal societies were stratified in the form of a pyramid with kings at the summit and serfs at the base. In between, there were various gradations of power ranging from territorial principalities to baronies or castellanies. The kings claimed descent from God. Through high priests (prelates) they received the insignia of their office and were anointed with consecrated oil which, according to Catholic liturgy, invested them with a sacred character. On the other hand, the various lords, princes, barons, and knights were personally and territorially subordinated to the kings. A differentiated cluster of powers, duties, and obligations went with each of these social groupings. Thus, for example, a lord had certain obligations not only to the king, but to the knights below him, who in turn had certain obligations to their master, i.e., the lord, and to the serfs below them. There was a clear-cut system of superordination, and a person was bound to another through the bonds of "vassalage." The bond of vassalage was very strong and permeated every facet of a person's life, including family relationships.

It should be noted, however, that this well-defined, orderly system did not operate in a well-defined, orderly manner. Often subordinates became more powerful than their masters and quite autonomous. William the Conqueror, for example, although a vassal to the King of France, established his own authority, invaded and conquered England, and set up a separate kingdom.

Education in feudal societies corresponded to the class system. Generally speaking, there were two major classes: the nobility, including the higher clergy; and the peasantry. The background of the nobles at the beginning of the feudal period was diverse, but gradually the "most noble" signified persons of birth, wealth, power, and supremacy of rank. Nobles owned land, treasures, and jewels; but they did not directly engage in economic activities. A noble's main function was as warrior, and he always fought on horseback. The education of the feudal nobility was largely a process of socialization. The young nobleman was "socialized" at home or in the lord's castle in the values and skills befitting a warrior-gentleman, namely, hunting, wrestling, riding, dancing, singing, general etiquette, courtly love, and genial behavior, as well as a modicum of literary knowledge.

High accomplishments in the field of scholarship or, indeed, a high degree of literary culture, were not characteristic of the feudal nobility. There were, of course, many exceptions and, as Marc Bloch has pointed out, "it was commonly deemed proper that a leader of men should have access to the treasurehouse of thoughts and memories to which the written word, that is to say Latin, alone provided the key . . ."[1] Nevertheless, it was not uncommon to find many illiterates among the noble class. The term "cultured gentlemen" belongs to a later period, not

[1] Marc Bloch, *Feudal Society*, tr. L. A. Manyon (London: Routledge & Kegan Paul, Ltd., 1961), p. 79.

the medieval feudal societies. Thus, unlike the Platonic ideal, institutional education did not perform the function of recruiting and selecting the ruling classes. A noble and a ruler were born into the noble and ruling class, and high culture—when it was pursued—was merely of a symbolic rather than a functional value. The criteria for status differentiation not only between nobleman and serf, but among nobles themselves, were mostly ascriptive, i.e., wealth and birth.

Formal education in the medieval feudal period was largely in the hands of the church. Through different types of schools (monastic, cathedral, parish, etc.), the church sought to instruct the clergy and the people in Christian beliefs, in morals, in the essentials of reading and arithmetic, and in the liberal arts. This form of education was regarded as important for the recruitment of priests and Christians to church membership. Of all classes of feudal societies the clergy were the most educated, although in some cases ignorant men managed to secure appointments to high ecclesiastical posts.

The medieval emperors, kings, and lords encouraged the educational efforts of the clergy, and in some instances—in the case of Charlemagne, for example—invited learned scholars to set up schools to instruct the clergy and laymen and to prepare them for various positions in the society. In general, the ruling elite relied heavily on the clergy for services which their own entourage could not supply. The clergy were employed as interpreters of the ideas of the great thinkers of the past and as guardians of political traditions.

Judged by modern standards, opportunities for formal education in the medieval period were limited. In the absence of a public system of education the masses of the people relied on the charitable efforts of the church for their education. Although through the church efforts many poor children received the rudiments of knowledge and some rose to high positions, the vast majority of the peasant laboring groups lived a life of poverty and ignorance.

With the expansion of trade and the growth of cities after the eleventh century, the system of apprenticeship became an important educational institution in the recruitment and training of skilled artisans to perform new occupational roles. During this period the Western university emerged as an educational institution whose major purpose was to recruit and select people for professional careers. The medieval university had clearly defined functions and a clearly defined curriculum consisting of the seven liberal arts (grammar, rhetoric, logic, arithmetic, geometry, astronomy, and music). It was essentially a professional school, training people to be clerics, teachers, theologians, lawyers, and doctors, i.e., the professional elite.

The period between the fourteenth and the seventeenth centuries witnessed the further expansion of trade and the growth of urban centers, with a concomitant rise of the middle classes. In addition, this was the period of the Renaissance and Reformation, and the gradual emergence of national states. All these factors had an impact on education. In the first place, the position of the church as the sole agency controlling education was threatened by lay bodies (towns, lay rulers, etc.). In the second place, the ideal of the educated man, and the content of his education underwent significant transformations. The pre-Renaissance ideal of the educated man was dominated by religious considerations and emphasized Christian humility, asceticism, saintly virtues, and other wordliness; on the other hand, the Renaissance ideal was that of the *uomo universale,* characterized by the possession of a combination of classical and Christian virtues. The content of education became heavily classical in its emphasis. Classical education and its assumptions emerged as the basic desiderata of the new ideal of man, the scholar-gentleman, and have dominated Western European education right up to the nineteenth century. This new classical orientation opened up new vistas in the conception of man and his role in the society. The Humanists sought to free the individual from the shackles of older forms of authority and to assert his own individuality.

Like the classical prototypes of Greece and Rome, formal education during the humanistic period, and as late as the eighteenth century, was largely intended for the upper classes of society. Vittorino da Feltre's famous school at Mantua, Italy, trained future scholars and elites in government, the church, and the military. It thus became a model of the Renaissance education for a gentlemanly class. Educational opportunities corresponded to the gradations of society. The masses continued to rely on voluntary efforts, but most of their education was provided through informal agencies, e.g., apprenticeship and the home. It is significant that the origins of European education, especially at the secondary and university levels, were essentially aristocratic. The primary concern was the education of an elite group. This was to be expected, since wealth and power were the privilege of the upper classes. But education for an elite group has been so much a part of the pedagogical and ideological tradition of Europe that it continues to be a powerful force today.

30

OTTOMAN ISLAMIC SOCIETY

The medieval feudal West affords only one illustration of a system of stratification and its relation to education prior to the emergence of modern national systems. Equally important, however, for an understanding of modern ideas and practices, is the institutional structure exemplified by the medieval Ottoman Islamic state.

A distinguishing characteristic of the feudal West was the existence of "estates," which were clearly defined and differentiated as well as almost hereditary social strata. The Ottoman society of the time was also socially differentiated and stratified, but it was not marked by the existence of a closed aristocracy based on wealth and birth, as the Western societies were. To be sure, there were great inequalities of power and wealth, and a bifurcation between the elite and the peasant masses; but, paradoxically, the Ottoman system, unlike that of the feudal West, maintained a comparatively fluid system of recruitment of talent.

At the very top of the Ottoman social pyramid was the ruling elite consisting of the Sultan and his personal clique, and the high military, civil, and ecclesiastical officials; at the very bottom were the peasants of Anatolia, Rumelia, and the other provinces of the Ottoman Empire. The administration of the empire was in the hands of the elite; the peasants, for all meaningful purposes, constituted a large nonparticipating mass. Yet the ruling elite did not form a self-perpetuating and closed caste. During the early centuries of the Ottoman Empire members of the nonreligious elite were recruited through the system of *devşirme* from the non-Moslem, mostly Christian, subjects on the basis more of merit than of wealth or birth. These young, promising *devşirme* were selected by specially trained representatives of the Sultan, and they were educated in the Sultan's Palace School (*Enderun Mektebi*) located in the middle of the seraglio at Constantinople. Within the Palace School promotion from one grade to the next depended on demonstrated competence and achievement in military and educational accomplishments. Upon graduation the most meritorious of the group were assigned high-level positions in the military and civil bureaucracies. This rather open system of recruitment, advancement, and placement applied also to the ecclesiastical branch of the polity, the *Ulema* group. It was not until the late eighteenth and the nineteenth centuries, that the high *Mollas* in this group developed into a closed religious aristocracy.

A distinguishing feature of the Ottoman system of career opportunities for elite status was the functional role of education. In all the branches of the government education and individual achievement were important conditions for occupational placement and for promotion. In the case of the military and the civil branches of the administration, the Palace School was a training ground and a selective agency for mobility and placement; in the case of the religious institution, this function was performed by the *medreses*, the higher religious colleges. As in the medieval feudal West, however, the masses received very little, if any, formal schooling, and what limited education they did receive was largely in the form of education for basic socialization.

The ideal of universal, compulsory, and public education is relatively modern. It is one of the basic solutions to the problem of recruiting children into the culture of a society. The form which this ideal took during and after the Reformation set the pattern for subsequent centuries, and even today vestiges of it are to be seen in certain European countries.

This was the two-track system whereby the masses had access to one type of schooling—an inferior kind—and the upper classes to another. The common people received their education in the vernacular and vocational schools, "common" schools, and the higher classes in literary-humanistic schools of which the Latin grammar school became the most typical example. This trend became more and more crystallized in the eighteenth and nineteenth centuries when in most countries the state assumed more responsibility for education. The example set by Austria and Prussia in the public provision and secularization of education was followed by the United States, France, England, and Russia.

Several conditions accounted for the increased importance placed upon schools as recruiting agencies in the society. One was the upsurge of nationalism, characteristic of the nineteenth century. The identification of people with common political and cultural ties and aspirations heightened the importance of schools as agents of political socialization and to imbue the young with the ideas and values of the national state. There is ample evidence in past and present societies to support this generalization. One of the first concerns of nations immediately after attaining independence is education. Education becomes the central agency for the development and maintenance of national consciousness. It becomes an instrument of the state to free the nation from foreign cultural and political ties and influences. This was true of America in the eighteenth and nineteenth centuries, of the states that won political independence from the Ottoman Empire, and of several Asian and African nations in the twentieth century.

The historical phenomenon known as the "Industrial Revolution" brought about several economic, social and intellectual changes and enlarged the schools' responsibilities. Industrialization meant diverse occupations requiring differentiated and specialized skills; it meant urbanization, the growth of factories and slums, a different social structure and major changes in intergroup relationships. To some, this revolution seemed to breed moral deterioration; to others it heightened the need for a more literate populace. Philanthropic endeavors in England extended educational opportunities to the poor, and by the end of the nineteenth century legislation for the compulsory education of the masses resulted. In the United States, industrialism hastened the growth of publicly supported and controlled common schools.

Growth of industrialization was a factor in the emergence of different political alignments, in a new type of educational differentiation, and in competing social ideologies. This was the period of the emergence of an industrial capitalism with a strong bourgeois middle class. In England and in the United States, under the protective cover of political and legal freedom, capitalism was left unhampered in maximizing its economic gains. This condition contributed to acute differences in the distribution of wealth. The laboring classes began to organize into what might be called a "fourth estate," and thus became an important new political and economic force. Societies of the West were rather sharply demarcated by upper, middle, and lower groups—each of which demanded its share in the benefits of the new social order and sought to guard jealously its gains.

In the United States, political and legal freedom meant the possession of certain inalienable rights, e.g., life, liberty, prosperity, and the pursuit of happiness. The natural rights theory fired the imaginations of the revolutionary generation, and immediate steps were taken to implement this idea. It was also assumed that freedom and equality could best be ensured through the enlightenment of the people. Thus, during the revolutionary period numerous plans for the establishment of a system of national education suited to the realities and genius of the new republic were formulated by liberal thinkers, such as Benjamin Rush, Robert Coram, Noah Webster, and Samuel Knox. However, it was not until the first half of the nineteenth century that a public common school system took form. Likewise, in England it was not until 1870 that the foundations of a national system of education were laid. Prior to that date the prevailing social philosophy was laissez-faire liberalism which placed heavier emphasis upon individual legal and political freedom than upon the creation of conditions for educational and economic equality. The liberal temper of the time called for the extension of the franchise, reform of local government, and abolition of certain privileges of the Established Church and of patronage in the civil services.

It would be wrong, however, to assume that the doctrines of political liberalism and legal equality in Europe and America resulted in equality of educational opportunity as well. The European educational systems of the nineteenth century corresponded rather closely to the prevailing social stratification patterns. The type and amount of education one had or could have depended to a large degree on one's social and economic background. Thus, for example, the education of the lower classes in France, Germany, and England usually ended at about the age of fourteen, and it was provided in socially inferior institutions, e.g., elementary schools in England, *écoles primaires* in France, and *Volksschulen* in Germany. On the other hand, the education of the middle and upper classes was provided in separate preparatory schools and it continued into secondary schools and finally into the universities. In France, the upper and middle classes had access to the *lycées* and the *collèges*, in England to endowed grammar schools, and in Germany into the *Mittelschulen* and the *Gymnasien*. One might say that in education there was institutional inequality. This was even truer of Russia, where society continued to be stratified on medieval feudal lines until well into the nineteenth century. At the very top there was a hereditary nobility who were educated in "cadet schools" and *lyceums*; beneath them were the small middle class, clergy, poorer urban dwellers, and artisans who sent their children to "elementary schools" (*shkoly gramotnosti*) and the gymnasia; and at the very bottom there was the large peasant group who, for the most part, sent their children to various types of popular institutions (schools of the *zemstvos*, church schools, *mektebes*, urban schools, etc.).

In all these countries the class barriers were rather rigid, especially between the lower, poorer classes and those above them. For example, the chances of the working segments of society to enter a grammar school, a *lycée*, or a Russian *gymnasium* were almost nonexistent, although by no means completely absent. In Germany, a lower-class child had good opportunities to move from the *Volksschule* to the *Mittelschule*, but almost none to the *Gymnasium*.

It should be noted, however, that the determinants of recruitment into the different schools were not the result of any legislative decrees. Theoretically, anyone could attend the *lycée*, the *Gymnasium*, or the grammar school, provided he possessed the requisite intellectual competence; indeed, some people from the lowest classes did. However, in addition to intellectual criteria, e.g., the passing of stringent examinations, especially in France and Germany, there were also social and economic criteria. For example, secondary schools charged fees which rendered attendance by the poorer classes rather difficult. Also there was little articulation between an elementary and a secondary school: the former, was more of a terminal institution and consequently the curriculum was in many respects different from that of the preparatory schools attached to the secondary schools. Each type of educational institution had clearly defined functions. Thus, the various elementary schools trained pupils in the basic skills of literacy and in certain vocational skills; the secondary schools prepared students for middle-level professional careers, for the universities, and thereby for high offices in the state, the church, and the higher professions.

In many respects the educational pattern of nineteenth century America was different from the European. The principle of corporate, public responsibility in education had its roots in the colonial period. During the time of the revolution, as mentioned earlier, several plans were proposed to establish a system of education, "republican" in form and spirit, compulsory, and free for all. It was assumed that political consensus in a democratic society was impossible without an enlightened citizenry. In the first half of the nineteenth century, this ideology found expression in the common school movement advocated by Horace Mann, Henry Barnard, James Carter, Calvin Stowe and others. The common school in America was not for the common people, as in Europe, but was common to all the people. Furthermore, the common school was envisaged as a "social leveler," i.e., as an institution which would blur social distinctions. By the time of the Civil War, this type of school had become a reality, and America, unlike the European nations, enlarged the base of recruitment and created a different framework for education. The reasons for these variations are many, but among them one must include the existence in America of a more fluid class structure, the absence of deeply entrenched traditional institutions, and the emerging influence of a frontier ideology.

During this period, characterized by the emergence of nationalism and a conscious effort on the part of the state to establish a publicly controlled and supported system of education, the Ottoman Islamic system retained most of its original elements. For example, the system of government continued to be theocratic and absolute, and popular education remained largely in the hands of the *Ulema*. Indeed, the major social groups became more solidified and the system of recruitment into the schools and the occupations lost its previous openness and fluidity. However, during the nineteenth century, especially during the *Tanzimat* (reorganization), there were already visible signs of change. Several attempts were made to place education under state agencies, and to set up a new organization of schools into primary, middle, and secondary categories. New Western-oriented institutions, e.g., the Imperial *lycée* at Galatasaray, were introduced. In spite of these innovative elements, it was not until the Revolution of 1923 that a major educational transformation took place.

34

SUMMARY

In this section we have examined the characteristic features of European feudal and the Ottoman Islamic societies and the changes that ensued through the nineteenth century. In feudal Europe, formal education corresponded to and reinforced the existing feudal estates. The church provided limited basic education to the masses of the people, whereas a more advanced type of education was confined to the nobility and the higher clergy. Social mobility through education was almost nonexistent. In contrast, the Ottoman Islamic society represented a fairly open system of recruitment, advancement, and placement, in spite of the fact that the system of government was absolute and theocratic. This, in and of itself, did not mean that the Ottoman society exhibited the characteristics attributed to democratic states. A poor child could through education become a Grand Vizier, one of the highest officials in the civil bureaucracy. Nevertheless, such a person continued to be regarded as the personal "slave" of the Sultan, who was the final authority in all major decisions. The Ottoman case points up an interesting observation, namely, that the existence of an open pattern of social recruitment and selection may be a necessary but not a sufficient condition for democracy. "Democracy" is a term that encompasses other important elements, including freedom of inquiry and choice, and a share in political power.

The complete breakdown of the feudal order, the revival of learning, the rise of commercialism and industrialism, and the emergence of modern national states were accompanied by changes in the nature and function of education. Formal schooling, especially at the primary level, became an important means of developing political consensus in the new societies. Hence, by the end of the nineteenth century most European countries and the United States had already introduced legislation for free, compulsory, and universal elementary education. However, the principle of universal education was not extended to include secondary schools, which continued to be selective institutions, and in Europe at least, retained some of the aristocratic features of the previous eras. In the European countries, elementary and secondary education constituted two almost separate systems corresponding to the prevailing gradations in the society. The various schools within this two-track arrangement had clearly defined functions and different curricula. The elementary schools provided the basic skills of literacy and some vocational training, and prepared for low-level occupations; the secondary schools offered a general academic course of study and prepared for the universities and for middle- and upper-level careers. In the United States the common school movement of the nineteenth century established the basis for an organically related system of education. In the opening decades of the twentieth century, the common school idea was pushed upward into the high school, which took the form of a multifunctional comprehensive institution.

Our review of the educational developments in Europe and the United States suggests the following generalizations: that highly-differentiated systems of education are found in highly-stratified societies; and that in such societies the various types and levels of schooling have clearly-defined functions. For example, in the European societies of this period we do not find the all-encompassing and often discordant purposes of the American high school; the English grammar school and the French *lycée* had the explicit function of preparing for the university or for specific occupations.

The process of industrialization, urbanization, and secularization gathered accelerated momentum in the twentieth century and brought about educational changes in all societies that were affected by them. In addition, the twentieth century has witnessed overwhelming events such as two world wars which created certain conditions conducive to educational change.

In elementary education there were at least two significant developments in most European countries. First, there was a change in the social status of education; and second, there was a change in the pedagogical theory underlying it. For instance, in Germany the *Grundschule*, a uniform elementary school, was introduced; in England, the Act of 1944 replaced the class-oriented elementary schools by primary schools for all; and similar measures were taken in France.

In Russia, as late as 1909, the idea of compulsory attendance was not yet firmly established. Ten years later, however, one of the main preoccupations of the Soviet revolutionary government in its program of radical social change was the organization of a free and compulsory system of education for both sexes up to the age of seventeen. The Soviet revolutionary thinkers

CONTEMPORARY SOCIETIES

4

conceived of compulsory education as an indispensable means of creating the Marxist-Leninist utopia. Thus, they sought to eliminate the previous structure by setting up a different type of school which, in the words of Lunacharsky, the first Soviet Commissar of Education, would be "the school of the proletarian class."

As these societies developed more complex economies, as political power was realigned to accommodate the pressures of new political groupings, and as new social ideologies emerged, compulsory attendance at the lowest level of education was found to be inadequate. The acquisition of basic literary skills, although necessary for political consensus and the general socialization of the individual, was found to be insufficient. The mechanization of all areas of the productive sector (agriculture, manufacturing, etc.) required technical knowledge and skills beyond those which were attained through the system of apprenticeship or the elementary schools. Such knowledge and skills became necessary not only for purposes of production, but also for the distribution of goods and services, and for living in general. In addition, increased urbanization, a phenomenon of industrialization, created certain psychological and social problems, e.g., increased crime rate, creation of slums, etc., which in turn called for more and better education. Finally, the great impetus given to democratic ideologies in the West during the periods following the two world wars accelerated the movement toward social equality and greater educational opportunities.

Thus, in most industrially developed societies the compulsory school-leaving age has been raised to include post-elementary education, and attempts have been made to broaden the social base of recruitment into secondary schools and institutions of higher learning. Together with changes in policies of recruitment into the educational institutions, emphasis has been placed upon the process of selection as well. More specifically, there have been changes in the methods of selection (examinations, tests, etc.), in the age level at which selection should take place, and in the form of selection (through allocation or elimination). Although changes in recruitment and selection have characterized most advanced societies, and although, in the main, such changes have been justified on the same ideological grounds, the style, and stratagems of these processes have varied according to historical traditions, economic, political, and religious conditions, material resources, and the general value structure of each society.

Although primary education continues to occupy the attention of educators and school reformers, it would be true to say that most pedagogical activity in developed societies has recently centered on secondary education. Numerous plans have been formulated affecting curriculum, methods of instruction, the organization and administration of schools, etc.

As shown earlier, the most important determinants of recruitment in the previous centuries were the economic and social position of parents. The twentieth century witnessed systematic attempts to shift these determinants from those of ascription to those of intelligence, achievement, and individual aptitudes, needs, and interests. This has been true not only of the United States, but of England, France, Germany, Sweden, and the Soviet Union. But each country has given different interpretations to these ideas, and the individual patterns and practices have varied. On the other hand, in no country, including America, have social and economic factors been eliminated, and there is evidence to show that children from high social-status groups have decidedly more advantages both for secondary and higher education.

In England, France, and Germany there is currently legislation affirming the responsibility of the State to provide formal education, not only at the primary stage, but for a number of years beyond it. In all three countries it is further decreed that there should be equality of educational opportunity, and that no child should be debarred from an education according to his ability, needs, and interests because of economic, social, or even intellectual reasons. In implementing this policy, emphasis has been placed upon public examinations in order to assess the abilities of the elementary school graduates and to place them in appropriate secondary institutions. All three countries have adopted a diversified system of secondary education, each constituent element of which provides different amounts and quality of education and performs clearly defined functions. But efforts to expand secondary education and to "democratize" it have been greatly influenced by the indigenous cultural traditions. Thus, in the plans for reorganization and change these nations have had to take into consideration the tradition of private education, the magical appeal of institutions like the grammar school, the *lycée*, and the *Gymnasium*, with their academic and intellectual bias, the idea that equality in education does not mean identity but variation, and the view that a democratic state cannot function properly unless it is guided by a well-educated and competent elite.

THE ENGLISH PATTERN

The tripartite system of secondary education in England, which was recommended after the passing of the 1944 Education Act, was justified on the grounds that since children differed in "tastes and abilities" their education must also differ.[1]

In order to gauge the tastes and abilities of the students and to select them for the appropriate type of school, the system of examinations known as the eleven-plus was more widely used. On the basis of the results of the eleven-plus, usually given upon completion of the elementary grades and with the parents' consent, students have been admitted to the Grammar Schools, the Technical Schools and the Modern Schools. Theoretically, students who were originally assigned to one type of school at the age of twelve or thirteen were transferred to another if their performance and inclination justified it. In practice, however, such transfer has been rare.

It should be stressed that since the Hadow Report of 1926, tripartitism and secondary school selection were not seen as antithetical to the principle of equality in education.[2] R. A. Butler, one of the architects of the 1944 act, agreed that "equal educational opportunities" was not "identical educational opportunities." Nonselectivity and nondiversity, according to

---

[1] Ministry of Education, *The New Secondary Education* (London: His Majesty's Stationery Office, 1947), Pamphlet No. 9, p. 22.

[2] Board of Education, *Report of the Consultative Committee on the Education of the Adolescent* (London: His Majesty's Stationery Office, 1926), pp. 78-79. Hereafter cited as the Hadow Report.

Butler, would stunt and retard the growth of the "uncommon child." [3]

The recruitment and training of leaders has always been central to British pedagogical theory and practice. In the nineteenth century leaders were recruited primarily from the upper segments of society, where intelligence, rationality and sobriety, as well as the social and personal characteristics for leadership were presumed to reside. With the increased importance placed upon education as a qualification for leadership, the school assumed a more positive role in the selection and training of leaders. The idea of a cadre of experts to lead and initiate policy in all walks of life—which, as we have seen earlier, has its prototype in the Platonic model—has been viewed as central to British democracy. This emphasis on the gifted or talented partly accounts for the lükewarm reception in England, at least by the Conservatives, of the comprehensive school idea. Many Englishmen are anxious lest comprehensiveness on a large scale should fail to develop the intelligence and "professional expertise" so necessary for the survival of British democracy. [4]

The 1944 act was passed by a coalition government (Conservative and Labour) in the name of democracy and social equality. However, since that time, especially during the fifties, tripartitism and the policy of selection at eleven-plus have been criticized by various groups, the most prominent of which has been the Labour Party. The critics have attacked both policies as inequalitarian, antipedagogical, and contrary to modern psychological findings. It has been maintained that early segregation on the basis of intelligence is contributing to the substitution of an aristocracy of brains, a meritocracy, for the traditional aristocracy of wealth and birth, and that this new aristocracy is no less antidemocratic and fraught with dangers than the previous. [5] The voices of the critics have at times reached a high pitch when research into the recruitment patterns of the grammar schools, purportedly based on ability criteria, showed that there is a disproportionate representation of certain social classes. Although the number of children from the working class attending grammar schools has increased, their chances have remained the same as before the passing of the Education Act of 1944. Furthermore, it has been found that there are marked differences among subgroups within the laboring class. And according to a more recent survey of the education of the working class children in a northern industrial city, the "sixth forms" are heavily represented by middle-class children. [6]

On the other hand, the selective procedures in the secondary schools,

39

[3] R. A. Butler, "Education: The View of a Conservative," *The Year Book of Education* (London: Evans Brothers, 1952), pp. 35-36.

[4] For an insightful analysis of the comprehensive school idea in England, see Edmund King, "Comprehensive Schools in England: Their Context," *Comparative Education Review*, III, No. 2 (October 1959), 13-14; and "Comprehensive Schools in England: Their Prospects," *Comparative Education Review*, III, No. 3 (February 1960), 21.

[5] For a witty discussion of this subject, see Michael Young, *The Rise of the Meritocracy 1870-2033: The New Elite of Our Social Revolution* (New York: Random House, 1959).

[6] Jean Floud, "Education and Social Class in the Welfare State," in *Looking Forward in Education*, ed. A. V. Judges (London: Faber & Faber, Ltd., 1955), p. 43; and Brian Jackson and Dennis Marsden, *Education and the Working Class: A Survey by the Institute of Community Studies* (London: Routledge & Kegan Paul, Ltd., 1962). Also see criticisms by Liberal Party spokesmen in *The Times* (London) *Educational Supplement*, December 15, 1961.

and tripartitism, have been defended by other individuals and groups, by the Conservative government, and by the influential *Times Educational Supplement*. In a recent editorial on the subject, the *Supplement* frankly stated that selection is unavoidable since, whether people like it or not, the English society was "a selective society." The *Supplement* underscored the basic rationale for selection and tripartitism, viz., that talent was all important in England, and that it must be given full rein, that no better and more equitable alternatives than the eleven-plus have been found, and that the tripartite system was in accord with "human nature." [7]

The class bias of the secondary school system has also been found to be related to the performance of grammar school children. Nevertheless, class differences in educational opportunity and school achievement could be accounted for by culturally determined ability differences. It was found that there were class differences in the children's test scores which sought to measure "grammar school intelligence"; that is, relative to the social composition of the male population over fifteen years of age, there was a higher proportion of middle class than working class children who possessed "grammar school intelligence." On the basis of this social distribution, it has been concluded that when intelligence, as measured by existing instruments, is taken as the basic criterion of selection into grammar schools, class discrimination is more apparent than real, and a boy's chances are almost entirely independent of his social background. [8]

Now it may be contended that since the tests used to measure "grammar school intelligence," and notably the IQ test, are themselves culturally biased, class differences in the results are to be expected. Hence, the force of the argument of an existing equality in education is considerably blunted. On the basis of this cultural bias criticism, some local education authorities substituted other kinds of tests for the existing IQ test. However, attempts to devise culture-free instruments have been generally unsuccessful. It would appear that as long as there are social and economic inequalities, any type of test will be culturally biased. In a democracy the complete elimination of such differences is difficult to achieve. There will always be differences in income distribution, education of parents and their place of residence, friends, and cultural and recreational activities. Furthermore, education may be conceived as a means by which society transmits certain values to the younger generation. Such values may indeed be those of one predominant social group, in which case children who are born in that group will have more advantages than the others. Likewise, education in industrially advanced societies sorts out people for specialized training leading to high social positions. This selective function of the schools would tend to place the culturally-deprived and laboring classes at a disadvantage.

While opportunities for all types of education may be open to all segments of the society, there must also exist the necessary student motivation, stimulation, and interest in order to take the fullest advantage of, and to gain the maximum benefit from these opportunities. When these psychological factors are also taken into consideration, the social composition of student bodies in selective secondary schools may not be a true

---

[7] "Selective Society," *The Times* (London) *Educational Supplement*, February 16, 1962, p. 355; see also March 30, 1962, p. 631.

[8] Floud, *op. cit.*, p. 44. Also see J. E. Floud, *et al.*, *Social Class and Educational Opportunity* (London: William Heinemann Limited, 1958), p. 58.

reflection of the availability of education for working-class children. It has been found, for example, that in a London borough inhabited by working class families, highly intelligent children who had received scholarships to enter secondary schools refused to accept them because of subculture pressures, i.e., family and peer group pressures.[9] Other evidence indicates that working class children had difficulties of adjustment to the social and academic demands of grammar schools. Problems of this nature are a factor in the dropout rate among working-class children, although in many instances withdrawal is contrary to the wishes of their parents.

THE AMERICAN PATTERN

As stated earlier, in the nineteenth century a uniform common elementary school was established as the basis of a public and universal system of education. By the end of the century the high school, a distinctly American type of secondary school, organically related to the elementary school, had developed. In theory this public system of schooling was free and accessible to all social strata. Yet, as late as 1890 access to education beyond the primary stage (usually ending at the ages of thirteen or fourteen) was extremely limited. In New England in 1892, less than 10 per cent of the children were able to receive any form of post-elementary education; and in the United States as a whole, less than 7 per cent of the eligible children were enrolled in secondary schools. Therefore, at the time of the closing of the frontier, the high school was a selective institution catering to a privileged minority who aspired to some sort of higher education and professional careers. Even the epoch-making *Report of the Committee of Ten* of 1893 perceived the main function of the secondary schools "to prepare for the duties of life that small proportion of all the children in the country who show themselves able to profit by an education prolonged to the eighteenth year, and whose parents are able to support them while they remain so long at school." [10]

The Committee of Ten was essentially concerned with curriculum matters and with the articulation of the secondary school with the college. On the question of the curriculum it recommended the well-known four-track arrangement (classical, Latin-scientific, modern languages, and English), each of which included in varying proportions what might be called academic subjects. In principle at least, the committee sought to break down the hegemony of classics and mathematics for purposes of college admission, and thus to allow for curriculum flexibility and diversity. In addition, it recommended that all subjects in the four tracks be considered of equivalent value and be taught to all students alike, regardless of whether students intended to go to college or enter the various walks of life directly.

This equivalence of academic subjects was applauded by some as cutting across the class idea of education, and criticized by others, notably by G. Stanley Hall, as failing to take into consideration differences in ability and vocational aspirations. Charles W. Eliot, the chairman of the com-

41

[9] See Michael Young and P. Willmott, *Family and Kinship in East London* (London: Routledge & Kegan Paul, Ltd., 1957), pp. 146, ff.

[10] *Report of the Committee of Ten on Secondary School Studies with the Reports of the Conferences Arranged by the Committee* (New York: American Book Company, 1894), p. 51.

mittee, defended the proposals on the ground that they were in line with American democratic ideals and practices. Eliot claimed that the Americans, in contrast to the Europeans, should not select and classify children into the various occupational categories (peasants, mechanics, professionals, etc.) at an early age. It should not be construed, however, that Eliot and his committee endorsed an equalitarian conception of secondary education or of the curriculum. The equivalence of subjects was restricted to the academic subjects, and what developed in the twentieth century under that concept cannot be attributed to the Committee of Ten. Moreover, although uniformity in standards was urged, the committee advocated a system of electives and expressed concern for what we now refer to as individual differences. Eliot in particular had no illusions about natural psychological and intellectual inequalities in children. A true democracy, according to him, must extend educational opportunities to all children and must tap the talent from all strata of society. The school must be adapted to the individual differences, even if in practice that meant early separation.

Yet, secondary education was not envisaged as universal for all children, but only "for those who show themselves able to profit by it." The idea that the secondary school should be for all students and that, accordingly, it should be multifunctional did not emerge in any systematic form until the appearance of the Cardinal Principles of Education, promulgated by the Committee on the Reorganization of Secondary Education, in 1918. By that time, several conditions—social, political and intellectual—had made new demands upon the school and its role in society: increased industrialization, urbanization, and immigration, accompanied by the progressive movement with its emphasis upon social reform (including the expansion of educational opportunities) made a selective and predominantly intellectual type of secondary education inappropriate. The nineteenth century concept of faculty psychology and its associated doctrines of mental discipline and transfer of training, which underlay the views of the Committee of Ten, were rejected by such thinkers as E. L. Thorndike, G. Stanley Hall, William James, and John Dewey. In addition, this period was characterized by a rapid growth in secondary school enrollment. Accordingly, the Commission on Reorganization of Secondary Education sought to broaden the nature and scope of education and to extend the functions of the secondary school in order to cater to the multifarious needs and abilities of the large, diverse school population. In its recommendations, it outlined the objectives of secondary education as health, worthy home membership, command of fundamental processes, vocation, civic education, ethical character, and worthy use of leisure; it endorsed the idea of a "comprehensive" program to be adopted in all secondary schools of the country.

The cardinal principles of education and the institutional framework through which they were to be realized reflected a shift in the psychological assumptions upon which learning was based and in the role of the school concerning the individual and the society. Henceforth, the secondary school was not to be a selective institution and a mere adjunct to the college, but rather a school common to all and serving a variety of individual and social needs. The concept of equality in education meant the right of every individual regardless of his racial, ethnic, religious, intellectual, and economic background, or status, to at least a high school education. In short, he emerging basic rationale of secondary education was essentially the ame as that of the common school in the nineteenth century. Until ecently, subsequent statements by various educational bodies refined and xpanded this idea of secondary education rather than modified it. In the ast few years, there has been considerable criticism of and reaction to the ll-encompassing functions of the comprehensive school. In 1961, the Educational Policies Commission of the National Education Association paid lip service to the "cardinal principles," but stressed the development of the rational powers as "the central purpose of American education." Before examining the recent criticisms and developments concerning the nature and function of the secondary school, it would be appropriate to look into some findings regarding recruitment, selection, and equality of educational opportunity.

Although there is currently in the United States compulsory legislation hat covers a substantial portion of secondary education, this aspect of recruitment in and of itself belies many variations in the level and amount of education received by American youth. Several factors have been found o influence a child's opportunities for an education beyond the primary chool level. As in the case of England, there is in the United States an unequal social distribution of intelligence as gauged by the usual IQ tests; lower-class children have been found to be overrepresented in the 100 and below IQ scores; and conversely, middle-class children preponderate in he higher ranges of measured intelligence. When we further consider that ntelligence has also been found to be positively correlated with amount and level of education, then it is clear that there are social disparities in educational opportunity. In short, social class as well as intelligence, are mportant factors not only in determining who will finish high school but also who will go to college. Havighurst and his associates have found that, within the highest intelligence-quartile group in River City, 33 per cent of male students belonged to the upper and upper-middle classes and only 11 per cent to the lower-lower class. Conversely, no student from the former social class was represented in the lowest intelligence quartile, but 41 per cent of the latter were found in this quartile. The disparities were much greater among female students. They also found that about four-fifths of students of both sexes from the upper and upper-middle classes went to college, but only 2 in 57 boys, and none of the girls from the lower-lower classes, did so.[11] In another study, involving high school graduates in Iowa, it was found that 80 per cent of children from the professional occupational category entered college, whereas only 18 per cent of children of farmers and laborers did so.[12]

We also have sufficient evidence to show that ethnic and religious background are important factors in differential patterns of recruitment into the schools and colleges, when both intelligence and economic factors are held constant. It seems that children from certain ethnic and religious groups (e.g., Jewish) have higher motivations and educational aspirations

43

[11] For a review of studies on these questions, see Robert J. Havighurst and Bernice L. Neugarten, *Society and Education* (Boston: Allyn and Bacon, Inc., 1962), pp. 227-35, and Havighurst, *et al.*, *Growing Up in River City* (New York: John Wiley & Sons, Inc., 1962), pp. 49-51. Also see Orville G. Brim, Jr., *Sociology and the Field of Education* (New York: Russell Sage Foundation, 1958), pp. 36-37.

[12] C. Wayne Gordon, "The Sociology of Education," in *Foundations of Education*, ed. George F. Kneller (New York: John Wiley & Sons, Inc., 1963), p. 410.

than other children. In one way or another, all these factors contribute t
what has been called "talent loss." The educational system sorts out an
trains the ablest middle- and upper-class children better than the abl
lower-class children.

Differences in social recruitment have also been found to exist in cur
riculum streams within the comprehensive school. The college preparator
curriculum, for example, tends to draw its students mainly from the highe
status groups, and the general and vocational curriculums from the lowe
status groups. It would be of interest in this connection to make som
comparisons with the English pattern of recruitment. We shall take as th
index of comparison what we have previously termed "class chances" fo
a high school and university education. On the basis of the data availabl
from these two countries, direct comparisons of access into secondar
schools are complicated because of differences in entering ages, in cur
riculum structures, and in the types of institutions. Our data for Englanc
are limited to the grammar school, while for the United States they cove
the entire comprehensive school. Nevertheless, it is still possible to make
some rather tentative generalizations.

In our section on the English pattern of recruitment and selection, we
stated that when measured intelligence is taken as the selection variable
for entrance into the grammar schools, working-class children who posses
the requisite intelligence have chances equal to those of middle-class chil
dren. In the United States, on the other hand, there are indications tha
working-class children who possess the intelligence for a college preparatory
curriculum (the closest equivalent to the English grammar school curricu
lum) have about the same, or more probably fewer, chances than their
counterparts in England. However, in order to arrive at more reliable es
timates of educational opportunity, we need to have more empirical re
search based on cross-national stable categories.

The apparent wastage of talent has lately been a major area of contro
versy in the United States. In addition, the recent years have witnessed
many criticisms against the high schools, their standards, their functions,
and their basic philosophy. The need for a re-appraisal of certain assump
tions upon which the school has been based has been strengthened by
changes in the domestic and international conditions, such as increased
specialization, mass general education, foreign political and economic com
petition, and other problems associated with the Cold War. These factors
have placed upon the schools the responsibility of selecting and preparing
a larger number of intellectually competent students for higher education
and for specific occupational roles. In order to facilitate this process, several
suggestions have been made and several programs have been initiated by
the national government and by private or semiprivate agencies. Thus, for
example, the much publicized and highly influential Conant Report on
the high schools recommended, among others, the strengthening of the
academic curriculum for the college-bound student; since 1955, the
National Merit Scholarship Corporation has granted over 6,000 scholarships
to talented students for higher education; the program of the National
Science Foundation aimed at the improvement of science and mathematics
teaching particularly in the secondary schools; and, of course, there are
the National Defense Education Act and many other programs supported
by the various foundations. In addition, various forms of public pressure
have been exerted upon the schools to strengthen their academic programs

and to provide adequate training and challenges for the gifted students. Research on the origins of students entering programs for the gifted has revealed that, like selective schools of the European countries, there are disparities in the patterns of social recruitment. It has been found that there are fewer children in the programs for the gifted from racial minority groups, low socio-economic classes, and nationality groups with low intellectual or educational aspirations.[13]

Judging by the current climate of opinion, early selection and differentiation do not seem to evoke the "antidemocratic" opprobrium of previous years. They are indeed very often justified on the grounds that, under the previous practices, the few gifted students were penalized and their minds were not stretched to the fullest, with the result that the basic idea of an education according to individual aptitude and needs was not fully realized. Yet in seeking to remedy this situation it is well to bear in mind the English experience where the excessive concern for the talented has recently aroused controversy concerning the basic issues about social equality and parity of educational provision. The complex factors of democracy and education are discussed in greater detail in Chapter 9.

THE FRENCH PATTERN

The liberal principles of equality of opportunity and of the full development of the individual's capacities and potentialities date from the French Revolution. Both the 1946 and 1958 constitutions reaffirmed the idea that "the nation guarantees to every child and adult equal opportunities to gain education, professional training and culture." As in England, however, the French notion of equal opportunities does not connote identical opportunities. French democracy, even more explicitly than the English, is based on the "rule of the best" theory, the term "best" signifying the intellectually best, the true *aristoi* in the Platonic meaning of the term. It is assumed that, once a carefully selected and trained "aristocracy of brains" is placed at the helm of the state craft, society will be guided wisely.

In the process of selection and training of the elite, education—especially that of the *lycée*—has since the revolution played a key role. Through a stringent system of examinations the *lycée* has sought to recruit the intellectually most competent people and to impart to them a body of knowledge and values best expressed by the French concept of *culture générale*.

The progress toward the attainment of equality of educational opportunity has been slow. Until 1930, the *lycées* charged tuition fees; this deprived certain children from gaining access to them. As in England and Germany, there was a dual track in France called the *dualisme scolaire*, with distinctive social and educational characteristics: an elementary track for the majority of the students, mostly recruited from rural and working classes; and an elementary-secondary track for the middle and upper classes. Secondary education, in fact, was exclusively defined in terms of the classical humanistic *lycée* and the *collège*. In the twentieth century, the *dualisme scolaire* gave way to the common school (*école unique*), which was first a five-year school and after the Berthoin Law of 1958-59 was extended to a seven-year school.

45

[13] James J. Gallagher, *Analysis of Research on the Education of Gifted Children* (State of Illinois: Office of the Superintendent of Public Instruction, 1960).

With the abolition of fees and the establishment of the *école unique* any student who possessed the requisite intellectual ability could in theor gain admission into the *lycée* and the *collège*. However, these institution continued to recruit most of their students from the middle and uppe echelons of society. Recruitment patterns of French secondary school have not received as much attention in France as they have in Englanc and the United States. The very few studies that have been made attes clearly to the fact that social and economic factors are important determi nants for access into the various types of post-elementary schools. Fo example, in 1950 Roger Gal found that the civil servants and the libera professions provided 25 per cent and 19 per cent, respectively, of the sec ondary school population (*lycée* and *collège*), whereas the workers and the farmers provided 13 per cent and 9 per cent. The disproportionate sec ondary school representation of the civil servants and professionals become: even more striking when it is viewed against the total number of peopl in each of the occupational categories. Gal established that there wer 810,000 officials in the civil and administrative services, and 750,000 in the liberal professions, as against 7,500,000 industrial and transport workers and 7,400,000 farmers.[14] In another study, A. Girard found that two-third: of the students in the upper elementary schools were children of agricul tural laborers, farmers, and workmen, but only one-third of those whc entered a secondary school around the age of 11 came from the same group. According to him, there were hardly any children from the highes! social groups in the upper elementary schools. Girard concluded:

Children of varying home backgrounds do not have equal chances o! selection at eleven or twelve or, in particular, of gaining admission tc secondary schools. For agricultural laborers' children, the chances ar slightly more than one in ten; whereas children from more fortunate homes have eight or nine chances in ten.[15]

Similar disparities were reported in 1956 to the National Assembly by the Minister of Education. According to that report, over 80 per cent o! the children of high government officials, executives, and professionals attended academic secondary schools, whereas only 8 per cent of workers' children did so. Three years later, the French Center for Sociologica] Studies reported that 31 per cent of the children in the first year of the academic secondary schools came from the occupational categories of farmers, workers, and artisans. Compared with the representation of the same group in 1936 (about 9 per cent), there appears to have been a sizable expansion of educational opportunity for these children. However, the same source indicates that the majority of these children were enrolled in the modern sections of the academic schools (which excluded Greek and Latin), and that there was a heavy dropout rate among them. Subse quent evidence shows that the classical schools continued to draw heavily from the professional and high administrative occupational groups.[16]

---

[14] Roger Gal, "France," *The Year Book of Education 1950* (London: Evans Brothers, 1950), pp. 410-25.

[15] A. Girard, "Selection for Secondary Education in France," A. H. Halsey, *et al.*, eds., *Education, Economy and Society* (New York: Free Press of Glencoe, Inc., 1961), p. 193.

[16] George A. Male, *Education in France* (Washington D. C.: U.S. Government Printing Office, 1963), pp. 81-84.

It was partly in recognition of this differential pattern of recruitment that the Law of 1959 created a two-year observation stage (*cycle d'observation*). The observation stage has statutorily at least lengthened the years of the *école unique* from five to seven. But in many cases the *école unique* continued to be a five-year school. Selection for secondary schools was postponed for two years in order to allow for a period of observation of a child's aptitudes, interests, and abilities and for better guidance concerning his future educational destination. Because of financial limitations, however, observation stages were, for the time being, to be attached to only two types of institutions: the colleges of general education (*collège d'enseignement général*) which were to replace the previous upper elementary classes (*cours complémentaires*); and the *lycées*.

Although, theoretically, any primary school graduate may enter an observation stage, in practice, there are constraining factors which operate against the automatic transfer of students from the lower level to the higher. First, *lycées* and *collèges* do not exist in all localities where there are elementary schools; consequently, for many children it involves considerable hardship to enter an observation stage. Second, observation stages at this time provide places for about 40–50 per cent of those who leave elementary school, which makes this extension of common schooling selective in itself. Students are screened for admission to the observation stages. The alternative for those who for some reason or another do not qualify, is to go to the "terminal classes" (*classes terminales*) which are essentially practical in their orientation and which lead to lower occupations. Third, there is a difference in the education offered in the two types of schools which have observation stages.

The training of the teachers in the colleges of general education compared with that of the teachers in the *lycées* is not as rigorous or as respected. Furthermore, the prestige attached to the *lycée* will continue to be an important factor in the type of observation stage chosen. Finally, the *lycées* and the colleges of general education are administered by different branches of government. This factor has reinforced the differences in prestige accorded to these types of institutions.

47

If one were to summarize the French contemporary pattern, one would have to agree with the Minister of Education who maintained that types and amounts of education in France are determined by social, geographical, and cultural factors. It is particularly significant to notice that rural children are at a tremendous disadvantage because of inadequate educational facilities in rural areas. Also, in France working class children have by tradition been employed at an early age. When all these considerations are taken into account, it is unlikely that the differential patterns of social recruitment into the schools will disappear.

THE SOVIET PATTERN

In the early nineteenth century, as we have seen, education in Russia corresponded in large measure to the existing social structure. At the very top, there were the highly aristocratic schools, like Czar Alexander's Lyceum at St. Petersburg, which were the preserve of a hereditary noble class, of the generals, and of some high government officials; below them there were the *gymnasia* which recruited their students mostly from the small middle class and from the clergy; at the very bottom there were several types of elementary schools (schools of the *zemstvos*, the *shkoly gramotnosti*, the church schools, the *mektebes*) for the peasant majority. The social and educational lines of this threefold school-society classification were rather sharply drawn, although there was a trickle of *gymnasium* graduates who could enter the higher schools of the nobility, and of graduates from the popular schools who could enter the *gymnasia*. By the end of the century, access to schools improved considerably, especially from the *gymnasium* to the university. However, there was still a close correlation between education and social class background, and access to schools was hampered by economic factors. In 1909 Darlington wrote that "nothing is done to pick out poor boys of good capacity attending the primary schools, in order to send them on with the help of bursaries, reduced fees or the like, to the secondary schools." [17]

Not only was access to the secondary schools restricted; there was also opposition to peasant boys attending secondary schools. Yet, in considering recruitment and selection in the Russian educational system of the prerevolutionary period, we must bear in mind the following considerations. First, even in an autocratic society like czarist Russia, the doors of the secondary schools and the institutions of higher learning were by no means entirely closed to the peasants, workers, and petty bourgeoisie; second, the universities, in particular, recruited and trained some of the most illustrious free-thinkers of czarist Russia, including the great *Zapadniki* (the Westernizers); and third, since the emancipation of the serfs in 1861, there was a great change in the pattern of social recruitment into post-primary educational institutions.

As compared with the generation preceding the 1897 Russian census, Anderson has found that social background as a factor influencing access into middle schools decreased in importance. Over a period of one generation, the representation of the noble–official group had dropped by one-fourth, that of the clergy by about one-half, but that of the peasant group had more than tripled. Similarly, within the same time span and using the same status categories, he found that the portion of the noble–official estate who had attended institutions of higher learning had declined from 86 per cent to 59 per cent, that of the clergy increased by one-half, while that of the peasant group multiplied eight times.[18] Other writers have estimated that between 1904 and 1914 the percentage of gentry and officials decreased from 43.8 to 32.3 in the boys' *Gymnasia* and from 30.6 to 22.6 in Real Schools, whereas the number of peasants increased from 12 per cent to 22 per cent and from 21.7 per cent to 32.1 per cent in the two types of schools, respectively.[19] These rather startling developments toward the closing decades of Imperial Russia may be attributed in part to the impetus given to industrialization, and to the relative emphasis on democratization. But they also show that the process of the expansion of educational opportunity, usually associated with the post-revolutionary period, was incipient at this time.

[17] Great Britain, Board of Education, "Educational Policy in Russia," *Special Reports on Educational Subjects* (London: His Majesty's Stationery Office, 1909), XXIII, 323.

[18] C. Arnold Anderson, "A Footnote to the Social History of Modern Russia: The Literacy and Educational Census of 1897," *Genus*, XII (1956), 1-18.

[19] Nicholas Hans and S. Hessen, *Educational Policy in Soviet Russia* (London: P. S. King and Son, Ltd., 1930), p. 97.

The ideology of the Bolshevik Revolution included, *inter alia,* the abolition of all social class differences and the establishment of a uniform and universal educational system free from any class encumbrances. In short, here was to be complete equalitarianism in all spheres of social and economic activity. To accomplish this, the economic basis of the society was transformed through such steps as nationalization, re-allocation of land holdings, leveling of wage differentials, etc. A campaign was waged against illiteracy, and educational steps were taken to extend opportunities to the working class and the peasants. Indeed, there was a conscious attempt to eliminate the opportunities held by the former "exploiting" classes.

To what extent the Soviets have attained the equalitarianism they have advocated is an open question. The available research in this field, although limited, points to a type of social structure not radically different from that of Western industrial societies. Inkeles and Bauer, for example, have found that there were not only classes—in the sense that their members shared typical or average conditions of life of sufficient importance to warrant class distinctions—but also a high degree of correlation in occupational ranking between the Soviet Union and the United States. In both countries the professional groups ranked higher than other groups, and the professions were the most desired occupations. The same writers found that there was a high correlation between level of education and occupation attained, and between occupational background of parents and opportunities for education.

It is true that the Soviets have generally been successful in expanding opportunities for education. After the revolution special schools like the *rabfacs* were set up with the express purpose of providing further education for the workers and the peasants. However, in examining this process, we must guard against hasty generalizations. In the decade following the revolution, the social composition of secondary schools, insofar as the peasant and working groups were concerned, was not substantially different from the preceding decade. Moreover, as the society developed economically and industrially and reached a higher degree of social stability, mechanisms were created which facilitated the growth of a new system of stratification and a new elite. This development, coupled with the traditional concept of intellectual selectivity, contributed to differential patterns of social recruitment, not unlike western industrial societies. Like the European educators, the Soviets have placed great faith in examinations of ability and achievement for purposes of selection, differentiation, and promotion.[20] As *per analogium,* the same factors restraining equality of opportunity seem to obtain here as well.

In sheer growth of the educational enterprise the Soviet gains have been quite spectacular. In the immediate prerevolutionary years fewer than 10 million persons were in Russian schools. Of this number, 8 million or about one-fifth of those of elementary-school age attended elementary schools; and 679,300 were in secondary educational institutions. It has also been estimated that 76 per cent of the entire population was illiterate. The Revolution of 1917 created havoc in education; enrollments reached their lowest ebb in 1922, when only 7.4 million persons attended the various types of schools. But after 1923, a steady increase was registered

49

[20] For a good discussion on these themes, see C. Arnold Anderson, "Educational Dilemmas in the U.S.S.R.," *The School Review,* LVII, No. 1 (Spring 1959), 26-44.

at all levels of education, reaching a peak in 1940–41, when over 35 million children were attending school. After that year there was a relative decline. In 1957–58, 30.6 million pupils were in the general system of pre-university education; of these 28.7 million were enrolled in elementary, seven-year, and secondary schools, and about 2 million in schools for young workers, rural youth, and adults.

As a result of the 1930 decree "On Universal Compulsory Education," prescribing a minimum of three years of schooling, there was a spectacular increase in elementary school enrollments (7 million between 1929 and 1931). After this initial spurt enrollments increased slowly. In 1955–56 there were 13.6 million children attending grades 1–4. The secondary school picture saw comparable increases, especially after the decrees in the 1940's, affecting primarily the urban and industrial areas. For example, in 1940–41 there were 10.8 million students in grades 5–8, and in 1950–51, 12 million. In 1955–56 total enrollment in these grades dropped to 9.3 million. At the higher grades of secondary education (8–10) there was a steady increase. In 1940–41, 2.3 million youth were enrolled in these grades, but in 1955–56 the number soared to 5.2 million.

We might indicate the growth in enrollments in different terms. In 1914–15 only about 20 per cent of children between the ages of 6 and 11 were attending schools; in 1959, 90 per cent of this age group were enrolled in grades 1–8. In the secondary schools (grades 9–12) 55 per cent (5.2 million) of the corresponding age group were at school.[21]

In assessing the pattern of recruitment in the Soviet Union one must consider the urban-rural and the "nationality" dimensions. While the school representation of the rural population has increased since the revolution, it is still disproportionately low relative to the urban population, especially in the secondary schools. In 1955–56, total school enrollment in rural areas was 16.1 million and in urban areas 12.0 million, while the corresponding population figures were 113.2 and 87.0 million respectively. While disparities in the over-all enrollment pattern may be observed, the greatest urban-rural disparities occur in the upper grades. According to one estimate, only 44 per cent of the students in the upper grades were in rural schools. Similarly, while over-all educational opportunities for the various nationalities have increased during the Soviet regime, in recent years disproportionate increases have been registered for the Russian Soviet Federated Socialist Republic (R.S.F.S.R.) and the Ukrainian Soviet Socialist Republic, especially in the higher grades. In these two republics the following increases were made: In 1950, the proportions of students enrolled in grades 8–10 were 4.3 and 4.0 per cent respectively; in 1955 the proportions increased to 18.8 and 20.0 per cent in the two republics. It should be pointed out that, while the figures for 1950 were below the

[21] It is interesting to note that the comparative statistics in the United States for the year 1959 were: 100 per cent enrollment in the elementary grades and 8 per cent in the secondary grades. At the university level, the comparative enrollments were 6 per cent for the Soviet Union and 24 per cent for the United States. It is quite clear that, compared to the United States, opportunities in the Soviet Union decrease as we ascend the educational ladder from the elementary school to the university. See Nicholas DeWitt, *Education and the Development of Human Resources: Soviet and American Effort*, Congress of the United States Joint Economic Committee (Washington, D. C.: Government Printing Office, 1962), p. 241.

national average, those for 1955 were above. These trends were not generally true of the other republics.[22]

An important part of the educational enterprise in the Soviet Union comes under the category of "professional education" such as secondary specialized schools, vocational schools, and semiprofessional schools, which also include what are known as *technicums*. Enrollment increases in such schools have been substantial. In 1914–15 only 54,300 persons were attending technical schools and other middle professional educational establishments, but in 1956–57 there were over 2 million people enrolled in such schools.[23]

Because of increased demand for semiprofessional education in the 50's in contrast to what prevailed in the 30's there was a surplus of candidates for admission. Consequently, the entrance requirements became more rigorous. Earlier, persons with less than seven years of schooling were admitted, but in recent years a prior seven-year schooling became the absolute minimum, and today the usual pattern is to recruit graduates of the ten-year schools. Recruitment into the semiprofessional schools is also influenced by other factors. Since the Reform of 1959, academic achievement has been replaced by employment experience for purposes of selection. Other selective factors include membership into the communist youth organizations and trade unions, and military service.[24]

Thus, even in an allegedly classless society, and in one which can legislate by *fiat* the amounts and types of education of younger people, we observe disparities concerning access into the schools, as in the other societies we have examined. That is, children of professional groups are found to have more "intelligence" or "school ability," they get more and better education, and they enter the most preferred positions in the society. In addition, other factors such as urban-rural origins, ethnicity, and political affiliations, play an important role in the process of selection.

51

THE TURKISH PATTERN

After the Revolution of 1923, Turkey embarked upon a program of educational reorganization and expansion. The reorganization and the present structure of the system are discussed elsewhere. Since 1923 there has been a dramatic increase in school enrollment.[25] In 1923, there were about 350,000 children enrolled in the primary schools, and of the total school population only about 3 per cent were enrolled in schools of all types. In 1960–61 enrollments in the primary schools rose to 3.4 million, and the over-all number of children at school rose to about 12 per cent. Yet,

22 Nicholas DeWitt, *Education and Professional Employment in the U.S.S.R.* (Washington, D. C.: Government Printing Office, 1961), pp. 142-45.
23 Robert Maxwell, ed., *Information U.S.S.R.* (Oxford: Pergamon Press, 1962), p. 411. DeWitt points out that 47 per cent of the students attending semiprofessional schools in 1960 were part-time programs (DeWitt, *ibid.*, p. 167). Also see Alexander G. Korol, *Soviet Education for Science and Technology* (Cambridge: Massachusetts Institute of Technology, 1957), pp. 106-7.
24 DeWitt, *ibid.*, pp. 168-69.
25 All the statistics in this section have been taken from reports published by the Research and Measurement Bureau of the National Ministry of Education and by the Office of Statistics of the Republic of Turkey, and from an empirical study conducted by one of the writers in 1962-63.

although today there is compulsory legislation concerning the primary stage of education, a sizable percentage of children, especially in the villages, are not in school. As late as 1952–53, more than half of the villages in Turkey were without schools, and about 33 per cent of all the children of primary school age received no formal education. The disparities in educational provision among girls is even greater. There are only half as many girls enrolled in primary schools as boys. In assessing the over-all provision of primary education, one should also bear in mind the high dropout rate within the various primary grades. This attrition has been a perennial problem in Turkey. For example, of the 240,900 students enrolled in the first grade in 1933–34, only 83,600 or 33 per cent were able to complete the fifth and final grade in 1938. According to the latest statistics of the Ministry of Education, only about 45 per cent of the children of the appropriate age groups are enrolled in the fifth grade, while over 90 per cent are enrolled in the first grade.

Of the total number of students who graduate from a primary school, a small percentage enter the middle level schools. In 1952–53, only 18 per cent of the boys and 14 per cent of the girls who finished a primary school entered the middle general school (orta); those who entered vocational schools were 7 per cent and 6 per cent, respectively. In 1958–59 there were 266,802 students who received primary school diplomas; of this number, about one-third entered the middle schools, and about 10 per cent entered other middle level schools.

A high dropout rate is also characteristic of the various grades in the orta schools, which are described in greater detail in chapter 7. One writer has estimated that in 1952–53 only 47 per cent of the students who entered these schools three years earlier were able to graduate.[26] On the basis of the latest figures available, we have estimated that today about 36 per cent of the students who enter the orta schools are not able to graduate.

Of the graduates of the orta schools, about one-third gain admission into the lises, which are essentially academic institutions leading to the universities and other institutions of higher learning, and to clerical occupations. As in the case of the lower levels of education, there is a high dropout rate in the lises. Taking a three-year period (an ordinary lise is a three-year school), we have estimated that, of the total number of students who entered the lises in 1959–60, only about half were enrolled in the third class of the lise in 1961–62. In general, it may be concluded that of the total first year students in these schools only about one-third are able to graduate. Similar high rates of attrition are to be found in the other types of middle and lise-level schools. Viewing the whole picture of the flow of students from one rung of the educational ladder to another, it has been estimated that of 100 primary school pupils, about 8 may expect to enter a middle school; and of those 8, about 2 may expect to enter a lise; of 100 middle school students, about 28 may expect to enter a lise; but of 100 lise students, about 86 may expect to enter an institution of higher learning.

It is quite clear from what has been said that graphically the Turkish educational system corresponds to a minaret-shaped pattern of recruitment and selection; enrollments diminish steadily and substantially from the primary school to the university level and are dramatically peaked and

---

[26] Richard C. Maynard, "The Lise and its Curriculum in the Turkish Educational System" (Ph.D. dissertation, The University of Chicago, Department of Education, June, 1961), p. 131.

onstricted at the summit. It is also of interest to note that once a student
has managed to reach the top grade of the *lise* he can virtually be assured
of entrance into the universities or other institutions of higher learning.
At least this was the case until the early 1960's. Indeed, students with a
ise diploma considered it a right that an appropriate place should be
found for them in the university. In 1962, however, a system of stand-
rdized testing was introduced for admission into Ankara University,
ventually to be used for entrance into all other universities and institu-
ions of higher learning. The students who were not successful in these
dmission tests marched in protest in the main streets of Ankara and sent
eputations to the government protesting against such screening procedures,
vhich took away their "right" of admission to the university. Subsequently,
ositions were found for them, but this incident points out that, unless
igher education expands in direct proportion to the increased enrollments
n the lower schools, discontent is likely to become exacerbated.

In examining the problem of educational opportunity, we should also
ook at available evidence on the social aspects of the selective process.
n our examination of the Ottoman nineteenth century background, we
tated that educational opportunities were circumscribed by social and
conomic factors. The *lise*, in particular, recruited students from the upper,
vealthier classes; the majority of the population who received any form
f education, religious or otherwise, attended lower schools. One of the
vowed aims of the Atatürk regime was to break down the sharp disparities
hat existed, and to allow for the better recruitment of the talent from all
egments of the population. The *lise* became the main institution for the
ducation of talented youth. Preliminary findings of a study conducted
n Turkey on this problem have revealed that about 40 per cent of the
tudents in the public *lises* and 52 per cent of those in private Turkish *lises*
re drawn from the professional, high technical, administrative, and clerical
occupations. The over-representation of these occupational groups is evi-
lent when we consider that they constitute only 5.6 per cent of the male
opulation of Turkey. Going down the occupational scale, 22.3 per cent
f the students in these schools have been found to be drawn from the
ategory of farmers, fishermen, and hunters, who constitute 62.3 per cent
f the male labor force. Clearly this indicates that there are disparities in
ocial access to these prestigious institutions. We have also found that the
ises draw more students from the more educated urban classes than from
he uneducated peasant groups. Our data show that children of educated
arents with urban backgrounds, who belong to the so-called "white collar"
groups, have greater chances for a *lise*-type of education than other groups
—a finding with which sociologists of education are quite familiar in
nost societies.

Yet it would be quite wrong to conclude that the *lise* in Turkey is exclusively an elite institution. We know that about 28 per cent of the students
n these schools are children of farmers, fishermen, hunters, unskilled
aborers, and semiskilled workers, almost all of whom are either totally
illiterate or semi-illiterate. If we include a proportion of those classified
as private traders and small business people, the proportion would prob-
bly be over one-third. In a sense, therefore, one might say that the *lise*
s as much a "popular" school as it is an elite one. If we compared this
attern of social recruitment with the prerevolutionary one, we would con-
lude that the social function of the *lise* has changed during the republican

period; and this, one might say, happened in spite of the fact that its curriculum content has remained substantially the same. This finding also compares favorably with the patterns of recruitment into the high status schools of the European societies we have examined. However, we must bear in mind that, although there seems to be a fluidity in the system of the inflow of students, certain top positions in the government, the military, and the government-operated industrial and commercial enterprises are filled with graduates of high status institutions, such as the Atatürk Boys School and the Galatasaray *lise* in Istanbul and the Political Science Faculty of the University of Ankara.[27]

SUMMARY

In the twentieth century, all societies we have examined have sought to expand educational opportunities through such means as compulsory attendance, reorganization of the educational structure, and more equitable methods of selection and differentiation. In the European societies and the United States the age of compulsory education has been extended to encompass a good portion of the secondary stage. In short, secondary education for all has become a major objective. In developing societies like Turkey, compulsory education even at the primary stage has not been attained in spite of the fact that it is an expressed political goal.

In the area of reorganization, at least two major patterns have emerged: the differentiated multi-track pattern of the European societies, and the comprehensive, single-track pattern of the United States. However, in recent years there have been several attempts to introduce changes in these arrangements. Some of these changes include (1) the extension of common schooling (e.g. the French *cycle d'observation*, and, one might add, the German *Förderstufe*) to give the student a better opportunity to demonstrate his talents and interests, and thus defer his choice of specialization; (2) the movement toward the establishment of comprehensive patterns of secondary schooling (e.g., England and, to some extent, Turkey); and (3) the setting up of alternative routes to higher education (e.g., the German *Zweite Weg*, and the Russian evening or alternating-shift secondary schools). The American pattern, however, displays some interesting features. It has been assumed that the ideal of secondary education for all can be realized best through the comprehensive school rather than through the European parallel tracks. Yet, while the European countries seem to be attempting to establish connecting links among such parallel tracks, some American changes tend to move in the opposite direction. Thus, for example, there has been a tendency in some schools to provide a separate type of education for the academically gifted students.

Our examination of contemporary societies indicates that in the twentieth century efforts have been made to eliminate or minimize ascriptive criteria in recruiting and selecting students for the various levels of education, and to maximize criteria of achievement and ability. As a means toward the attainment of this goal, a system of objective examinations has been introduced, and the general policy, particularly in the European countries, has

[27] This is a pattern not dissimilar from that of Japan, where certain high jobs in the ministries are occupied by graduates of such schools as the First High School of Tokyo and Tokyo University.

been to allocate students to different educational streams on the basis of the results of these examinations. Moreover, success in such types of examinations entitled the individual to an education from which he was previously debarred, because of his social or economic background. Thus, examinations were expected to perform allocative and equalizing functions. While it is true that the system of examinations has introduced a new dimension into the selective process, it can also be argued that no instrument has been found to be devoid of cultural and other biases.

In this chapter it has been shown that considerable progress has been made in breaking down social class and other barriers concerning access to certain levels and types of education. However, in no society have these factors been completely eliminated. Academic education tends to draw a disproportionate number of students from the middle and upper classes. Nevertheless, it would also be true to say that inequalities in access to education because of social, economic, and cultural factors vary from one country to another. Of all the advanced societies we have examined, the French pattern seems to be the most socially selective, although in terms of over-all expansion in the lower- and upper-secondary schools it has made the most striking progress within the decade of the 1950's.

As stated earlier, compulsory attendance has not been attained in Turkey. Yet, relative growth of education since the Revolution of 1923 has been quite dramatic. Furthermore, it is interesting to note that, although enrollments in the secondary schools are small compared to those of the other countries, the social composition of the student body in such schools is not dissimilar. The Turkish *lise*, for example, like the English grammar school, draws a sizable percentage of its students from the lower socioeconomic classes. Yet, the Turkish pattern displays characteristics that are also different from the European and American patterns, and more similar to those of developing countries in Africa and Asia. First, over-all opportunities for an education beyond the primary level are extremely limited, and the proportion of primary school graduates who enter a *lise* is extremely small; and secondly, the schools in Turkey occupy a more central position in the social mobility than comparable institutions in Western societies. Finally, because of imbalances between the growth of secondary education and the distribution of occupations, there is unemployment and under-employment among secondary school graduates.

PART THREE   THE STRUCTURE OF
SYSTEMS OF EDUCATION

ENGLAND

The English tradition of education until
well into the nineteenth century rested on
the principles of voluntary effort carried
out mostly by religious bodies and parental
responsibility. It was not until 1870,
through the famous Forster Act, that the State
assumed more positive responsibility over
popular education, thereby laying
the foundations for a national system of
education. The 1870 act created the dual system
of schools, one run by the religious
denominations, and the other by the
newly-established School Boards. As the School
Boards set up more and more schools at the
elementary stage, another type of duality
emerged: the elementary schools and the
secondary schools.
Secondary education in the nineteenth century
was *sui generis*; it was provided in endowed
grammar schools, private and proprietary schools,
and in the famous public schools (not public
in the American meaning of the term), and
functioned separately from the public
elementary schools. Most of these schools were
classically-oriented in their curriculum, and
they were expensive. Consequently, they drew
their students from the higher echelons of

DEVELOPED
WESTERN
SOCIETIES

5

society, and their main function was preparation for the universities and the higher professions.

Administratively, the educational system at the close of the nineteenth century was confusing. In recognition of what at the time was referred to as an "educational muddle," the government in 1894 appointed a Royal Commission under the chairmanship of James Bryce, charged with the responsibility of making recommendations for a better organization of education. In 1899 and 1902 two Education Acts were passed which in part were based on the recommendations of the Bryce Commission. According to the 1899 act, a central Board of Education was established which merged the powers of the existing Education Department, the Science and Art Department, and the Charity Commission. The new board was charged with the "superintendence of matters relating to education in England and Wales." The Balfour Act of 1902 was more comprehensive in its administrative provisions. School Boards were to be replaced by Local Education Authorities (L.E.A.'s) drawn from the councils of counties, county boroughs, the boroughs, and the urban districts.

There are at least two noteworthy features about these two legislative measures. In the first place, an administrative framework was established which laid the foundations for a national system of elementary and secondary education. In the second place, the dual system of voluntary and public school continued and indeed became a permanent feature of the English educational system. Like the 1870 act, the Balfour Act did not replace voluntary schools but aimed at "filling the gaps" left by voluntary effort. Moreover, continuing expenses of these schools, now called "non-provided" schools, were henceforth to be met by the L.E.A.'s.

The partnership between church and state in the provision of education has continued into the twentieth century and to some extent characterizes the Engish system of education today. Since 1902, however, there have been important shifts in the respective roles of these two institutions and in the general conception of the state system of education. The Liberal policy after 1906 aimed at the expansion of opportunities at the secondary level and the articulation between elementary and secondary education. Thus the so-called free-place system was initiated, whereby 25 per cent of the secondary school places were to be allocated free of charge to children from the elementary schools after they passed the same qualifying examinations as fee-paying students. After World War I, and largely as a result of the conditions and needs created by it, the Liberal government was able to pass the Fisher Act of 1918, which extended the responsibilities of the local education authorities in the provision and support of both elementary and secondary education and made attendance in schools compulsory up to the age of fourteen (normally the end of the elementary stage). It also made the L.E.A.'s responsible for providing central schools, and central or special classes for the more intelligent children who desired an education beyond the age of fourteen.

During the war years and in the 1920's, there was increasing concern over the expansion of education, and the doctrine of secondary education for all acquired added significance. In 1926, the famous Hadow Report officially advanced the idea of secondary education for all, that is, that all normal children should avail themselves of some form of education after the primary stage, and that such a type of education should go by the general name of "secondary." In addition, the Hadow Committee

57

laid out the framework for the organization of secondary education. It recommended a separation or segregation at the age of eleven-plus, and the allocation of students into different institutional forms after that stage. The different types of secondary schools were to be (1) grammar schools with a leaving age of at least 16, (2) selective central schools with a leaving age of 15, (3) non-selective central schools for those not admitted to selective schools, and (4) senior classes, central departments, or higher top schools for advanced instruction beyond eleven-plus. According to the report, the selective and nonselective schools were to be called "modern schools," as distinguished from the "grammar schools." The Hadow Committee also recommended that the compulsory school-leaving age be raised to fifteen and that the different types of secondary schools should enjoy "parity of esteem." [1]

The recommendations of the Hadow Committee were not fully implemented. Successive governments were not able to pass any substantive legislation which would raise the school-leaving age as the Committee recommended or which would confer secondary status to schools other than the grammar schools. In 1938 the Spens Report carried the Hadow idea of secondary education for all even further by including technical schools. It recommended a tripartite arrangement of secondary schools into grammar, modern, and technical with variations in curriculum emphasis, but it stressed "parity of esteeem" for all schools.

The tripartite arrangement recommended by the Spens Committee was reinforced in 1943 by the Report of the Committee of the Secondary Examinations Council which had been appointed by the President of the Board of Education in 1941. The Norwood Report, as this document is commonly known, justified such an arrangement on the grounds that there was a threefold typology of students—the bookish-intellectual, the technical, and the practical—and that the tripartite concept was in accord with recognized practice. Like the Spens Committee, the Norwood Report rejected the multilateral school idea, accepted the age of eleven-plus as suitable for transfer from the primary to the secondary school, and asserted that the first two years of the three types of secondary schools should be "diagnostic." [2]

The subsequent development of English educational policy was based on the recommendations of the aforementioned committees. In 1943, the government issued the White Paper, which endorsed the tripartite system of secondary schools and proposed comprehensive reforms based on the principle that "the child is the center of education and that so far as is humanly possible, all children should receive the type of education for which they are best adapted." In words reminiscent of previous pronouncements, the White Paper averred that it was "just as important to achieve diversity as it is to ensure equality of educational opportunity." [3] One year later a comprehensive Education Act was passed by a coalition government, laying the administrative framework of the present system of English education.

---

[1] The Hadow Report, *op. cit.*, p. 72.
[2] Board of Education, *Curriculum and Examinations in Secondary Schools* (London: His Majesty's Stationery Office, 1943), pp. 2-3, 18-19.
[3] Board of Education, *Educational Reconstruction* (London: His Majesty's Stationery Office, 1943), pp. 3-9.

The Education Act of 1944 provided that public education in England hould be under the charge of a Minister whose duty was "to promote the ducation of the people of England and Wales and the progressive development of institutions devoted to that purpose, and to secure the effective execution by local authorities, under his direction and control, of the national policy for providing a varied and comprehensive educational ervice in every area." [4] The powers granted to the Minister of Education were extensive. He is authorized to compel local education authorities to maintain high standards and to provide educational opportunities for all children according to their different ages, abilities, and aptitudes. In the performance of his duties, the minister is assisted by a Parliamentary Secretary, who, like the minister, is a member of the government and sits in Parliament. Under the minister there is a large staff of permanent civil servants divided into the central administrative officers and Her Majesty's Inspectors (H.M.I.'s). The work of the inspectorate lies mostly with the areas of the local education authorities. It provides an important link between the central and the local units of administration, and its functions are advisory. The inspectors, who reside in the districts assigned them, inspect and report to the Minister of Education on the efficiency of schools, advise the minister and the L.E.A.'s on general problems of educational policy, assist the minister in the compilation of pamphlets and handbooks for the benefit of administrators and teachers, organize professional conferences, and so on. The inspectors are not authorized to rate teachers as is the custom, for example, in Turkey. They are usually drawn from the teaching profession and are believed to be men of high ability and training.

In matters of educational theory and practice the minister is also advised by two Central Advisory Councils, one for England and the other for Wales. These two bodies have replaced the previous Consultative Committee, but for the most part perform the same function, except that on their own initiative they make suggestions and recommendations to the minister.

The proposals to strengthen the central administration and the powers given to the minister caused concern and disquietude among those who took pride in the relative autonomy of the local bodies and the delicate nature of partnership between the central and local authorities. Fears that the new arrangements would destroy this partnership were allayed by several factors. In the first place, the Minister of Education, being a Member of Parliament, is accountable for his actions to that body, and *a fortiori* to the public; in the second place, the ministry does not provide, own or control schools, nor does it employ or dismiss teachers; in the third place, the minister does not dictate to headmasters or to teachers the content or method of instruction, nor does he prescribe syllabi or textbooks. In matters of curriculum, the Ministry of Education issues handbooks, pamphlets, and circulars that embody "suggestions" for the consideration of teachers, etc. It should be re-emphasized, however, that the ministry's role is not "advisory" or "negative" in all matters. Those schools which are classified as "controlled" or "maintained" schools, i.e., those that draw considerable funds from the national treasury, must conform

59

[4] *Education Act, 1944* (7 & 8 Geo. 6. Chapter 31), Part I, Section 1 (1).

to certain standards in terms of equipment and general efficiency; other wise funds may be withdrawn or withheld. Moreover, the Minister of Education has the power to compel local authorities to provide an education for all children in their respective localities.

At the local level, public education is in the hands of the L.E.A.'s, drawn from county councils and county boroughs. According to the 1944 Education Act, the total number of L.E.A.'s was reduced from the existing 315 to 146 by eliminating the previous municipal boroughs and rural districts. The councils, which are the locally elected units of government in many services, perform their educational functions through education committees, the majority of which must be council members. About one-third of the members of an education committee are appointed (co-opted), and the committee includes people who have had special experience or interest in education. Each education committee operates through sub-committees that conduct studies, make recommendations, and report to the education committee. It appoints a chief education officer (often called Director of Education, Education Officer or Secretary for Education), who must be approved by the Minister of Education and who is comparable to the county or district school superintendent in the United States.

Each L.E.A. is required by law to provide "efficient" education and sufficient educational opportunities through all the stages of the statutory system of education, viz., primary, secondary, and further. It surveys the educational needs of its locality, formulates "development plans," appoints and employs teachers, makes general recommendations concerning curriculum and programs, and is responsible for about 40 per cent of the total educational expenditures. This amount is raised from local taxation; the remainder (about 60 per cent) is paid by the central government in the form of grants, after approval of a budget submitted by the L.E.A. It is appropriate to mention also that, although the L.E.A.'s are responsible for making recommendations concerning curriculums and methods of instruction, final decision in such matters rests with the head teachers of schools. The English pattern of administration and control in the main presents a unique case of a partnership between the central and the local authorities. Although through the power of the purse the Ministry of Education exercises control over the L.E.A.'s, these local units of administration retain a great deal of autonomy, and can initiate and implement policy. Moreover, the individual head teacher has an unusual freedom of action in matters pertaining to the curriculum and the use of textbooks.

One of the persistent areas of controversy surrounding educational reform in England since the latter part of the nineteenth century was the place of the voluntary schools, most of which had been schools run by the religious denominations, in the general system of education. The issue revolved around the role of public authorities (central and local) in the governance and support of these schools. Although during the entire period since the Education Act of 1870 there were voices raised against the very existence of such schools, all legislative measures, as well as the overwhelming body of public opinion, supported the continuation of these schools and the dual system of education. The Education Act of 1944 was no exception. The number of voluntary schools and of pupils attending them, particularly in the case of those run by non-Catholic groups, had, by the 1940's, considerably decreased. Yet such institutions provided an education for not less than 25 per cent of the children of elementary school age. Moreover, their existence rested on tradition and on some long-cherished assumptions and beliefs. The Church of England, in particular, had a long standing involvement in popular education. There were questions of freedom of conscience and of a partnership between religious bodies and the state. Hence, the White Paper of 1943 expressed a widely held view when it said that voluntary schools should not be abolished. By then it was equally obvious, however, that any partnership between church and state would give the latter greater authority and responsibility over national education; for education was far too important for the national growth and development to rest on a mere partnership, or on mere superintendence and supervision.

The Education Act of 1944 classified voluntary schools into three categories: controlled, aided, and special agreement schools. Controlled schools were to be supported entirely by the L.E.A.'s, which were also responsible for the appointment and dismissal of teachers, but were subject to consultation by the managers about the appointment of a head teacher and teachers responsible for religious instruction (called "reserved teachers"). The managers of aided schools were to be responsible for half the cost of structural improvement and external repairs, and for the appointment of teachers. Special agreement schools were schools that made proposals under a previous Act (Act of 1936). In such cases the L.E.A. paid not less than 50 per cent and not more than 75 per cent of the capital costs, and appointed and dismissed teachers, "subject to the managers to be satisfied as to the fitness and competence of the reserved teachers." In all these types of voluntary schools government participation or "control" encompasses supervision so that standards concerning instruction and equipment should be maintained or brought up to date. In addition, in the case of the controlled schools, two-thirds of the managers are appointed by the L.E.A.'s; in that of the others, two-thirds are appointed in accordance with the trust deed and only one-third by the L.E.A.'s.

ORGANIZATION OF THE SCHOOLS

The 1944 act stipulated that the statutory system of public education should be organized "in three progressive stages to be known as primary education, secondary education, and further education"; the L.E.A.'s in their turn were obligated to provide "efficient education throughout those stages . . . to meet the needs of the population of their area." It was further stated that primary and secondary education should be provided in separate schools, and that nursery schools and special schools for the handicapped should be established.

About 95 out of 100 children in England begin their schooling in a state primary school that covers the years from the age of five to about eleven; the rest enter preparatory schools of various kinds run by private individuals or agencies. Primary education, whether state-supported or not, is compulsory, and for those attending state schools, free. In addition to classroom instruction, primary school children receive the benefits of many social-welfare services which are carried out by the School Health Service, a cooperative program between the Ministry of Health and the Ministry of Education, in collaboration with the L.E.A.'s.

After 1944, the Ministry of Education, which was responsible for the implementation of the Education Act's provisions, established the tripartite system of secondary education, viz., grammar schools, modern schools, and technical schools. At about the age of 11 most primary school children are subjected to a comprehensive examination (the eleven-plus), and are subsequently channelled into one of three types of secondary schools. Compulsory and free education extends up to the age of 15; for those who show ability and desire to continue, free education extends to the age of 18.

Of all primary school children who enter the three types of secondary schools, about 20 per cent go into grammar schools, about 50 per cent into modern schools, and about 10 per cent into technical schools. The remaining are distributed in schools (all-age schools) which cater for all children from the age of five to fifteen.[5] It should be emphasized, however, that such figures vary from one section of the country to another. The available grammar school places in England and Wales vary from about 10 to 45 per cent and, according to the Crowther Report of 1959, over 40 per cent of the L.E.A.'s do not provide technical schools. Moreover, statistical information is confounded by the fact that some L.E.A.'s provide technical streams in modern schools and grammar streams in bilateral, multilateral, or comprehensive schools. According to the Crowther Report, in 1958 there were 1,414 grammar (including direct grant schools) schools, with an enrollment of 681,976 pupils; 3,890 modern (including "selective central," and "intermediate") schools, with an enrollment of 1.5 million pupils; and 279 technical schools, with an enrollment of 95,194 pupils. In addition, there were 2,297 "all-age" schools, with 120,189 pupils; 54 bilateral and multilateral schools, with 32,747 pupils; and 86 comprehensive schools, with 75,050 students.[6]

The secondary grammar school is an academic institution *par excellence*. It is an outgrowth of the traditional grammar school, and it belongs to the same category as the French *lycée* and the German *Gymnasium*. In its official pronouncement setting up the tripartite system, the Ministry of Education stated in no unequivocal terms that the grammar school was a selective institution and that the grammar school course demanded "disciplined thought and the capacity to wrestle successfully with intellectual questions." The grammar schools have provided and continue to provide the largest percentage of students who continue their education after the age of 15 and in the "sixth forms," (about the ages of 17 and 18); who are successful in the General Certificate of Education examinations; who win scholarships; and who enter the universities, the professions, and other higher types of employment. Of the total number of students at age 15, 50.6 per cent were, in 1958, enrolled in maintained grammar schools and direct grant schools, 15 per cent in modern schools, 12 per cent in independent private schools, 8.6 per cent in maintained technical schools and 3 per cent in comprehensive schools. Of those students who were at school at the age of 17 in the same year, 70 per cent were in the first cate-

---

[5] G. A. N. Lowndes, *The British Educational System* (London: Hutchinson's University Library, 1955), pp. 13-15.

[6] These figures represent total enrollments between the ages of 11 and 18. Ministry of Education, *15 to 18*. (London: Her Majesty's Stationery Office, 1959), p. 17. A Report of the Central Advisory Council for Education, Vol. I. Hereafter cited as Crowther Report.

gory (grammar and direct grant), less than 4 per cent in technical schools, and none in modern schools.[7]

The secondary grammar school is the pride of the English, and the most sought-after school by parents for their children. It is also the school most often singled out by foreigners, especially Americans, as exemplifying academic rigor, emphasis on intellectual accomplishments, and the like. Supporters of this institution have acclaimed its impressive record in various awards (scholarships, exhibitions, university prizes, etc.) as well as in what one writer referred to as "invisible exports," i.e., the development of such qualities as character and spirit, which are necessary for leadership in the society. Others, however, have raised questions and, as we noted in Part Two of this book, there is currently a great deal of controversy surrounding the grammar school, the methods of selection into it, the types of students who attend it, and its place in a society that is increasingly emphasizing a more equalitarian approach to education and to a democratic polity.

The first thing we should note about the secondary technical school is that it is not technical in the usual meaning of the term. The Spens Committee and the Ministry of Education were quite explicit that such an institution should not be in any sense narrowly vocational or a trade school. To paraphrase and quote the ministry's words, it is the school which selects "a minority of able children who are likely to make their best response" when the curriculum is so designed to assimilate scientific principles by selecting particular spheres of industry or commerce.

In terms of over-all enrollments in the tripartite system of schools, the technical schools serve a small proportion of the children of secondary school age. Students are admitted into them at the age of 11, although transfer is possible at the age of 13. At the age of 16, the normal school-leaving age, technical school students might enter a craft, an apprenticeship, or a junior clerical post in an office linked with apprenticeships; alternately, they might sit for the General Certificate of Education and continue their training in a technical college leading to a certificate by a professional body (civil, mechanical, or electrical engineering, chemistry, etc.); some may in fact go to the universities.

Although high hopes were expressed when the technical school was proposed, the general response of local education authorities, educators, and others has been rather mixed and ambivalent. It is the least developed school in the famous institutional triad, and its growth as a separate school has been atrophied. Some authorities have completely rejected both the school and its underlying rationale. They have argued that there is no such thing as a separate scientific, technical, or mechanical aptitude that can be established at the age of 11, and what technical or scientific orientation is needed at the secondary level could easily be provided in conjunction with other schools, e.g., grammar, modern, or the various types of comprehensive schools. Another charge against the technical school has been that it has failed, in the main, to recruit students of the high ability that originally had been anticipated.[8]

63

[7] These percentages were computed from statistics provided by the Crowther Report. *Ibid.*, p. 200.
[8] For a more detailed analysis of the reaction to the technical school, see Olive Banks, *Parity and Prestige in English Secondary Education* (London: Routledge & Kegan Paul, Ltd., 1955), pp. 151-67.

The modern school has been envisaged consistently as an institution with a more practical bias. It has been thought of as meant for students who want to continue their education beyond the elementary stage, but who do not possess the requisite intelligence or interest to withstand the "stern intellectual discipline" afforded by the grammar school. According to the ministry's recommendations, the differentiating characteristic of the modern school vis-à-vis other secondary schools must be "its very broad outlook and objective"; it must provide a series of courses for children of widely different "ability, aptitude and social background"; it must cater to the needs of intelligent boys and girls with "a marked practical bent," as well as those of backward children; and it must have as its overriding aim "a good all-round secondary education, not focused primarily on the traditional subjects, . . . but developing out of the interests of the children." [9]

The secondary modern schools provide schooling for the majority of children between the ages of 11 and 15. The largest number of modern school children (70 to 75 per cent) leave school after the completion of the normal four-year course; they enter minor clerical occupations, work in factories and shops, become bus drivers, telephone operators, and the like; or they take employment on farms. A small percentage of the more intellectually able or ambitious children (between 10 and 15 per cent) may continue their education either in their own schools or elsewhere. They may sit for the General Certificate of Education, and they may even find themselves in universities or other institutions of higher learning.

Some writers have seen advantages in the modern school. Not working under the shadow of examinations as the grammar schools do, the teachers in a modern school have more freedom to experiment with new ideas and practices, and can help the pupils develop their potentialities. Further, modern schools are more likely to draw their students from a cross section of the population in terms of ability and social background. Also, the modern school affords an opportunity for the "late bloomer" to pursue his academic or other intellectual interests. At the same time, however, it has become the focus of intense controversy. The advocates of equalitarianism contend that it clearly discriminates against the child of modest means and brains, and that the education provided in it is not equivalent to that in the grammar or technical schools; and this in spite of the often expressed policy that there should be "parity of esteem" among all types of schools. Under the existing structure, and considering (1) the differences in the rewards that accrue from attendance at the various kinds of institutions, and (2) parental pressures, the modern schools are forced to assume responsibilities and perform functions which lie outside their official purview. In some cases the modern school is forced to provide strictly academic streams in order to compete favorably with the grammar school in the university entrance examinations; in others, it provides technical streams.

There are, finally, two other categories of schools that need to be mentioned: the independent and the comprehensive schools. There are about 5,000 independent schools with an enrollment of about a half-million students. Such schools vary in standards and functions: some are similar to the maintained grammar schools, others are similar to the modern

[9] Ministry of Education, *The New Secondary Education*, Pamphlet No. 9 (London: His Majesty's Stationery Office, 1947), p. 29.

and still others fall short of the standards of both. But among this group of schools there are the famous and, in many respects, typically English public schools like Eton, Harrow, Winchester, etc. Considering their number and the percentage of children attending them (not more than 3 per cent of all British children) they occupy a pivotal position in English education and society. We discuss the function of these schools in the recruitment and training of political leaders in Part Four of this book. It is sufficient to mention here that, for the most part, they are the preserve of the more affluent and politically powerful classes of society; they provide about 40 per cent of the entrants to the prestigious universities of Oxford and Cambridge; and generally admission to them carries the stamp of gentility, affluence, respectability, and power. Inevitably they have their partisan supporters who marshal the accomplishments of these schools and the weight of a long-standing tradition as reasons for their continuation. But they have been the target of serious as well as humorous criticism. Some see them as elegant anachronisms, as part of the "Establishment," defined by one writer as "the present-day institutional museum of Britain's past greatness" and by others, more jokingly, as "the source of irony on the theme of social climbing (dear to the hearts of class-ridden English) as well as pomposity, conceit, homosexuality, religion and philistinism." [10] To social equalitarians they stick out as a sore thumb in a society that takes pride in being democratic. John Vaizey condemned them both on social and educational grounds.[11] But few, if any, have disputed the fact that the "great public schools" have in the past played and continue to play a most significant social role in English society; that as a subculture they constitute almost a separate world of their own; and that at least some are schools with superb and exacting intellectual standards.

In sharp contrast to the public schools in rationale and scope are the relatively few but increasingly common comprehensive schools—perhaps the most daring recent experiment in English education. We have already referred to these types of schools in the previous part of this study. Dominated by the more socialistic (in the English sense) groups, the comprehensive schools are envisaged as a possible solution to the class-character of English education. It would be quite inaccurate, however, to view the comprehensive schools as an instrument of political propaganda. They are also seen as an answer to the evils associated with early selection and the eleven-plus examination, and as a means to blur social distinctions reinforced by different types and amounts of education.

Like tripartitism and the eleven-plus, comprehensive schools have been the center of controversy. Those who have been against their expansion claim that since their size must be large if they are to be effective, standards will be lowered, there will be difficulties in staffing, and bright students and the individual will be lost. Underlying the melee of arguments for or against such schools is a fundamental conflict in English social ideology, a conflict between an elitist form of democracy or a more equalitarian one; and a pedagogical conflict between maintaining standards of excellence on the one hand, and educating everybody on the other.

A political scientist characterized the English school system as "a series of high steps," compared to the American, which he described as

[10] Hugh Thomas, ed., *The Establishment* (London: Anthony Blond, 1929), p. 23.
[11] *Ibid.*, p. 46.

"a sloping pyramid." The same writer observed that this series of step (the breaks at the ages of 11, 16, and 18) and the schools emphasize "cultural norms concerning inequality," something which is regarded by the English as not only natural, but often desirable. The various dif ferentiating features of the English schools not only reflect basic assump tions about who should rule and who should not, or status differentiation in the society, but they also reinforce such distinctions and, in fact, seek to impart to the young the differential social and political roles they are expected to perform in the society after leaving school. Speaking spe cifically about the political culture, Richard Rose stated that "nearly al the schools, within their own school community, stress a hierarchica system of authority, training youths for different but complementary role as leader and follower." [12]

The twentieth century witnessed a change not only in the social statu of the elementary or primary school, but also in the pedagogical theory underlying this level of education. As a result of developments in psychol ogy of learning and teaching and philosophy of education, the curriculum and the methods of instruction have shifted. As in the United States and indeed in many other countries of the world, in England there ha been a shift toward a more *pedocentric* (child-centered) approach, in the sense that attempts have been made to base the curriculum and methods on an understanding of child nature, development, and needs. In addition primary education is today perceived as a stage in a continuous educational process, not as a terminal institution. These developments in the English pedagogical mind have been accompanied by changes in the content of instruction, in the activities in which the child engages, and in the methods of teaching. The traditional aims of teaching the essentials of literacy and computation remain fundamental; but the teaching methods have changed radically. Children even sit differently in the classrooms. They arrange shapes and colors and engage in "projects." They are exposed to sophisti cated concepts about time, the physical and biological environment, and justice and injustice.

Since the middle of the last century, when Herbert Spencer asked "What Knowledge is of Most Worth?" there has been considerable con troversy surrounding the curriculum of the secondary schools, and various changes have taken place. In the period that followed the Hadow Report of 1926, attempts were made to incorporate literary, scientific, and prac tical elements in the curriculum of the various types of secondary schools The three types of schools in the tripartite system are distinguished, espe cially after a relatively common two-year core (ages 11 to 13), by their emphasis in one of the three aforementioned elements. The common cur riculum includes history, English, geography, mathematics, general science art, music, drawing, handicraft, physical education, etc. The differentiating features between the grammar and the modern school, in so far as this basic core of subjects is concerned, are (a) the inclusion of Latin in the case of the former, (b) the fact that one would find more "integrated" courses in the modern schools, e.g., social studies, and (c) that in modern

66

[12] See Richard Rose, *Politics in England* (Boston: Little, Brown & Co., 1964) pp. 65-72.

schools there is a greater emphasis placed upon the practical subjects. The common curriculum of the technical schools is about the same as that of the grammar schools.

Beyond this common stage, however, there is greater differentiation stemming from the fact that schools prepare for different goals—educational and/or vocational. In his third and fourth year, a grammar school boy will take English, French, mathematics, physics, scripture, physical training, and games, plus three additional subjects chosen from prescribed combinations of Greek, Latin, German, history, geography, chemistry, biology, art, music, mechanical drawing, and workshop. Beyond their fourth year, grammar school boys are regrouped according to ability, and they follow shorter more general courses or take subjects leading to the ordinary or advanced level of the General Certificate of Education. At the end of the fifth year, those who choose to continue their education and demonstrate competence to do so enter the "Sixth Form"—a highly specialized, university preparatory course, leading to the advanced level of the General Certificate of Education. Within the Sixth Form, there is intensive concentration in one of several streams (classical, mathematical, scientific, linguistic). Thus, according to one writer, specialization in mathematics and physics at Westminister School entails the following weekly timetable in the first year: not counting games and physical education, 12 periods of mathematics, 7 of physics, 2 of genetics, 4 of English, 3 of French, 1 of art, and 1 of divinity; in the second year, the weekly periods of mathematics and physics are increased to constitute over 70 per cent of the total hours of instruction.[13]

Until the age of 15, children in the modern schools generally study the same subjects, except for variations in the number of periods devoted to each and in the school's inclusion of a grammar stream. In some schools, a foreign language is also included in the general course. According to the recommendations of the Ministry, the practical subjects of the curriculum should include "physical education, art, music, handicraft, housecraft and various kinds of craft work, and—wherever possible—gardening and animal husbandry." The Ministry, however, has been explicit in stating that it does not prescribe the subjects of the curriculum nor the time spent on each; this decision is left to the local authorities, the school managers, and the teachers. Hence, there are considerable variations in the overall curriculum of the modern schools, which render any description in terms of subjects and allotted time quite impossible. In a gallant effort to do so, the recent Newsom Report estimated that the percentage-time allotment in the four-year curriculum of a typical modern school for boys was distributed as follows: humanities (English, religious instruction, history, geography, miscellaneous) 39 per cent ; science and mathematics, 24 per cent; practical subjects (art, music, physical education, wood and metal work, technical drawing) 37 per cent. In the case of a typical school for girls, the distribution was: humanities, 39 per cent; science and mathematics, 22 per cent; and practical subjects (art, music, physical education, housecraft, needlework) 39 per cent. In some schools, common subjects may include rural science (5 per cent of the total hours); shorthand and

[13] A. Harry Passow, *Secondary Education for All: The English Approach* (Columbus, Ohio: Ohio State University Press, 1961), p. 129.

typing (20 per cent); and a foreign language (11 per cent), depending on the specific "bias" or "emphasis" of the school.[14]

As noted earlier, the dosage of general subjects in a technical school is basically the same as that in a grammar school. From the ages of 13 to 15, the same dosage is increased, and technological or commercial subjects are introduced. In addition, there may be a "bias" in one of the following areas: science, engineering, social services, commerce, or art. Many technical schools prepare for the same type of examinations as do the grammar schools, and the most able students in them enter "Sixth Forms." Some technical schools—like the Cheney School (Oxford)—are more practical in their curriculum orientation; after the common two-year general course, they offer programs for building trades and engineering, for arts and crafts, and for commercial purposes.[15]

In discussing the curriculum content of English schools, it is interesting to note that the Education Act of 1944 made no provisions as to what the schools should include, except in matters of religious observance and instruction. The religious rapprochement or concordat reached at that time—and in force today—provides for a "collective act of worship" and for religious instruction in all state-aided schools. Such worship and instruction is subject, however, to the Conscience Clause, which allows parents to withdraw their children from participation if they so desire. Religious instruction varies, but according to the 1944 act, it must not be "distinctive of any particular denomination" and must be conducted "in accordance with a nonsectarian 'agreed syllabus' . . . drawn up by representatives from the various important religions in each area, from the teachers' associations, and from the L.E.A." The arrangements agreed upon in 1944 marked the solution of a problem that has been the source of intensive controversy in the development of English educational policy since the nineteenth century.

WEST GERMANY

Since the unification of Germany in 1871, the educational history of the country (not including that of East Germany after World War II) can be roughly divided into four periods: (1) The period of the Empire (1870-1918); (2) The period of the Weimar Republic (1919-1933); (3) Education under the Third Reich (1933-1945); (4) Education in the German Federal Republic (1945- to present). During the Imperial period, the three-track system of education was firmly established, and it set the basic pattern for schooling in modern Germany. Under that system, there were three types of schools: the *Volksschule* for the masses; the *Mittelschule* for the middle groups (in terms of ability and social class); and the *Gymnasium* for the upper classes or the ablest students. The *Volksschule* and the *Mittelschule* provided terminal education and generally prepared students for minor positions in industry and/or business. Those graduates of the *Gymnasium* who qualified for the final comprehensive examination (*Abitur*) were eligible for entrance into the university.

[14] Ministry of Education, *Half Our Future.* (London: Her Majesty's Stationery Office, 1963), p. 237. A Report of the Central Advisory Council for Education. Hereafter cited as Newsom Report.

[15] Passow, *op. cit.*, p. 152.

The curriculum of the school was classical-humanistic in its orientation; however, under a new plan, two additional academic types of schools were introduced: the *Realschule,* which emphasized science and mathematics and the *Oberrealschule,* which stressed modern foreign languages.

During the period of the Weimar Republic, in an effort to democratize the schools and provide a common education for all, the *Grundschule* (or the basic elementary school) was introduced. Transfer to higher schools was allowed only after completing the work of the fourth grade. A new secondary course was introduced that allowed the student to complete his education in six years (in the *Aufbauschule*) and made it possible for youth in the rural areas to attend school. The *Deutsche Oberschule* was a new type of *Gymnasium* that emphasized German language, history, literature, and science rather than classical studies and languages. Under the Third Reich, the *Deutsche Oberschule* became the dominant secondary school; its administrators tried to inculcate in youth the ideas of Nazism and national socialism and to train loyal and efficient subjects. During this period, in an attempt to solidify, unify, and control educational practice, a National Ministry of Education was created and vested with vast powers—including the selection of school curricula, teaching procedures, and textbooks in the various communities. After the defeat of Germany in 1945, the national ministry was dissolved and each *Land* was vested with the authority to exercise control over its own educational system.

ADMINISTRATION AND CONTROL

Today the Federal Republic of Germany is divided into ten states (*Länder*) plus West Berlin, which is usually treated as a state although as an administrative unit, it constitutes a separate category. Educationally, each state is autonomous with its own minister of education, who is responsible for the administration, supervision, and financing of schools, as well as for the formulation of educational policy. The six larger states have an intermediary administrative unit with its own offices, which mainly supervises the instructional programs in the elementary, middle, and vocational schools. At the local level, there are county (*Landkreis*) or city (*Stadtkreis*) units, which supervise schools under their jurisdiction. A state supervisor (*Schulrat*), appointed by the Minister, sees that the school district operates efficiently and that State educational policy is implemented. The local unit functions in close cooperation with the local governmental authorities, i.e., the heads of the county governments or the city mayors.

In the absence of a central national ministry of education, each state retains autonomy in educational and cultural matters. However, at the federal level there are certain agencies that are instrumental in policy decisions affecting the individual states. One such agency, located in Bonn, is the "Permanent Conference of Ministers of Education," which consists of the ten state ministers of education and the representative of West Berlin. The conference has three standing committees (Universities, Elementary and Secondary Schools, and Culture Committees), and it makes recommendations on educational matters to the state authorities. By and large, the conference has tried to bring about some uniformity among the various states concerning school entrance requirements, transfer of students from one state to another, and teacher certification. In this way, problems of transfer created as a result of different educational standards among states have been somewhat alleviated. Nevertheless, it should be stressed that the conference has only advisory powers and that its recommendations are in no way binding unless, on the initiative of the minister, they are enacted into law by the state legislature.

In 1953, the German Committee for Education and Instruction was formed by joint action of the Ministry of Interior and the Conference of Ministers of Education. This is another advisory and research organization, consisting of twenty members who are appointed by the two aforementioned parent agencies for a five-year term. The members are selected from all walks of life, but usually teachers, university professors, and scientists form the core of the agency. In 1959, this body prepared a "Master Plan" (the *Rahmenplan*) to reorganize the entire educational system in Germany. The *Rahmenplan* and its implications for the future of Germany will be discussed in another section in more detail.

Public-school financing is mainly a joint task of the state and the local community. As a general rule, each state is responsible for institutions of higher learning and for vocational and teacher training schools; the local school district (or municipality) is responsible for elementary, middle, and secondary schools. When public schools offer vocational and technical subjects, they often receive combined support from the state and local unit. The state usually supports personnel costs (teacher salaries, pensions, etc.) whereas the local unit contributes to the material costs (construction and maintenance of buildings, libraries, instructional facilities, etc.) In *Baden-Württemberg*, for example, the local community contributes 30 per cent of personnel costs to elementary schools and pays for all material expenses. In Berlin and Hamburg, all material and personnel costs are underwritten by the government; textbooks and tuition are free. In all other states, the system of combined support prevails.

Within the school, the director supervises the instructional program, the teaching staff, and the physical plant. In the past, he enjoyed "dictatorial" powers; however, under the federal system of West Germany, a "teachers' conference" was created, through which the views of the faculty were being expressed. In some states, such as Bremen and Hamburg, the "conference" is a decision-making body and the director is obligated to carry out its policies.

It is interesting to note that Lindegren found many similarities in administrative practices in German and American schools.[16] In both systems, education rests with individual states. The educational ministers in Germany meet in a Permanent Conference of Ministers of Education and try to exchange views on educational problems and to bring about some uniformity in school standards. According to Lindegren, the Council of Chief State School Officers in the United States performs a similar function.

ORGANIZATION OF THE SCHOOLS

Before World War I, German education—like French education—was dualistic. The upper segments of society followed a different educational track from the rest of the population. The Weimar Constitution of 1919

---

[16] Alina M. Lindegren, *Germany Revisited: Education in the Federal Republic*, Bulletin No. 12, U.S. Department of Health, Education, and Welfare, Office of Education (Washington, D. C.: Government Printing Office, 1957), p. 13.

sought to bridge the gap between elementary and secondary education by introducing a system of common primary schools and by increasing opportunities for able lower-class children to enter secondary schools and ultimately the universities. Traditionally, secondary education was dominated by the classical-humanistic *Gymnasium*, whose main function was the selection and training of intellectually competent students for entrance into the university, the professions, and the civil service. The social and educational functions of the *Gymnasium* were essentially similar to those of the French *lycée* and the English grammar school. As in those systems, however, it was not impossible for a clever working-class child to gain admission into the *Gymnasium*.

After World War II, the occupying powers issued a directive that embodied the basic democratic doctrine of equality of opportunity. In addition, this directive provided that there should be compulsory education from the ages of six to fifteen; that such education should form a comprehensive pattern organized into two consecutive levels of instruction, namely, elementary and secondary; and that tuition, textbooks, maintenance grants, etc. should be free of charge in all educational institutions.

The directive was interpreted in different ways. A unified common school system was not adopted and what resulted was not a radical modification of the traditional pattern. In February, 1955, at Düsseldorf, the Minister Presidents of the West German states approved the proposals presented by the Conference of Ministers of Education for the unification of education. In their agreement, there were specific recommendations for the expansion of educational opportunities. In general, the unified plan envisaged a four-year elementary school, followed by two alternatives: a six-year middle school, which might be shortened into a five-, four-, or three-year middle school after completion of elementary grades five, six, or seven, respectively; and a nine-year, long-type secondary school of three kinds— classical language *Gymnasium*, modern language *Gymnasium*, and mathematics-natural science *Gymnasium*.

Under the present system, all children attend a common elementary school (*Grundschule*) before entering a more specialized course of study, which to a large extent determines their occupation and social position. After completing the course in the *Grundschule*, a pupil has three avenues open to him. (1) He may continue in the eight-year elementary school (*Volksschule*) and upon graduation attend a part-time vocational school (*Berufsschule*) or a full-time vocational school (*Fachschule*). In most states school attendance is compulsory until the age of eighteen, for those who do not attend full-time schools. (2) He may attend a middle school (*Mittelschule*), which combines an academic and a practical curriculum through grade ten. Upon completion of this course, the student receives a middle-level maturity certificate, which enables him to find employment in the lower business or in governmental occupations. (3) If the student is successful in his entrance examination, he may continue his education in the prestigious *Gymnasium*, which is the gateway to the university or to positions of considerable economic and social importance. In the *Gymnasium*, a student may opt one of three streams: ancient language, modern language, or mathematics-science.

The tripartite classification into the *Volksschule*, the *Mittelschule* and the various types of *Gymnasia* does not vary substantially from the English tripartite classification. The Germans, like the English, have elaborate methods of selection, except that the age at which selection takes place is more frequently at about ten-plus. Also, according to one writer at least, the Germans are trying to make these selective examinations as flexible and as "humane" as possible.

The organizational structure of the German educational system came under attack in the late fifties and early sixties. It was claimed that the system perpetuated the conditions of social inequality, and that children of middle- or upper-class families had better opportunities for advanced education and for professional careers than children from low socio-economic backgrounds. In theory, selection does not take place until after the *Grundschule*. But in practice, parental pressure—reflecting a socio-economic bias—influences the child's educational choices beginning with the first grade. It is estimated that about 30 per cent of children in the basic schools or *Grundschulen* go on to middle or secondary schools.

As in England, the selective procedures and the differentiated institutional structure to which they lead have been criticized as being undemocratic, as tending to turn the school "into a shunting yard for careers and social status," and as being too demanding on the children's intellectual capacities.[17] Although we lack adequate data on the social composition of the student bodies in the various types of post-primary schools, the scattered information we have points to the persistence of ascriptive as well as achievement criteria in the process of selection and differentiation. It is argued that these conditions contribute to social inequality and waste in manpower resources, that four years of basic elementary schooling are not sufficient to provide maximum development of individual potential, and that the different educational arrangements under the federal system create an educational chaos. For instance, there were several types of secondary schools—13-year schools, 9-year schools, 6-year schools, and 2-year schools—each specializing in different fields. In addition, there were urban schools and rural schools differing in organization and selection procedures.

As a result of such criticisms, a committee established in the 1950's proposed the *Rahmenplan* (master plan) for the unification of the diverse practices in organization and selection.[18] The *Rahmenplan* rejected the notion of a common secondary school similar to the American comprehensive secondary school. Instead, it proposed a two-year middle stage called *Förderstufe*—somewhat similar to the French *cycle d'observation*—for all children finishing a four-year *Grundschule*. Beyond this stage, it suggested three main types of institutions: the *Hauptschule* (upper elementary, formerly known as the *Volksschule*), a three- or four-year school with a practical curriculum for the majority of the students; the *Realschule*, a five-year school providing a terminal education for students of average ability and leading to lower-grade, white-collar occupations; and a two-track academic *Gymnasium*, one a seven-year school for the highly intelligent students and the other a nine-year school, starting immediately after the *Grundschule*, for the very small percentage of exceptional children.

According to some observers of the German educational scene, the *Rahmenplan* did not introduce any revolutionary changes in the system.

---

[17] Willi Koelle, "Selection Procedures in the Schools of the Federal Republic of Germany," *The Year Book of Education*, 1962, p. 265.

[18] For an interpretive account of this plan, see Ursula Kirkpatrick, "The Rahmenplan for West German School Reform." *Comparative Education Review*, IV, No. 1 (June 1960), 18-25.

The traditional tripartite structure was retained. Vocational, evening, and private schools were not discussed in the proposal. The strictly academic, inflexible nature of the curriculum was maintained. Emphasis continued to be placed on classical and humanistic studies, so that the student would be imbued with the values of great traditions of European civilization. The educational system would still tend to discriminate against children of the lower-economic strata, who generally would not pursue an education in the *Gymnasium* or even in the Middle Schools. Although such criticisms of the *Rahmenplan* may be justified, one could question the extent to which changes in the organization of the schools and in the curriculum may—in and of themselves—bring about radical social reform, especially in a society that historically has been characterized by aristocratic modes of thought and institutions.

On the other hand, several points in the *Rahmenplan* constitute a definite improvement over the previous pattern. First of all, the several types of secondary schools are brought within a unified educational structure which, for example, minimizes the problems associated with student transfers from one state to another. The *Förderstufe* extends the common educational experience of most of the children to six years; and it provides a two-year diagnostic period, mostly for the benefit of "late bloomers".[19] The *Rahmenplan* also suggested alternative routes to higher education. Under the plan known as *Zweite Weg* (second road), students who attend part-time vocational schools could take extra work in the newly created "colleges" (*Abendgymnasien*), which would prepare them for the university entrance examinations. Thus, the gap that has existed between academic and vocational education may be bridged, and students of low socio-economic status may be given more opportunity for social advancement.

While the merits and demerits of the *Rahmenplan* were still being discussed, one of the larger organizations of teachers—the *Arbeitsgemeinschaft Deutscher Lehrerverbände*—which is comprised mostly of elementary- and middle-school teachers proposed a new scheme known as the *Bremerplan*. The proposal, presented in the early 1960's, incorporates the main aims of the *Rahmenplan*—e.g., to increase the nation's manpower capability and to allow for a more equitable distribution of educational opportunity—but it goes much further than the *Rahmenplan* in its suggestions for implementing these goals. Under the *Rahmenplan*, the transition grades (*Förderstufe*) are not designed for all students (the bright students are exempted). Under the *Bremerplan*, all children—regardless of their intelligence and social background—attend the same transition grades, which serve both diagnostic and social purposes. Also, the latter plan argues that the Main School (*Hauptschule*) or Senior Elementary School (*Volksschuloberstufe*) should be extended to include grades seven through ten and that the curriculum should incorporate more vocational subjects.

The *Rahmenplan* proposed two types of academic secondary schools, the 9-year *Gymnasium* (grades five through thirteen) and the 7-year *Gymnasium* (grades seven through thirteen). The *Bremerplan* advocated only one type of *Gymnasium*, the 7-year *Gymnasium*, which has three curriculum streams: classical language; modern language; and mathematics-science. The *Bremerplan* claimed to provide the individual with better

---

[19] This practice has been attacked by many *Gymnasium* teachers who feel that it will lead to a lowering of standards in the *Gymnasium*.

chances to pursue a course of study consistent with his intellectual competence and career interests.

One will have to admit that the *Bremerplan* goes much further than the *Rahmenplan* in its recommendations for educational reform. It makes a strong case for common educational experiences in the transitional diagnostic stage, it emphasizes vocational education in addition to the classical-humanistic subjects, and it makes provisions for individual differences. A German educator concluded his comparison of the two plans with the following perceptive remarks: "In some respects, the Teachers' Association's plan is more courageous and advises steps that are more revolutionary in character; but its general outline also fails to suggest a thorough change of the old model of German education." [20]

CURRICULUM

The major aim of the elementary school is to provide experiences to help each child develop to his fullest capacity and understand his physical and social environment. The most important subject in the elementary-school curriculum is *Heimatkunde,* which deals with topics familiar to the child—home, church, school, farm, factory, etc.[21] Local traditions and myths are taught and are often supplemented by excursions and field trips to places of historical and cultural interest. By and large, the curriculum of the *Volksschule* embraces all the subjects taught in American schools—including reading, writing, arithmetic, geography, history, nature studies, singing, and drawing. In addition, religious education—Protestant and Catholic—constitutes an essential ingredient of the curriculum. Religion is endorsed by the state government and is frequently taught by a clergyman. State syllabi have detailed information on the content and method of instruction. According to several official pronouncements, the school is responsible for the upbringing of children in accordance with Christian principles. Although church and state are separate, in some of the states there are statutory provisions to the effect that the German school is a Christian school. The federal constitution stipulates that "religious instruction is to be part of the normal program of the schools . . ."

The *Schulbehörde* (Office of Education) in each state issues a teacher's manual that outlines the curriculum of the elementary and secondary schools and sets forth "guiding principles" on matters relating to organization, selection, and sequence of subjects. The teacher has considerable freedom in selecting his textbooks and methods of instruction.

With the exception of religion, which is taught in the elementary school and throughout the nine years of the secondary school, one finds that the curriculum of the German *Gymnasium* reflects the pattern prevalent in most European secondary schools. Allowing for the particular emphasis in the three *Gymnasium* tracks (humanistic, modern language, or scientific), the general curriculum includes the entire spectrum of subjects— German, social studies (civics, geography, history), English, French, Latin, physics, chemistry, biology, music, fine arts, and physical education. Elec-

[20] Herbert Enderwitz, "Two German Educational Reform Schemes: The Rahmenplan and the Bremerplan," *Comparative Education Review,* VII, No. 1 (June 1963), 47-50.

[21] This program is comparable to elementary-school programs in the United States, where they generally operate under the principle of the "expanding environment," i.e., the study proceeds from the familiar to the less familiar.

tives within each track are very rare; when available, they are usually offered in the senior grades of the *Gymnasium.*

German language and literature receive major attention at the secondary level in terms of both intensity and allotment of time. In addition, foreign writers such as Gogol, Hemingway, and Shaw are carefully studied. At the lower grades, grammar and composition are stressed.

Instruction in Latin begins in the fifth grade and continues through the senior grades of the secondary school. Classical Greek receives lesser emphasis, but its study is compulsory only in the humanistic *Gymnasium.* In addition to the classics, modern foreign languages—especially English and French—are required subjects in most states. In the upper grades, the most important goal of language instruction is to know and appreciate the cultural heritage and the spirit of the English and French people.

The curriculum in mathematics and science is very demanding. Beginning with simple fractions and decimals in grade 6, the student studies trigonometry and calculus in grades 12 and 13. Physics, chemistry, and biology are taught as separate subjects and contain topics such as thermodynamics, the periodic system of elements, and morphology and physiology of plants. In contradistinction to Soviet practice, no special provisions are made in the German *Gymnasium* to relate scientific knowledge and skills to practical situations in industry.

In the field of history and social studies, European history is treated chronologically; each grade deals with consecutive epochs, e.g., students begin with the Greco-Roman civilization in grade 7 and end with modern Europe in grade 13. Geography, which has an important place in the curriculum, deals with German and European landscape. A course in political education, introduced on the advice of the Allied Powers after the War, aims at inculcating modern democratic values in German youth. Moreover, an attempt is made to examine critically the ugly episodes of recent German history, despite some resentment against this practice. Whether these forms of political education achieve the professed democratic goals of the Federal Republic or not has been a topic of debate in current literature. Obviously, as in the case of Japan, it is unreasonable to expect that deep-seated sentiments and feelings toward the nation and its history will be eradicated over a short period of time through a course in civic education.

In sum, the educational system in West Germany still retains the traditional curriculum pattern that has historically characterized European education. It is conceivable, however, that the need to understand and utilize modern technology will be increasingly reflected in school programs. The educational plan introduced in 1959 is only a beginning in the modernization of German public education.

THE UNITED STATES OF AMERICA

With the "transit of civilization," the early immigrants transplanted English ideas and practices about education to the colonies of the New World. Dame schools, writing schools, Latin grammar schools, and a college were soon established to train future religious and civic leaders by transmitting the values the Puritan settlers espoused and the religious practices they could not exercise freely at home. Yet, unavoidably, the conditions of the new environment created the need for certain changes and adaptations. Unlike England, Massachusetts as early as 1642 and 1647 enacted laws compelling parents to send their children to school and town officials and communities to provide teachers and facilities for them. In addition, public authorities were called upon to assume responsibility in the education of young children. Thus, education in the United States became a community function early in its history.

Another strand in the American tradition that had important ramifications for education has been the existence of religious and cultural pluralism. There has never been an established church responsible for education in the English sense. Although some states did have established churches, there was generally considerable variation and competition among religious denominations. The very existence of religious diversity was a contributing factor in the subsequent separation of church and state, with its implications for education—e.g., the place of religious instruction in schools, the public support of parochial schools, etc.

The absence of deeply entrenched traditional institutions is another characteristic of American culture. Although the majority of the early settlers came from England, there was an absence of the aristocratic institutional patterns that pervaded and regulated English life and education. The absence of such traditional constraints facilitated a frontier type of life and the creation of new institutions and outlooks. Beginning with the eighteenth century and acquiring increased proportions in the nineteenth century, the elements of practicalism and equalitarianism became activating forces in the evolution of educational policy.

In the latter part of the eighteenth century, the liberal doctrine and spirit of the Enlightenment fired the imagination of the revolutionary thinkers and education was conceived to be a necessary instrument for the creation and maintenance of a viable democratic society. In a well-known statement, Jefferson epitomized the new democratic ideal and faith in education as follows: "If a nation expects to be ignorant and free in a state of civilization, it expects what never was and never will be. . . . There is no safe deposit [for the functions of government] but with the people themselves; nor can they be safe with them without information."

It should be noted that such important documents as the Declaration of Independence and the Constitution of the United States and its Bill of Rights made no explicit reference to education. Implicitly, however, the Tenth Amendment makes education the responsibility of the individual state rather than of the federal government. It is also significant to note that since then education has been thought of as an indispensable means to realize the political and social goals of the Revolution. In contrast to the prevalent European pattern, the citizen of the "first new nation" viewed education as a right rather than as a privilege.

Two of the outstanding educational features of the first half of the nineteenth century were the emergence of the common school and the growth of the academies. The common school, grounded in the social and political milieu of the Jacksonian era, was envisaged as a school common to all, not for common people in the European sense. It was regarded as a social equalizer, capable of breaking down sharp social divisions created by economic, social, and cultural differences. It was considered a necessary safeguard of the rights and freedoms of the individual and the society; and it was viewed as an important agency of social and moral improvement, as well as an agency for developing American patriotism. The common school was the first stage of education; it provided the rudiments of knowledge (reading, writing, spelling, arithmetic, and possibly geography, history, and grammar) and moral—but not sectarian—instruction. By 1850, the common-school movement had taken roots. Such schools were supported by permanent school funds established for this purpose, or by direct taxation. By this time also, public control—either by the local community or by the individual state—had become an established practice.

The academy movement may be traced to Benjamin Franklin's Academy of Philadelphia. By the middle of the nineteenth century, the number of academies increased to phenomenal proportions. In part a protest against the prevalent Latin school, the academy, in addition to preparing for college, sought to train a diverse social group for the "business of life." The curriculum of the academies was varied and flexible depending on the interest of the students who attended them and on the financial resources of the school. Most academies were private, and their standards ranged from those of an elementary school to those of a college. Some had an academic bias, others a practical one.

The academy opened up opportunities for men and women who could not find a place in the Latin grammar schools. It became the "people's college." Yet, the academy was a "stopgap." It performed a necessary function in a growing industrial and practically-oriented society and it laid much of the groundwork for the high school; however, with the increasing emphasis placed upon public support and control of education, the possibilities of its becoming the universal pattern of American education were limited. Already in 1820, a subcommittee of the Boston School Committee was asked to investigate the possibility of establishing a seminary for young men who would complete "a good English education" and enter "the departments of commercial life." This led to the setting up of the English classical school, soon changed to the English high school.

The high school idea spread; by the Civil War, there were more than 300 high schools over the country, the majority being in the Eastern states, especially in Massachusetts. By the opening years of the twentieth century, their numbers soared to over 7,000, contrasted to a very sharp decrease of academies.

The early high schools were established by transforming existing academies, by adding to the grades of the common school, or by setting up completely new institutions. Unlike the European and other countries, the emergence of the high school as a publicly supported and controlled institution was enmeshed in local and state politics rather than in national politics. Moreover, as the movement was gaining ground, the high school was envisaged as a logical sequel to the common elementary school and as a school that would recruit students from all the social strata. This fundamental shift in the conception of secondary education in the United States took place during the opening decades of this century, and culminated in the famous report of the Commission on the Reorganization of Secondary Education of 1918. Some of the ideas embodied in this document are discussed in a following section. Suffice to mention here that, according to this report, secondary education should consider the needs of the society it serves, the diverse characteristics of the students, and the available knowledge of educational theory and practice. A type of school that aimed at the intellectual development of a selected group of adolescents would not be consonant with the needs of a diverse high school population, nor of the complex new social order. To accomplish the goals suggested, the commission endorsed the idea of a "comprehensive program" and urged its adoption "in all the secondary schools in the nation."

Essentially, the new conception of secondary education was the common school ideal extended into the high school. Since the appearance of the Cardinal Principles of Education, the ideal has mainly remained the same. Subsequent policy statements by various bodies refined and expanded rather than modified it. It was only in the period after World War II that certain assumptions about secondary education and the comprehensive school came under attack.

The United States does not have a national system of education administered and controlled by a department or a ministry of the national government. Rather, the legal responsibility for regulating and maintaining public schools is given to the individual states. The legal cornerstone for a state system of education is cemented in the Tenth Amendment to the Constitution, which says: "The powers not delegated to the United States by the Constitution, nor prohibited by it to the states, are reserved to the states respectively, or to the people." According to this provision, state legislatures have unlimited power provided that there is no conflict with the Federal Constitution or with the constitution of the individual state.

Each of the fifty states maintains a state department of education, which usually consists of a state board of education, a chief state-school officer, and his staff. In the majority of the states, the members of the board are appointed by the governor; in others, they are elected by popular vote. The most important duties of the state boards of education include: the distribution of state or federal funds for the support of school districts; the establishment of criteria relating to accreditation of schools, certification of teachers, curriculum development, building construction, and student health and safety; and the development of general school policies.

The policies of the state legislatures and of the state boards of education are executed by the chief school officer, who is often known as superintendent, commissioner, or director. As of 1961, the chief school officer was appointed by the state board of education in 23 states; the rest have used other procedures of selection, e.g., gubernatorial appointment or popular election. The main functions of the chief school officer are: the general supervision of schools; the interpretation of school laws; the submission of reports to the board and to the legislature about the status and needs of the schools; and the preparation of a budget regarding the appropriation of state funds to the various local school districts.

Although at the state level the board of education and its chief executive have the overall responsibility for maintaining and regulating public education, the local school district is responsible for the day-to-day operation of the schools within the district. There are more than 40,000 such school districts, which are political entities created by the states. Each school district has its own board of education and school superintendent; each district has been traditionally considered a symbol of local autonomy, because it has been delegated considerable authority by the state legislature and its membership is drawn from local lay people.

Local autonomy was characteristic of the administration of schools in New England during the Colonial period, and it gradually became the dominant pattern throughout the United States. The movement for independent boards in charge of the local schools was generally accompanied by provisions for compulsory attendance, taxation for support of public schools, and control and maintenance of schools. The changes that have taken place in American society over a period of about 300 years raise certain questions concerning the effectiveness of an autonomous school board at the grass-roots level and its contribution to the democratization of American public education. It has been argued, for example, that decentralization and local control of education has resulted in numerous school districts (about 125,000 in 1933 and about 103,000 at the close of World War II), many of which have not been economical and efficient to operate, thus providing limited educational opportunities for children attending them. Recently, the movement for consolidation or redistricting attempted to solve the problem of many school districts that were too small, and it succeeded in reducing the number to about 35,000 in 1962, many of which had a relatively sounder fiscal and educational basis.

The typical American school board has about five members who represent both sexes and all professions. In most districts, school-board members are elected through nonpartisan elections, but at least one board in seven is appointed by city administrators. Less than 15 per cent of school districts pay a nominal salary to their school board members; in the remaining 85 per cent, school members are not compensated for their services. The main duties of the school board, which are established by law, are as follows: (1) to carry out the directives issued by the state legislature and the state board of education; (2) to formulate policies and rules in conjunction with school management; (3) to interpret school policies and decisions on crucial issues; (4) occasionally, to adjudicate cases concerning grievances, appeals, or teacher and pupil dismissals; (5) to evaluate school practices and identify problems; (6) when necessary, to function in an administrative capacity. The main task of the school board, however, is the selection and appointment of a chief executive officer or superintendent of schools, who acts as the interstitial or intermediary between the representatives of the people and the school staff.

The superintendent of schools is often a very powerful individual who has control over the destinies of thousands of children, teachers, and personnel, directly or indirectly involved with schools. Although he is accountable to the board and subject to removal by it and although in most states he does not have legal tenure, he discharges a number of important functions in connection with his position as the chief local officer. Some of these functions are: (1) to nominate (in effect to hire) new administrators, teachers, and other employees; (2) to recommend suspension of teachers whose performance has not been satisfactory; (3) to prepare courses of study as authorized by the board, and to supervise curriculum revision; (4) to supervise the maintenance of the school plant and the purchase of new equipment, etc.; and (5) to prepare the school budget and submit it to the board for approval. One of the most crucial problems faced by superintendents is to maintain harmonious relations with the board and, at the same time, to represent the teaching profession. Their position is extremely delicate since they perform a dual function as employees and employers. A traditional bone of contention between superintendents and school boards has been the nature of the authority legally vested in them. As a general rule, the board is supposed to formulate broad educational policy in the district; the superintendent is expected to administer the schools within the framework of the policy guidelines. However, because it is often difficult to distinguish between policies and rules and regulations, the lines of demarcation between the two are often muddled and jurisdictional problems result. The jurisdictional problem is probably the most significant contributing factor to the high turnover of superintendents, who—on the average—stay in one place about six years and are sometimes referred to as the "itinerant schoolmasters." Callahan, reviewing the actions of school administrators in the twentieth century, pointed out that they contributed to an American educational tragedy when, trying to counteract their vulnerability to the pressures of the board and the community, they resorted to a businesslike scientific management of the school. In emphasizing the efficiency of business corporations, they lost track of the crucial educational objectives and intellectual concerns of the school.[22]

Within each separate school—whether elementary, junior high, or senior high—the principal operates as the chief administrative officer. According to a 1958 survey of the National Educational Association, the average school principal's time is divided among such tasks as supervision, administration, clerical work, teaching, and community relations. Actually, about 65 per cent of his time is spent on supervision of instruction and administration of the school; the remaining time is devoted to the other activities. Although there are schools where the principal exercises his duties in a very authoritarian way, there are as many or more schools where he consults with his faculty on crucial issues. Unlike the school superintendent, both principal and teacher can attain academic tenure.

Although there is no centralized office at the national level responsible for basic educational policy and administration of school districts, the federal government influences educational activity in many ways. First of all, the U.S. Office of Education in the Department of Health, Education, and Welfare—initially established in 1867—operates as a dissemination center in education; it collects information and statistics on the conditions of the schools. Secondly, through the U.S. Office of Education and other agencies, federal funds are distributed to the states in support of certain programs. Under the National Defense Education Act of 1958, for example, the states were given federal monies to strengthen the mathematics, science, foreign language, and guidance programs. Similarly, monies were allocated to colleges and universities to conduct summer institutes for the training of teachers and counselors. A recent law passed by Congress provided for direct contributions to school districts in which enrollments increased as a result of federal activity. These grants were used for operating the schools, for teachers' salaries, and for school construction. State and local educational policy may also be influenced by decisions of the Supreme Court of the United States, as, for example, in the famous Brown v. Board of Education decision of 1954, concerning the legality of the separate but equal doctrine. The Supreme Court ruled that the separation of schools and facilities on racial grounds was unconstitutional. This decision has laid the legal basis for school desegregation and continues

[22] Raymond E. Callahan, *Education and the Cult of Efficiency* (Chicago: University of Chicago Press, 1962).

to be invoked in cases where racial segregation is practiced. The Supreme Court also has adjudicated on matters affecting religion in schools—for example, whether prayers, public transportation for parochial-school children, provision of free textbooks for parochial-school children, etc. are in accord with the provisions of the Constitution.

In addition to the influence exerted on the schools by various agencies of the federal government, some private and semiprivate organizations—such as the College Entrance Examination Board, the National Merit Scholarship Corporation, and the National Science Foundation—have had a considerable impact upon educational programs. A recent survey of the programs developed under the foregoing organizations and the U.S. Office of Education, which has administered the National Defense Education Act, summarized their influence as having "(1) changed courses offered in science, mathematics, and foreign language; (2) altered guidance programs; (3) created a vast external testing program; (4) changed college admissions procedures; (5) established a new pattern of in-service education for teachers; (6) altered school-plant planning and construction; and (7) given the public a new measuring stick with which to evaluate schools." [23] One should also remember that teacher-organizations like the National Education Association, the various national and regional accrediting agencies, citizens' lay groups like the Parent-Teacher Associations, textbook writers and publishers, etc. in one way or another, influence the schools. All these direct and indirect influences contribute to a relative uniformity and standardization of school programs throughout the United States. However, many differences in the quality of the schools still exist in the various geographic regions of the country.

Public school expenditures are underwritten by the states and the local communities. During the 1961-62 school year, for example, 40.2 per cent of the total school revenue came from state sources; 56.1 per cent was derived from local sources; and 3.7 per cent came from the federal government. In recent years, the amount of money spent on public education was approximately 15 billion dollars (the cost of higher education was about 5 billion dollars), as compared with 50 billion dollars for military preparations.

In 1959, the President's Science Advisory Committee recommended that public expenditures in education be doubled to keep pace with rising school enrollments, longer attendance, and the emphasis on quality instruction. A relatively small per cent of the national income is spent for education (about 3.5 per cent), compared to that spent by the Soviet Union, England, and other countries (about 5 to 10 per cent). The relatively small percentage of the national income spent on education, may be explained partly by the fact that the main financial responsibility for the schools is borne by the states and local communities. In absolute figures, of course, the amount of money invested in education is greater than that of several other countries.

As mentioned before, the school budget is prepared by the school superintendent and his staff, and it is submitted to the local school board for consideration and approval. The school board conducts an open hearing on the budget in order to give members of the community the opportunity to express their views. Since a good portion of educational funds

[23] Roald F. Campbell and Robert A. Bunnell, "Differential Impact of National Programs on Secondary Schools," *School Review* LXXI, No. 4 (1963), 464.

is derived from local-school district taxes—e.g., property taxes—the adoption of the budget entails concomitant tax assessments on the community.

Unlike many of the European schools, the organizational structure of the schools in the United States is rather simple: an elementary school is followed by a secondary comprehensive school for all. However, there are certain variations in the organizational patterns of the local school districts —the so-called 6-3-3, 6-2-4, 6-6, or 8-4 patterns. A 6-2-4 pattern, for example, has a six-year elementary school, followed by a two-year junior high school and a four-year high school. In the majority of cases, such schools form separate units and operate under different school administrators. About one-third of the school districts are organized on the 6-3-3 principle, one-fourth are on the 8-4 plan, and one-sixth on the 6-2-4 plan. As a general rule, the first type of school organization is prevalent in large urban centers, while the latter types are most widely found in smaller communities. Such factors as local tradition, availability of facilities and equipment, and means of transportation seem to influence the organization of a particular system. In a period of thirty years, the general trend in school organization throughout the country has been from the 8-4 pattern to the 6-6 and 6-3-3 patterns. For example, of the 14,300 secondary schools in 1920, 94 per cent were on the 8-4 plan and only 5 per cent were on the 6-6 plan. By 1959, the percentage of schools falling under the 8-4 category was reduced to about 24 per cent; the schools in the 6-6 category increased to 42 per cent of the total number, which was about 24,000. Also, during this period, there has been a dramatic increase in the number of junior high schools. In 1959, these schools comprised 21 per cent of the total number of secondary schools. These junior high schools were created to meet what many educators referred to as the unique emotional, physical, social, and intellectual needs of the pre- and early adolescent. Mainly as a result of this belief, the junior high school generally provides an exploratory three-year stage—somewhat like the *cycle d'observation* in France—which gives the young the opportunity to try out certain subjects, discover their talents and interests, and begin to think about a career.

The great majority of the students in the United States attend a public secondary school, or as it is commonly known, a comprehensive high school. In contrast to the prevailing pattern in France, England, Germany, and other European nations, the American educational system—actually represented by the comprehensive school—is multifunctional. The system provides common learnings for all; but at the same time, it offers both skills that can be used in finding gainful employment after graduation and academic programs leading to advanced studies in a university or college. The school is expected to educate the gifted, the slow learners, the mentally retarded, the culturally deprived, and to function as an agency of assimilation of immigrants or their children.

Between 1920 and 1960, there has been a general increase in enrollments. For instance, 93.2 per cent of the twelve-year old group was enrolled in schools in 1920; by 1960, the percentage went up to 97.5. The most dramatic increases, however, took place among youth in the 16 to 20 age group. While only 50.8 per cent of the sixteen-year old group was attending school in 1920, 86.3 per cent was attending in 1960, equaling a significant increase of 35.5 per cent over a forty-year period.

The general picture of educational attainment in the early 1960's was as follows: dropouts, 30 per cent; high school graduates with no post-secondary schooling, 35 per cent; those attending a noncollegiate post-secondary school, 7 per cent; those with some college, 14 per cent; and college graduates, 14 per cent. This fairly advanced level of educational attainment may be explained in part by the fact that 47 states, Puerto Rico, and the District of Columbia have school attendance laws that, in the main, are enforced. In 36 states, 7 years is the required minimum age for attending a school; in 38 states, the maximum compulsory age of attendance is 16. Another explanation is that formal education in an industrially and economically advanced society such as the United States becomes a necessary prerequisite for occupational placement. For example, while only 14.1 per cent of the high school graduates in 1962 were unemployed, 28.6 per cent of the young people who had dropped out were in the same category. Thus, without a high school diploma, the chances to be unemployed are practically doubled. Moreover, economic affluence makes it possible for the country to forego the benefits of juvenile employment and thus keep children at school for a longer period of time.

CURRICULUM

Although European influences and forces peculiar to North America played a role in shaping the American public school, many contemporary practices may be traced to the activities of national committees around the turn of the century. For example, the famous Committee of Ten—chaired by Charles W. Eliot, then president of Harvard—in its report to the National Education Association in 1893 recommended that: (1) high schools offer four programs, classical, Latin-scientific, modern languages, and English; (2) no differentiation be made between college-preparatory and terminal programs; (3) electives be introduced to allow for some flexibility and for individual differences; and (4) intellectual disciplining would be the best training for life or for college.[24] Although the report generally reflected the humanistic-literary tradition, it recognized that modern languages and scientific subjects should have an increasingly important place in the curriculum. The report is also significant in that it did not recommend a dual program (college-preparatory and terminal), which would allocate pupils on the basis of ability and, probably, discriminate against those with a low socio-economic background. Twenty-five years later—as the United States entered a new era of urbanization and industrialization and as new immigrants began to arrive en masse—another national committee, known as the Commission on the Reorganization of Secondary Education proposed changes in the programs and purpose of the schools. The report of this commission, issued in 1918 and known as *Cardinal Principles of Secondary Education*, was based on a rationale similar to Herbert Spencer's in that it emphasized the activities of the individual for complete living. The new educational goals, or principles, were stated as: health, command of fundamental processes, worthy home-membership, vocation, civic education, worthy use of leisure, and ethical character. These principles were supposed to apply to all levels of education—elementary, secondary, and higher—and each school subject was

---

[24] For a comprehensive discussion of the composition and activities of the national committees between 1880 and 1920, see Edward A. Krug, *The Shaping of the American High School* (New York: Harper and Row, Publishers, 1964).

supposed to relate to these educational objectives. Thus, the commission gave a green light to those who wanted to introduce vocational subjects and citizenship education into the curriculum. In sum, the report emphasized the unifying task of the schools; it reaffirmed the idea of the comprehensive high school; it provided for individual differences to be cultivated in differentiated curricula (e.g., agricultural, business, household-arts); it stressed good citizenship values, including loyalty to school, state, and nation; and it argued for universal secondary education.[25] The objectives of vocational education and social efficiency were echoed in a statement on the "Imperative Educational Needs of Youth," published in 1944 by the Educational Policies Commission of the NEA. The need to develop "saleable" skills and to understand the rights and duties of citizens in a democracy figured prominently in the statement.[26]

In subsequent years, the questions of what the purpose of the schools should be and what programs they should emphasize were debated with vigor. Critics of American public education—like Arthur E. Bestor (professor of history), Robert Hutchins (then Chancellor of the University of Chicago), and Hyman Rickover (Admiral of the United States Navy)—have accused the schools of promoting mediocrity, of emphasizing "life adjustment," and of neglecting their fundamental intellectual tasks. In the fifties, titles like *Why Johnny Can't Read, Schools Without Scholars, Quackery in the Public Schools,* and the like, provided rallying symbols for vitriolic attacks against the schools. The champions of the public schools responded by pointing out that the schools were doing more than an adequate job in educating all the people, in providing differentiated instruction to accommodate varied talents and interests, and in equipping the young with the knowledge and skills necessary to meet the demands of a complex industrial society. Basing his arguments on statistical evidence, a well-known educator upheld the accomplishments and quality of the American public schools, and he concluded: "In 50 years the integrity of our country has stood firm through many harsh tests. In depression and war the graduates of our schools and colleges have proved that, while a few of us may be petty or mean, the average American is someone to be proud of . . . *we have more often succeeded than failed as a people, and a substantial measure of credit for this success is due to the effectiveness of public education.*" [27]

While the debate continues in one form or another, the basic aim of the American schools is maximum education for all. Keeping this goal in mind, let us briefly examine the curriculum in the contemporary-American educational scene.

At the outset, it should be stated that although educational provision is the responsibility of the states, it is accurate to say that there are more

[25] *Ibid.,* pp. 389-405.

[26] Educational Policies Commission, *Education for All American Youth* (Washington, D. C.: National Education Association, 1944), pp. 225-26. The E.P.C. recommended the distribution of secondary school subjects as follows: common learnings, 33.3 per cent; vocational preparation, 33.3 per cent; electives, 16.7 per cent; and health and physical education, 16.7 per cent.

[27] Harold G. Shane, "We Can be Proud of the Facts," in *The Great Debate: Our Schools in Crisis,* C. Winfield Scott, Clyde M. Hill, and Hobert W. Burns, eds. (Englewood Cliffs, N.J.: Prentice-Hall, Inc., 1959), p. 139. Reprinted from *The Nation's Schools* (September 1957). Copyright 1957, The Modern Hospital Publishing Co., Inc., Chicago. All rights reserved. With permission.

imilarities in the curricula among the fifty states than one would expect. One could easily identify a pattern of elementary and secondary education that would be representative of the nation as a whole. In the elementary school, for example, although the three R's are still emphasized, social studies, science, the arts, and even foreign languages are standard offerings. The ways these subjects are organized and taught, however, vary somewhat. The most prevalent arrangements in the elementary school are the subject-, broad-fields-, and experience-centered curricula. The subject-centered curriculum replicates the college or upper-secondary-school pattern, where subjects retain their identity and are taught separately. The broad-fields organization, sometimes known as "fused," combines related subjects into wide areas. For instance, civics, geography, history, economics, and sociology are included in the social studies area; grammar, reading, speech, spelling and writing are included in the language-arts program. The experience or activities curriculum is organized around interests or "felt needs" of children. The program is not planned in the traditional sense to include conventional subject matter; rather, certain subjects are examined in connection with "problems" that arise in class. Also, the prevalent arrangement in the elementary school—especially in the primary grades—is the 'self-contained" classroom where, with the possible exception of physical education and music, one teacher is responsible for all instructional activities. With some variations, the general trend in curriculum organization is toward developmental-activity programs in the first three grades of the elementary school and broad-fields or departmentalized programs in grades four through six or eight.

Since 1929, the following major changes in the elementary school have been observed: (1) a trend toward a unified approach in the organization of subject matter; (2) an emphasis on relating school work with life problems; (3) an attempt to introduce problem-solving procedures and stimulate student initiative and discussion in the classroom; (4) the use of new materials and classroom aids, e.g., radio, film, television; (5) a stress on individual differences; (6) improvement of standards of instruction and caliber of teachers; and (7) a trend toward flexible scheduling, so that the student may develop at his own pace. A more recent innovation is the nongraded elementary school which eliminates the rigidity of grades, etc., and stresses mainly developmental tasks as a criterion for promotion.

In the secondary school, the curriculum organization varies according to level. For example, the "core" or the unified-subject pattern is found in about 20 per cent of the junior high schools. This type of curriculum assumes a core of common learnings, and it is arranged in blocks of time where a group of related subjects and activities may be introduced. The subject-centered organization still characterizes many junior high schools and the majority of the senior high schools. Notwithstanding the varying curriculum patterns, a junior high school program usually includes mathematics, science, language arts, social studies. In the ninth grade, it provides some electives, e.g., foreign languages and art appreciation, thus enabling the student to make the transition from the junior high to the senior high and to begin to pursue his special interests.

Actually, the junior high school program is essentially diagnostic in purpose; it is supposed to provide student guidance and opportunity and to identify student talent through testing.

The senior-comprehensive high school—which usually includes grades ten, eleven, and twelve—offers programs for students with various educational and vocational interests. The student may major in certain subjects or combinations of subjects within such typical programs as general, college-preparatory, terminal-business, or terminal-industrial. It should be understood, however, that although a student might major in a terminal-business curriculum, his career choice, unlike most of the European schools, is not final. If he decides to continue his education, he may remove his deficiencies before entering a college, he may find a college that will admit him conditionally, or he may even be admitted into certain institutions of higher learning without any conditions attached. Regardless of his major or curriculum stream, however, there are certain subjects that are required of all students. These subjects are generally in the areas of English, social studies, mathematics, and general science. Another important feature that differentiates American high schools from schools in other countries is the system of electives. For instance, an American student who is a high school junior (usually age 16) and majors in business has a choice of electives from a number of subjects: algebra, French, German, Spanish, bookkeeping, typing, stenography, commercial law, economics, practical physics, practical chemistry, etc. Electives available to all, regardless of curriculum stream or major, could range from public speaking and art to advanced general music, technical drawing, or driver education.

High school credit is usually given in "Carnegie units." Each unit represents at least 120 clock hours of work in the classroom in one school year; normally, a student is required to complete a minimum of four Carnegie units a year. The Carnegie unit of measuring academic credit was adopted in 1909 by the Carnegie Foundation for the Advancement of Teaching, which sought to standardize the criteria for college admission. In recent years, the Carnegie unit has come under criticism mainly because it discriminates against "nonacademic" subjects, contributes to the inflexibility of school programs and class schedules, and emphasizes quantitative rather than qualitative aspects of school work.

The "great debate" of the fifties on the nature and scope of secondary schools culminated in the publication of the famous Conant Report in 1959. James B. Conant, former president of Harvard University, through a private research grant, attempted to assess the status of the comprehensive high school. His report concluded that very few comprehensive schools in the United States were actually meeting their objectives in the sense of offering general education for all, adequate elective programs, and a satisfactory curriculum for college-bound students. In the main, Conant attributed the failure of the schools to the existence of a disproportionate number of small high schools. He found that about 14,184 out of 21,000 public high schools had a graduating class of less than 100 students. According to Conant, such schools were too small to offer satisfactory programs at reasonable costs. Conant's recommendations emphasized the importance of individualized programs and common programs for all (i.e., four years of English, three or four years of social studies, one year of mathematics, and one year of science). Furthermore, Conant suggested rigorous and rich programs for the academically talented and the highly gifted and diversified programs for the development of marketable skills, e.g., typing and general secretarial work for girls or vocational agriculture for boys.[28] Conant's recommendations, although subject to several criticisms, seem to have had an impact on American public education.

Although the school curriculum is legally the responsibility of the individual state and local agencies, private organizations—like the one that financed Conant's investigation—have assumed a leading role in the shaping of the high school curriculum. The Chamber of Commerce, the Parent-Teacher Association, the League of Women Voters, the National Education Association, the AFL-CIO, and other lay or professional organizations operate as pressure groups in influencing the decisions of national and state agencies and, at the local level, of school boards and superintendents of schools. Also, there has been a revival of national study groups, seeking to influence education on a nationwide basis. For example, the last decade has witnessed the emergence of such groups as the Physical Science Study Committee, the School Mathematics Study Group, the Chemical Education Material Study, and the government-financed "Project English" and "Project Social Studies," which sought mainly to strengthen specific areas in the curriculum. The underlying goal of these study groups has been to reinstate the importance of studying a subject qua subject, without necessarily relating it to practical or vocational considerations. The almost hysterical attempts to strengthen the curriculum of the public school were largely due to the launching of the Russian Sputnik and to the feeling among certain groups that American hegemony in the world was beginning to fade away. What many people failed to consider was the possibility that it was not so much that the American schools were weaker than before, but that other nations were able to pay more attention to education and to improve the caliber of their schools and that the inevitable changing conditions at home and abroad necessitated an educational appraisal.

87

[28] James B. Conant, *The American High School Today* (New York: McGraw-Hill Book Company, 1959).

Confucianism, as a social and political philosophy, played a major role in the history of Japanese education. The Confucian principles —emphasizing filial piety, orderly life, loyalty, obedience, and benevolence—were introduced in Japan around the twelfth century, when the warrior gentry (samurai) rose to power and instituted a feudal regime. The military tradition developed during this time; legitimized by the Confucian doctrine, it resulted in vesting the emperor with ultimate moral, spiritual, and political power. All subjects were to be obedient and loyal to the sovereign. At the end of the twelfth century, the power of the emperor gradually declined and was taken over by the shogun, a military dictator who commanded a large army and who was the highest authority among the feudal lords. Until 1861, when Emperor Meiji restored the powers of his office, the institution of the shogunate functioned as the government of Japan.

Up to this period, the most important schools were the clan schools and the private temple schools (*Terakoya*). The clan schools were supported by the feudal fiefs and offered a curriculum based on Confucian principles of morality and samurai etiquette. Great emphasis

88

DEVELOPED NONWESTERN SOCIETIES

6

as placed on the Chinese classics, and caligraphy was considered an important subject designed to train character and develop aesthetic values. The clan schools in general aimed at preparing young men for positions of leadership in the government or in the military. The *Terakoya* schools, in addition to Confucian ethics and the military arts, taught practical subjects such as arithmetic and business. For the most part, these schools provided a means for the rising merchant class to train their offspring for positions in commerce.

Educational modernization in Japan may be said to begin with the Meiji restoration in 1868, and it is divided into three general periods: (1) the period of systematization and nationalization of education (1872-1939); (2) the wartime period (1940-45); (3) the period of democratization (1946 to the present). During the first period, a Department of Education was created to plan and supervise a nationwide system of education. In 1872, the "Government Order of Education" (the *Gakusei*) was promulgated in order to unify educational institutions at all levels and thereby accelerate the transition from a feudal society to a nation-ate. Under the new order, the nation was to be divided into eight university districts, each one having a number of middle (secondary) and elementary schools. During this initial period, the Japanese adopted the French system of educational administration—with a central ministry of education and prefectures.

It was at this time, also, that American educators were brought in to introduce new curriculum-practices and new methods of teaching. David Murray, an American college professor, was employed by the Japanese to help in the reorganization of the national system of education. Murray helped plan new courses of study and offered advice on the construction of school buildings. Encouraged by the government, several Japanese educators went to America and Europe to study modern pedagogical practices. Through them and the advisors at home, Pestalozzian and Herbartian ideas were introduced.

In the 1880's, however, there was a general reaction to the liberal ideas from the West; the main emphasis turned toward developing nationalism and increasing governmental control of education. The "Imperial Rescript" of 1890 reaffirmed the traditional values of filial piety, loyalty, obedience to superiors, and total submission to the Emperor. A required course in morals (*shusin*) was introduced, with its focus on Shinto ideology (emperor and ancestor worship).

The nationalistic, emperor-centered philosophy of education generally prevailed until the end of World War II, although during the period immediately following World War I there were some sporadic attempts to introduce liberal educational practices based on John Dewey, William Kilpatrick, and others. During the 1930's, there was a tremendous upsurge of a militaristic-chauvinistic type of nationalism, which pervaded the entire curriculum of the schools. The ministry, through a tight system of inspection and control, supervised all phases of public education to make sure that the goals embodied in the *Basic Principles of the National Polity*, issued in 1937, were realized. In accordance with this document, patriotism and a mystical devotion to the emperor were the ultimate virtues to be inculcated in all youth.

During the wartime period, the militarist group assumed dictatorial powers over all phases of life. A new Education Order issued in March,

1941, asserted the importance of imbuing the students with ideas about the moral mission of the Empire; it emphasized the need for self-sacrifice for the benefit of the state and the Emperor. The government continued to use the device of issuing Imperial Rescripts to bypass the Diet or any other bodies that expressed popular sentiment in its policy of deliberate thought-control. The Ministry of Education (Mombusho), headed by a minister appointed by the Emperor, had an elaborate bureaucratic machinery to enforce its policy. The permanent vice-minister of education was in charge of a secretariat and eight bureaus, through which he exercised control over personnel, school buildings, curricula, and textbooks. The Bureau of Thought Supervision was created in 1929, and reinforced in 1939, to combat "alien" ideas and movements among students. The implementation of national educational policy was the responsibility of the prefectural governor who, aided by a large staff, exercised surveillance over the schools in his jurisdiction.[1] A large corps of inspectors and superintendents responsible to the national ministry of education supervised the schools and made sure that local officials executed the imperial policy.

After the defeat of Japan in 1945, the course of educational history entered a new phase. Under the guidance of the Supreme Command for the Allied Powers and its special section on Civil Information and Education, a reform-plan, aimed at democratization and demilitarization of the educational system, was introduced. The new educational philosophy, endorsed by the Occupation Forces, was incorporated in a directive entitled, "Administration of the Educational System of Japan," issued October 22, 1945. There, it was specifically stated that the dissemination of militaristic and ultranationalistic doctrines was proscribed. The new objectives of the school were to develop educated, peaceful, and democratic citizens; new programs and textbooks were to be developed to reflect the democratic spirit. Subsequent directives provided that there be screening of teachers and that Shinto religion be separated from the state.

In March, 1946, a United States Education Mission consisting of twenty-seven distinguished educators visited Japan in order to acquire first-hand knowledge of pressing educational problems. In its report, the Mission recommended a general decentralization of the educational system. The Ministry of Education and its agencies were to perform advisory functions; and following the American tradition, school boards were to be elected by the people in the prefecture or the local community. These boards became responsible for appointing school superintendents, outlining the educational aims of the community, and preparing the school budget.

The new Constitution, adopted in 1946, revoked several previous Imperial rescripts and government orders and guaranteed certain basic rights and freedoms: life, liberty, and the pursuit of happiness (Article 13); equality before the law (Article 14); freedom of religion (Article 20); academic freedom (Article 23); and equal education according to ability (Article 26). The Constitutional guarantees were further expanded and

---

[1] Before the war, there were three types of schools: (1) grammar schools; (2) schools created by the prefecture or local unit; and (3) private schools. All of the schools were regulated by the national government.

[2] This Article stipulated that the state refrain from religious education.

amplified in the Fundamental Law of Education, passed by the Diet in 1947, which marked the first time in Japanese history that educational policy was legislated by a representative body. In addition, under this new law, nine years of free-compulsory education were required.

The directives issued by the Occupation Forces, the report of the advisory committee, the Constitution of 1946, and the Fundamental Law of Education furnished the legal framework within which major educational reform took place.

In contrast to the situation prevailing until 1945, the early postwar period was generally characterized by administrative decentralization of education. Under the Board of Education Law passed in 1948, which was influenced by the United States Education Mission, two types of school boards were created: (1) prefectural boards of education with six out of seven members popularly elected; and (2) local boards of education (for cities, towns, or villages) with four out of five members elected. The most important duties of the boards at both levels were to appoint school superintendents, principals, and teachers, and to prepare the budget for submission to the assembly by the state (prefectural) governor or mayor. Prefectural boards, of which there were forty-six, were empowered to certify teachers and authorize textbooks for public school use. The local school boards were responsible for school programs, the establishment and maintenance of school buildings, and the in-service training of teachers. The functions of the National Ministry changed drastically—from an agency exercising total control and supervision of education to one designed to offer professional advice and financial aid to the local communities. According to the Ministry of Education Establishment Law of 1949, the Division of Superintendents and Inspectors was dissolved. Hence, the Ministry retained its Secretariat and its five bureaus (Elementary and Secondary Education, Social Education, Higher Education, Research, and Administration), to which a Bureau of Physical Education was later added. As a consequence of this reorganization, the number of staff members was reduced.

91

The system of elected local and prefectural school boards did not work as well as expected. First of all, the majority of the board members lacked the necessary experience to handle problems relating to the creation, maintenance, and supervision of public institutions. Many of them wanted to expand their policy-making power to include tasks normally falling under the jurisdiction of the teachers and administrators. Secondly, many teachers inescapably committed to represent the professional interests of Japan Teachers' Union were elected to the various boards, thus defeating the idea of impartiality in the negotiation of teachers' contracts and promotions. Also, board members received remuneration for their services. For many, the position became a lucrative preoccupation—they were able to vote themselves sizable salaries and expense accounts. Finally, the local school boards (as distinguished from their American counterparts) were not financially autonomous; they depended upon the local assembly for funds. Consequently, local boards, played in the hands of the political party or interest group that happened to be in power. Obviously, superimposing a foreign school plan on another culture without taking into consideration the peculiarities of that culture does not solve existing problems; in many cases, it creates new and more serious social conflicts and dislocations. This question will be discussed in greater detail in another chapter.

In its search for ways to remedy the defects of the existing situation, the government reverted to a pattern resembling prewar arrangements. Under the new law of 1956, members of the prefectural and municipal (or village) school boards were to be appointed by the governor or mayor, respectively, with the consent of the appropriate assembly, rather than elected by the people. There was to be no control by any one single party. The Minister of Education was given the power to veto decisions made by the school boards. At the prefectural level, superintendents were to be appointed by the board with the consent of the Minister; at the local level, their appointment required the approval of the prefectural board. All elementary and secondary school teachers were to be appointed by the prefectural board.

Under the new system, the Ministry of Education—through its sections and bureaus—performs both advisory and supervisory functions; and it approves the establishment of prefectural colleges and universities, including private universities. The Ministry also controls and maintains what are known as "National Schools," namely, national colleges and universities and national upper-secondary schools. The relationship of the Ministry to the other schools—the prefectural and municipal schools—and to their boards is theoretically mainly advisory. However, the central government has assumed major responsibility in the setting of standards in matters of personnel and in determining the amount of direct-school subsidies.

In each of the prefectures, the board of education is in charge of the upper-secondary schools and special schools for the handicapped. In 1960-61, there were 5,959 upper-secondary schools and 225 special schools. In addition, the board's authority extends over museums, public libraries, etc. At the municipal level, the board is mainly responsible for elementary and lower-secondary schools. In 1960-61, there were 26,858 and 12,986 schools, respectively.[3] Moreover, the municipal boards supervise cultural and civic centers, such as citizens' public halls, libraries, and recreation places. According to a recent report of the Ministry, the more specific duties of the local school boards are: (1) establishment, maintenance, and closing of schools; (2) curriculum construction and revision; (3) adoption of textbooks; (4) appointment and dismissal of teachers; (5) purchasing of instructional materials; and (6) in-service training of teachers.

Supervision of instruction is exercised by both national and state agencies. The Ministry issues directives to the boards; regularly supervises schools through a system of curriculum specialists and/or outstanding university professors, serving on part-time basis; holds conferences and workshops for teachers, consultants, and administrators; and publishes syllabi and handbooks for teachers. The prefectures, on their part, supervise local boards through consultants, who are experienced teachers specializing in a particular field of study. Finally, in each school, the principals themselves perform supervisory functions over their staff; since 1957, they have been responsible for the evaluation and rating of teachers' performances. The reports of the principals concerning a teacher's character and competence are submitted to the appropriate board or agency. This practice

[3] Ministry of Education, *Japan: Education in 1960,* Annual Report of the Ministry of Education for the Year Ending March 31, 1960 (March 1962), p. 13.

has become highly controversial and has brought about sit-down and hunger strikes, sponsored by Japan Teachers' Union.

Because there is no special school tax, the national government underwrites a significant portion of the educational expenditures. The prefectural governments subsidize city and village schools. The local governmental units support and maintain public elementary and lower-secondary schools; payements of teachers' salaries are shared on an equal basis by the national and prefectural governments. The main source of revenue consists of taxes levied at the national and local levels, supplemented by money from miscellaneous sources such as donations, museum-admission fees, examination fees, etc. Bonds and short-term loans are authorized for the construction of buildings. The national government subsidizes education in three different ways: (1) through direct operation of national schools; (2) through allocations of monies to prefectures, municipalities, private schools, and research organizations; and (3) through local finance-equalization grants. In 1959-60, the distribution of public expenditures for compulsory education at the three levels—national, prefectural, and municipal —was 32 per cent, 38 per cent, and 23 per cent, respectively. In 1959-60, 521,148 million yen (1,448 million dollars) were spent for public education. This sum constituted 5.2 per cent of the national income and 21.1 per cent of the national and local public expenditures.[4]

From our discussion so far, it is clear that Japan's central government takes more than an active role in the administration and finance of education. According to Anderson, a recent observer of the Japanese educational scene, the present system has departed drastically from the early postwar pattern. Anderson feels that the introduction of time-schedules concerning standards of achievement, the new emphasis on military drill in physical-education courses, the uniformity of curriculum guides handed down by the state and national authorities, and the restrictions concerning discussion of controversial issues in the schools are "reminiscent of the uniform, controlled curriculum-making of former days." [5]

93

The position of the two major political parties on the current educational structure presents us with an interesting side light. The socialist and, generally, the leftist organizations—including Japan Teachers' Union—are strong advocates of the continuation of the educational system introduced by the American Occupation Forces. The conservative organizations, led by Liberal-Democrats, want to revise existing policies in order to bring about a higher degree of national control and to reintroduce some of the values of the past.

ORGANIZATION OF THE SCHOOLS

Compulsory education was introduced in Japan during the latter part of the nineteenth century. The code of 1872 stipulated that each village and town provide compulsory, free education for four years regardless of social class or sex. In 1908, compulsory public education was raised to six years and all but a very small percentage of children (about 5 per cent) completed elementary school.

[4] Ministry of Education, *Education in Japan: Graphic Presentation*, 1961, pp. 43-44.
[5] Ronald S. Anderson, "Japan," in *Comparative Educational Administration*, Theodore L. Reller and Edgar L. Morphet, eds. (Englewood Cliffs, N.J.: Prentice-Hall, Inc., 1962), pp. 271-72.

The school system before World War II was organized in terms of five tracks beyond a six-year elementary stage. Of these, the most prestigious was the academic track, which led to the university and to high positions in the government and in the professions. It consisted of five years in a middle school, three years in a higher school, and three years in a university. At each successive level, there were stiff entrance examinations that selected only a small number of students for further education. According to one report, only one-half of 1 per cent of children entering elementary school were able to finish a university. Among the thirty-two Government Higher Schools in this category, there was the famous First Higher School in Tokyo, a supraelite institution and the most important school for entrance into Imperial Tokyo University. The overwhelming majority of the students (about 72 per cent) in the middle schools terminated their education at that level.

A second educational track was designed especially for girls. It consisted of four- or five-year high schools and of three higher normal schools for the few very academically talented. In accordance with Confucian principles, a girl's place was at home as a wife and a mother. Consequently, the education of girls was different from that of boys—there was less emphasis on the basic subjects, but more on homemaking, decorative arts (flower arrangement, tea ceremony, etc.), and child care. Other institutions, such as private girls' colleges (of which some were missionary schools), offered additional work in language and literature.

A normal school (teacher-training) track provided the third educational alternative. This was designed to prepare teachers imbued with loyalty and devotion to the Emperor and the nation. The period of training in such schools varied according to the areas in which the teacher wished to specialize. For instance, the youth-normal school stressed vocational subjects for teachers in youth schools and offered a two-year course to those who had successfully completed eleven years of education. The government usually paid the expense of students in the normal schools; in return, a teacher was required to offer his services over a certain number of years.

The technical-school track included a five-year program of vocational education at the secondary level and a three- to five-year course at the higher level in technical institutes. The vocational-secondary schools enrolled about 10 per cent of elementary school graduates and trained them for low-grade positions in agriculture, commerce, and industry. This track —like its European counterparts—was held in very low esteem because of the traditional Japanese attitude, which looked down upon people doing menial jobs.

Finally, the Youth Schools offered another possibility for education beyond the elementary school in the form of part-time and full-time vocational education for laboring youth. The course of study ranged from two to seven years and emphasized subjects dealing with agriculture, industry, and fisheries. During World War II, there were about 15,000 of these schools throughout the country, especially in rural areas; many of them were production units in the war effort. At this time, they also came under the supervision of the army and they were used to instill feelings of nationalism and militarism.

The multi-track system provided the means for selection and differentiation of students. Moreover, within this institutional framework, there were some exclusive and high-status schools that prepared for the prestigious universities and, thereby, for positions in the professions and the civil service. For instance, graduates of Tokyo First Higher School were given top priority for admission into Tokyo Imperial University, which in turn was the main source of supply for executive and judicial posts in the government. The alumni clubs of Tokyo Imperial University and other similar institutions—e.g., Kyoto, Waseda, and Keio—exercised considerable influence regarding recruitment into the national ministries and other governmental and private organizations. Thus, the educational system before and during World War II reinforced the prevailing social-class structure of Japan; and directly or indirectly, it restricted the circulation of social elites through its control of recruitment patterns in secondary schools and universities. Vestiges of this system still exist in Japan.

As mentioned before, on the recommendation of the United States Education Mission, the Japanese reorganized their schools from a multi-track to a single-track system. Under the Constitution of 1946 and the Fundamental Law of Education of 1947, all children are entitled to an equal educational opportunity, regardless of "race, creed, sex, social status, economic position, or family origin." In its organization, the new system resembles the American system in that it is based on 6–3–3–4 plan. The six-year elementary schools and the three-year lower-secondary schools (or junior high schools) now provide compulsory education for all. The previous higher schools, preparatory schools, and technical schools have been merged into comprehensive upper-secondary schools for all. At the top of the educational ladder are the universities or colleges, which offer specialized four-year programs. In addition, some universities offer graduate work leading to the M.A. or Ph.D. degree. In their attempt to liberalize education and offer opportunities to working youth, part-time and correspondence schools at the upper-secondary level have been created. The part-time schools are mainly located in cities and offer specialized subjects in agriculture for boys or in homemaking for girls.

After completing their nine years of compulsory education, students wishing to continue in the upper-secondary schools must take an entrance examination. In these schools, students may elect such streams as general education, business, industry, agriculture, and the like. In 1959, approximately 55 per cent of those who completed the compulsory stage continued their education in the upper-secondary schools; of those who graduated from the upper-secondary schools, about 16 per cent went on to a college or university.[6] It is claimed that the proportion of upper-secondary school graduates who continue their education in institutions of higher learning is considerably higher in Japan than in other countries, except the United States.

Compared with the prewar situation, Japan has recently made significant strides toward the expansion of educational opportunities for all. Certain other government measures facilitated the process of democratizing education. One of these measures was the creation of school attendance districts in the prefectures; students are obligated to attend the school nearest their home. This regulation has removed the prestige attached to some schools and has created practical conditions for a more equal type of education. Other measures included the establishment of part-time schools, coeducational schools, new universities and junior colleges, and the grant-

---

[6] See, Ministry of Education, *Youth Education in a Changing Society: Japan*, March, 1961, pp. 50-52.

ing of scholarships to needy students. These governmental policies have encountered a great deal of opposition from students, parents, administrators, and teachers of high-status institutions. In many instances, the government, under pressure, relaxed its rules and tried to accommodate the interests of the competing pressure groups.

The reforms introduced in 1946 by the Allied Forces of Occupation had important effects on the curriculum of the elementary and secondary schools. The wartime course in moral education, which sought to inculcate in youth an unquestioned loyalty and devotion to the Emperor, was eliminated. History, geography, and morals as separate subjects were replaced by a unified course in social studies, where the key theme was responsible citizenship in a democratic society. Innovations were introduced in the science and mathematics programs, an attempt was made to promote independent study by allowing free study periods, and vocational subjects—especially courses in homemaking—were given added emphasis.

Today the Ministry of Education is legally responsible for setting curriculum standards in elementary and secondary schools. The Ministry publishes and distributes courses of study that outline the organization and sequence of required and elective subjects. In 1958, there was a major curriculum revision, the main goals of which were expressed as follows: "(1) to strengthen moral education; (2) to improve pupils' basic abilities; (3) to improve scientific and technical education; (4) to improve geography and history education; (5) to develop aesthetic emotions and to promote health and safety instructions; (6) to strengthen instruction in line with pupils' future careers and individual qualities in lower-secondary schools." [7] In accordance with an officially prescribed timetable, the curriculum of the elementary school includes Japanese language, social studies, arithmetic, science, music, art and handicrafts, homemaking, physical education, and moral education. In the same table, the Ministry of Education specifies the time allotted to each subject in each grade. For example, Japanese language is given a total of 238 instructional hours in the first grade (or about 7 hours a week) and 245 hours in the sixth. Moral education is taught for one period each week throughout the elementary school grades. Homemaking is introduced in the fifth grade and continues throughout the secondary school.

In the lower-secondary schools—the equivalent of the American junior high schools—in addition to the required subjects, which are the same as those in the elementary schools, there are a number of electives. The elective subjects emphasize vocational education and include courses in agriculture, industry, commerce, fisheries, and homemaking, as well as foreign language, music, and fine arts. Of the foreign languages, English seems to be the most popular. The course in moral education, which is supposed to build moral character and to foster socially approved behavior, is required; it is supplemented by extracurricular activities, such as pupil assemblies and clubs.

The study of the Japanese language is one of the most important, and perhaps most difficult subjects. It has also aroused considerable controversy in recent years. There are four systems of writing in Japan—Kanji,

[7] Ministry of Education, *Revised Curriculum in Japan for Elementary and Lower Secondary Schools*, Japan, 1960, pp. 3-6.

Katakana, Hiragana, and Romaji. Kanji, which was borrowed from China, is similar to picture-writing. At the compulsory level, a pupil is expected to know about 1,850 characters or ideographs. A university graduate is supposed to have mastered about 4,000, out of the 15,000 that are ordinarily found in a Japanese dictionary. Katakana and Hiragana have a Japanese origin and are systems of phonograms, each comprising 48 characters. Romaji is made up of Roman letters to express Japanese words. This system of writing is taught in the third and subsequent grades.

In social studies, the pattern is similar to that prevailing in the United States. In the elementary schools, the content centers in the study of the child's home, school, and community and gradually expands to encompass the national and international community. In the lower-secondary schools, the social studies are offered as separate subjects—geography, history, and social science.

Moral instruction has been the subject of much controversy in Japan since its reintroduction in 1958. Oshiba traced the origins of the notorious *shushin* (moral education), which emphasized national legends and reverence for the Emperor.[8] In later years, the course became ritualistic and was similar to ordinary religious services. After the wave of militarism in the 1930's, *shushin* was used as a convenient instrument to inculcate loyalty and patriotism, measured by the willingness of the populace to sacrifice their lives for the Emperor. When Japan was occupied by the Allied Forces, courses in *shushin* were suspended and "social studies" was introduced into the curriculum. The role of the school, as interpreted by the American consultants, was to lay the grounds for youths' participation in the building of a new moral order. As in the American tradition, it was assumed that morals are "caught" in the school rather than taught through formal instruction.[9]

The controversy reached a culminating point in 1958 when the Ministry, reacting to various pressures, reintroduced moral education in the curriculum. The main reason given for this action was that social studies, American style, de-emphasized nationalism and patriotism and resulted in a moral and social anarchy. The democratic values of the Americans were alien to Japanese students. It was also claimed that social studies, which stressed problem-solving methods, resulted in fragmentary knowledge of basic historical and geographical facts. In supporting its action, the Ministry referred to a governmental survey taken in 1957, in which it was reported that of the 3,000 people over 20 years of age polled, 70 per cent expressed a desire to have a course in morals restored in the schools.[10] It is doubtful whether this finding is representative of the feelings of the total population of Japan; the growing discontent and expressed dissatisfaction of teachers' organizations and labor unions seem to contradict the Ministry's claims.

Although the separate course in moral education purports to provide a content or orientation different from that included in *shushin* and

97

[8] Mamoru Oshiba, "Moral Education in Japan," *School Review* LXIX (Summer 1961), 227-44.
[9] Don Adams, "Rebirth of Moral Education in Japan," *Comparative Education Review* 4 (June, 1960), 61-64.
[10] R. S. Anderson, *Japan: Three Epochs of Modern Education*, Bulletin No. 11, U.S. Department of Health, Education, and Welfare (Washington, D. C.: Government Printing Office, 1959), p. 115.

although it is very similar to the American "Problems of Democracy" course in its emphasis upon good citizenship, there has been opposition to it from American advisers, who perhaps think that it will retrogress to its prewar status. Whether, as the Japanese contend, the course will offset rising juvenile delinquency and major social conflicts among the youth is doubtful. On the other hand, the American assumption that the transplanting of an American-patterned social-studies program in a society with a rich and deep-seated historical tradition will solve the ills of contemporary Japan is equally untenable.

Science education in the elementary schools includes the study of biological, physical, and natural phenomena; in the lower-secondary schools, it includes chemistry, physics, biology, and earth science. Mathematics includes arithmetic in the elementary school and subjects ranging from algebra to plane geometry and trigonometry in the lower-secondary schools.

The Japanese stress subjects in industrial arts or homemaking that are designed "to guide pupils to learn the fundamentals of technology necessary for life, acquire appreciation for the pleasure of creating and producing, and learn to understand modern technology, so that the solid attitude towards life is fostered." [11] Apparently, they are conscious of the need for functional education to meet the demands of a rapidly expanding economy.

The curriculum of the upper-secondary school is prescribed in the course of study issued by the Ministry of Education in 1960. A minimum of 85 credits (one credit is given for 35 hours of instruction over one academic year) is required for graduation. These credits are distributed among courses in the student's area of specialization and in general education, such as Japanese language and classics, social studies, mathematics, science, and foreign language. A student may follow a general educational path (Type A course) or an academic one (Type B course), with emphasis upon Japanese language, social studies, mathematics, science, and foreign language. The general education course is more flexible and includes fifteen hours of electives for boys and thirteen for girls; the academic course—the college preparatory course—leaves very little room for electives. In addition, the upper-secondary school offers a vocational curriculum with three major areas of specialization: industry, business, and agriculture. In turn, within each of these areas, there is further specialization. For example, within the mechanical course, there are five subareas of concentration: machine technology; supervision and management in machine shop; machine design and research; prime mover; industrial measurement and automatic control. It should be noted, however, that general education continues to be a major component, even within the specialized vocational streams. For example, in the machine-technology stream, the student is expected to complete 56 credit hours in general education and 52 hours in industrial education—a total of 111 credit hours, including three hours of homeroom or extra-curriculum activities. Graduates of vocational streams may occupy positions in industry, business, agriculture, or mining, or they may continue their education in a junior technical college.

Requirements in the general education stream are as follows: a minimum of twelve credit hours in modern Japanese language and classics; thirteen hours in history and the social sciences (ethics, political science, economics, and geography); nine credits in theoretical and applied mathematics; twelve credits in the sciences; six credits chosen from music, fine

[11] *Revised Curriculum in Japan*, p. 56.

arts, handicrafts, and calligraphy; and nine credits in modern foreign languages.

Despite the many postwar changes, the class character of the curriculum has not been completely eliminated; the academic tracks, by and large, continue to attract students from the upper socio-economic strata, who aspire to high government and business posts; full-time or part-time vocational schools attract mostly children from lower-status groups. Furthermore, some educational institutions—the feeder schools—continue to maintain their prewar prestigious position and to hold the key to good universities and certain higher occupations. The vicious competition for entrance into the high-status institutions has created many social and psychological problems; in some cases, it has even resulted in suicide.

As stated earlier, there is a general movement toward recentralization of educational authority. Notwithstanding the existence of local and prefectural school boards, the Ministry of Education still exercises a great deal of control over school buildings, program-development, staffing, and promotion of teachers. In the area of the curriculum, it can be said that very little consideration is given to local needs and to special interests of students. Although there are provisions for electives, the courses that really count are rigidly prescribed by the Ministry. On the other hand, by virtue of certain uniform policies and standards, the aura associated with certain institutions and certain curricula has been somewhat reduced. Furthermore, it appears that educational authorities in Japan have become more conscious of their national needs; much like the authorities in the Soviet Union, they are trying to provide a functional education for all.

THE SOVIET UNION

The roots of the Soviet school predate important events such as the Bolshevik Revolution in 1917 and the Emancipation of the Serfs in 1861. The doctrines of Greek Orthodox Christianity—the established religion until the Revolution—coupled with the arbitrary rule of the Russian princes and tsars gave Russian education a religious, mystical, and autocratic bent. Early Russian schools, organized on an informal basis, were attached to monasteries and churches; they aimed at the training of a small segment of the society for the priesthood. In the fifteenth and sixteenth centuries, when Russia began to emerge as a separate sovereign state, cultural and educational activities became more widespread. Under Ivan the Great, for example, several famous cathedrals were built, and Italian and German masters began to teach Russians practical skills. In subsequent years, enlightened rulers—such as Peter the Great and Catherine II—attached great importance to education and tried to emulate the educational practices of western Europe, especially those of Britain and Germany. It is interesting to observe that the first secular schools established during Peter's reign were a school of mathematics and navigation and a school of engineering and artillery. In addition, during Peter's regime, each province was asked to establish and maintain two elementary schools. Although this plan did not succeed and the schools continued to remain under the control of the church, the stage was set for increasing participation in school affairs on the part of the state and local community. This policy was followed by Catherine the Great, who set up Boards of Public Assistance, the functions of which were to build and maintain schools in towns and villages. The idea of compulsory education was still premature, however, and Catherine's plan did not materialize.

During these formative years of Russian development, the educational system generally reflected the conditions of Russian society and the conservative ideas of the ruling class. The purpose of the school—whether under the church or the state—was to foster an unquestioned loyalty to the tsar and the great Russian traditions, to maintain the autocratic regime and to perpetuate the existing class structure.

In the nineteenth century, the Russian rulers reacted against the French revolutionary ideas of equality, liberty, and fraternity, and the development of the modern European nation-state. Under Uvarov, Nicholas' Minister of Education, the traditional principles of Russian education—religion, autocracy, and nationality—were faithfully adhered to and reinforced. In this respect, a parallel with modern Soviet education may be drawn if one were to substitute Marxism-Leninism for faith, party for authority, and love of the motherland for nationality. By suppressing Western liberal ideas and technological developments, Uvarov may have delayed the industrial and economic development of his country. During this period, the universities lost their academic autonomy; church history and church law were made compulsory in all educational institutions, certain subjects such as natural science, social science, and philosophy were regarded with suspicion; and foreigners and people who had studied in Europe were distrusted.

In spite of constraining governmental measures, liberal ideas about government, society, and education gained momentum and began to spread in the major Russian cities. The Russian liberal thinkers of this period—e.g., Belinsky, Hertzen, Chernyshevsky, and Dobroliubov—emphasized the idea of social justice and respect for individual dignity and sought to cultivate the humanity of man through education. Such ideas were expressed in the activities of Konstantin D. Ushinsky, who founded the Russian primary school and teacher-training institutions.

Two other elements that have gone into the making of modern Soviet ideology were the economic and social theories of Karl Marx and the revolutionism of certain nineteenth century Russian thinkers. From Karl Marx, apart from a developmental theory of society based on changed modes of production, the Soviets obtained several ideas about society and education. Marx had argued that social organization and ideologies reflect the socio-economic conditions prevalent at the time. Hence, a change in the "super-structure" occurs when there is a concomitant change in the "objective conditions," within which he included educational provision. Marx also argued that in capitalist societies, there were several inherent "contradictions" expressed in education—e.g., unequal educational opportunities based on social class and geographical location (urban-rural), separation of theory and practice resulting in the "creation of pure theory and bad practice" and another separation between intellectual and physical labor with high specialization in the former. While the Soviets have based their social and educational theory on these Marxian principles, having incorporated many of them in their constitution and in their plans for educational development (polytechnical education, expansion of opportunities, combinations of manual and mental work), they have not been able to eliminate most of the "capitalist contradictions." [12]

From revolutionary thinkers such as Peter Zaichnevsky, Peter Tkachev, Sergei Nechaiev, and Mikhail Bakunin, the Soviets acquired a revolutionary absolutism, a revolutionary Machiavellianism, and generally "a tradition of revolutions by a highly organized and disciplined minority of intellectuals committed to a utopian vision of the ideal society." [13]

Following the Bolshevik revolution, Lunacharsky expressed the Soviet paradoxical policy as one aimed at creating a classless educational system, dominated by the proletarian class, and constructing a new type of school, oriented toward productivity. Thus, existing schools were abolished, the classical languages were declared nonobligatory, the mastery of academic subjects was relegated to a subordinate position, and under the slogan of "socially useful labor," a Unified Workers' School or Unified Labor School was established.

This type of school, which was the foundation of the Soviet educational system, comprised three sections: a four-year elementary section; a three-year middle section; and a two-year higher section. In addition, special institutions like the *Rabfacs* were set up to recruit people from the working classes for high positions in society; and such organizations as the *Young Pioneers* and the *Komsomol* were instituted to capture the youth and socialize them according to the Communist ideology.

The Unified Labor School was an experiment in pedagogy and social theory, pedagogical in that it sought to weave into a Soviet pattern various threads of progressive educational ideas and practices, and social in that it sought to create a new Soviet man and a new Soviet society. The controlling purpose was to eliminate social-class divisions and to give labor a dignified place in the society.

When after 1928 the Soviet Union embarked upon a series of five-year plans aimed at the complete industrialization of the country, the progressive-experimental or the *"romantic"* phase came to an end. The Unified Labor School developed into the polytechnical school, based on a systematic and firm mastery of the sciences—specifically physics, chemistry, and mathematics. Strict schedules of study and discipline were introduced; and a sentimental, permissive type of psychology known as pedology gave way to a more positive, purposeful psychology aimed at the creation of Soviet men who would "internalize" the Party line and who would, "like ideal bureaucrats, execute with energy and competence whatever tasks are set for them from above." [14]

In 1934, the nine-year sequence of the Unified Labor School was replaced by a ten-year system organized as follows: an elementary stage of four years; a middle or "incomplete" stage of three years; and a senior or "complete" secondary stage of three years. In a sense, this organization resembled the American elementary-junior high-senior high pattern of schooling. However, the Soviet system also resembled the German tripartite and selective structure, in that it consisted of three types of schools: four-year

[12] Maurice J. Shore, *Soviet Education* (New York: Philosophical Library, 1947), pp. 19-41.
[13] George S. Counts, *The Challenge of Soviet Education* (New York: McGraw-Hill Book Company, 1957), pp. 11 ff.
[14] W. W. Rostow, *et al.*, *The Dynamics of Soviet Society* (New York: New American Library of World Literature, Inc., Mentor Books, 1954), p. 109.

elementary schools; seven-year elementary-middle schools; and ten-year elementary-middle-senior schools. An important characteristic of this plan was that after a system of selective examinations, students could proceed from one type of school and level of education to another. Thus, for example, a child finishing a four-year school could transfer to a seven-year or a ten-year school, depending on his educational and vocational goals; similarly, a graduate of a seven-year school could transfer to a ten-year school. This restructuring of the system coincided with the reintroduction of high standards and rigorous terminal examinations, which culminated in 1944 in a maturity examination (similar to the German *Abitur*), covering the entire ten-year course.

ADMINISTRATION AND CONTROL

As the system is organized today, there is no overall national agency in charge of elementary and secondary schools. The Soviet Union consists of fifteen republics, each of which has a central ministry of education. Each ministry of education exercises its control over schools through regional and local departments of education. It issues directives concerning textbooks, courses of study, and methods of instruction; it supervises school construction and expenditures. Each republic ministry executes the decrees of the Council of Ministers of the U.S.S.R., which, in turn, implements the policy of the Central Committee of the Communist Party. Usually, the ministry of education of RSFSR, which is one of the fifteen Soviet Republics, sets the pattern for others to follow; it provides the standards for textbook writing, curriculum development, selective examinations, and the like. The RSFSR Academy of Pedagogical Sciences operates as a major research and dissemination center in education, and it indirectly influences education throughout the country. The remaining fourteen ministries adapt the instructional programs proposed by Moscow, the center of RSFSR, to the linguistic peculiarities of their respective regions. Other ministries—e.g., transportation, labor, etc.—and regional or local economic councils participate in the supervision of vocational and skilled-labor training programs. At the local level, the local educational agency (the RONO) cannot independently formulate educational policy or deal with educational issues concerning the local community. Its main responsibility is to prepare budgets and estimate enrollments and staff requirements. Local control of education, so familiar to the United States, is generally unknown in the Soviet Union. At the central level, the Communist Party controls education through the Council of Ministers and at the local level, through the party cells.

The highly centralized administrative structure, which exists at all levels (local, regional, republic, national), is replicated in each department of education and within primary and secondary schools under its jurisdiction. The head of each department of education, assisted by his staff, coordinates the activity of the schools in the district and appoints a principal or director for each school. The school director has administrative powers over his teachers and students, and he sees that the school meets the specifications of higher authorities. This rather rigid organization characterizes all Soviet schools. Teachers do not have a voice in the affairs of the school, although recent visitors have observed a degree of flexibility in methods of instruction. The work of both director and teacher is closely supervised by an inspector who is responsible to the district or city board of education.

Educational expenditures are underwritten by the state. The funds originate from the national budget, which derives its revenue from taxation. In 1937, total expenditures for educational-cultural activities amounted to 15.5 per cent of the annual budget. In 1960, the percentage earmarked for such activities was estimated to be about 13.8. Educational funds are allocated according to the norms of the State Planning Committee and the Ministry of Finance. Each educational unit proposes a budget based on the prescribed norms. A 1956 decree of the Council of Ministers abolished all tuition fees for secondary and high institutions. Stipends and scholarships for university students are based on merit and financial need. As DeWitt has pointed out, "stipends are, in effect, the production incentives of the Soviet educational systems." [15]

The conditions prevailing in the Russian political and administrative machinery tend to strengthen the powers of the bureaucracy and to inhibit educational leadership and the initiative of local authorities and school personnel. On the other hand, under the present system, the schools tend to respond faster to national emergencies and are used more effectively in the national interest. For example, through the system of stipends, students are channeled into fields that are currently in demand. The emphasis in the last decade on technical and professional skills—as opposed to programs of general education—and the consequent changes in educational practice have been facilitated by the centralized locus of decision-making.

ORGANIZATION OF THE SCHOOLS

The reorganization act of 1959 drastically changed the aims, organization, and curriculum of the primary and secondary schools. The four-year, seven-year, and ten-year schools were replaced by general-education-labor-polytechnical schools at three sublevels: the eight-year school (primary-secondary education for grades 1–8, inclusive of elementary education for grades 1–4 and junior-secondary education for grades 5–8); the three-year regular secondary school or evening-shift secondary school (beyond the eight-year school, including grades 9–11); and the eleven-year school (a complete secondary general-labor school, from grades 1 to 11). In addition, there are urban and rural *vocational-technical schools* that accept graduates from the eight-year schools and conduct both day and evening classes. Likewise, the schools commonly known as *technicums*, which are semi-professional training establishments, offer two- to four-year vocational curricula for graduates of the eight-year or eleven-year schools. The military and national security authorities have their own schools, which administratively remain outside the formal educational structure.

The movement for educational reform was initiated by Stalin in the early 1950's, mainly as a result of the great need for specialized jobs created by accelerated industrial and economic productivity. Prior to this period, the Soviet school concentrated on general academic education because of the abundance of people interested in manual and technical training. The manpower demands created by World War II losses, by a drop in the birth rate, and by the increased rate of economic growth forced the Soviet leaders to declare that children should receive a "functional" education—an education directly related to gainful employment. The whole movement found a powerful supporter in Khrushchev, who set the tone for subsequent structural changes in an address to the *Komsomol* in 1958. Khrush-

[15] DeWitt, *op. cit.*, p. 67.

chev criticized the existing system, because it separated school work from life and theory from practice; he attacked the prevailing attitude among students and parents to downgrade manual training and to place high esteem on academic education. He proposed to reorganize the structure and function of the Soviet schools in order to accommodate all children and to prepare them for socially useful labor. This principle was reiterated in 1959 in the theses of the Central Committee of the Communist Party and the Council of Ministers of the U.S.S.R. Among other things, the theses stated that "the task of the reconstruction of the school is the recognition that at a certain age all young people should be included in socially useful work and that their instruction in the foundations of science should be related to productive work in industry or agriculture. Hence the necessity of a correct correlation in the secondary school of general, polytechnical, and a vocational education . . ." [16]

One may summarize the major changes proposed in the 1959 act as follows: [17] (1) it made provisions to combine academic work with productive labor at all educational levels; (2) it created the eight-year school to replace the seven-year school, and it made eight years of attendance compulsory; (3) it provided that on leaving the eight-year school, young people could enter productive work in industrial and agricultural establishments or continue their study in a secondary labor-polytechnical school or a specialized secondary school; (4) it stipulated that the schools should strive to develop the new Soviet man, the man who has a high respect for labor and socially useful activity, a total devotion and loyalty to Marxism-Leninism and communist morality, and a love of the motherland; (5) it placed great emphasis on specialized fields like science, mathematics, and engineering, and reduced the requirements in the humanities and the social sciences; [18] (6) with regard to nationality schools—e.g., schools in the various republics and autonomous regions other than the RSFSR, it allowed parents to choose the language of instruction for their children, which may now be offered either in Russian or in the native tongue; and (7) in matters of ideology, the act tried to steer a middle course between historical interpretation, emphasizing great men (commonly known as the cult of personality), and sociological approaches, stressing social institutions and impersonal forces.

The new educational system attempts to strike a balance between higher and lower skills and to channel youth into such fields as conditions warrant. The Soviets operate under the assumption that once the conditions of inequality are removed e.g., the differential rewards and esteem of various types of schooling and the low prestige of labor, the society will reach the Marxist ideal, "from each according to his ability, to each according to his needs." Whether the present system will, in fact, remove social barriers remains to be seen.

[16] For a full text of the theses, see G. S. Counts, *Khrushchev and the Central Committee Speak on Education* (Pittsburgh: University of Pittsburgh Press, 1959).

[17] As this book went into production, the Soviet government announced a reduction of the 11-year system to 10 years of education. The reduction mainly affected the period of polytechnical training. *The New York Times*, August 13, 1964, p. 1.

[18] Counts, *op. cit.*, p. 41. This, perhaps, confirms the hypothesis that the Soviet Union has reached a substantial enough degree of social and political stability, as well as group conformity, not to warrant disproportionate instruction or catechism in political and ideological subjects.

In theory, each republic is autonomous; however, in practice, basic curriculum decisions concerning content and method in primary and secondary schools are made by the political leaders and the RSFSR Ministry of Education. A high degree of uniformity prevails in the educational programs of all the constituent republics and ethnic regions. Since World War II, the total hours of instruction have increased from 9,554 in 1947 to 12,828 in 1959 and another grade has been added to the ten-year school, thus further increasing the total number of instructional hours. Furthermore, a shift in the allocation of time devoted to each of the major subject areas has taken place. In the year immediately prior to the Reform Act, the percentage of time allotted to the various subjects was as follows: academic subjects, 44 per cent; scientific subjects, 31 per cent; and applied subjects, 25 per cent. After the 1959 Reform Act, the distribution was 38, 29, and 33 per cent, respectively.[19] It is obvious that the offerings reflect the major aim of the Soviets to de-emphasize humanistic and purely academic training and to stress the theoretical and practical nature of scientific fields.

The curriculum of the elementary school, with minor local revisions, is the same throughout the Soviet Union. Beginning with grade one, pupils are taught Russian, arithmetic, music, and physical culture, with main emphasis placed on the Russian language, history, and literature. It is expected that during their formative years, the youth should develop national identification and political awareness. "Labor" activities, which are part of the curriculum, consist of learning how to use scissors and sewing machines in the case of girls, and simple implements and tools in the case of boys. Pupils are often assigned simple chores around the school, such as cleaning up the classroom or collecting scrap metal, so that they may begin to internalize the idea of socially useful labor. The organization of the self-contained classroom (one teacher responsible for virtually all subjects) prevails until the fourth grade. Beginning with the fifth grade, each subject is taught by a teacher-specialist. In grades five through eight, the Russian classics and selected contemporary Soviet literary works are studied; and skills in reading, spelling, and essay writing are stressed. A prevalent theme throughout school instruction is the glorification of the modern Soviet State and contempt for bourgeois culture. In grades nine to eleven, prerevolutionary writers such as Pushkin, Turgenev, Tolstoi, and Chekov are studied in depth. Western literary figures such as Shakespeare, Goethe, and Mark Twain also receive some attention. The teaching of history begins in grades two and three and continues throughout the secondary school grades, with major emphasis on the history of the U.S.S.R. In the senior grades, a course in political education, stressing the Marxist-Leninist theory, was introduced in 1960; another in the Soviet Constitution was reinstated as a separate subject under the new program. History and other school subjects are used to inculcate in youth "the spirit of communist dedication to ideas and morality, intolerance toward bourgeois ideology, socialist patriotism and proletarian internationalism, and deep respect for labor." [20]

[19] DeWitt, op. cit., p. 108.
[20] Quoted by Marin Pundeff in "History in Soviet Education Since 1958," *Harvard Educational Review* XXXII, No. 1 (1962), 71.

Science subjects, mathematics, and foreign languages are introduced in the elementary grades and continue to occupy an important place in the curriculum of the eleven-year school. Of the foreign languages, German and English seem to be the most popular. In the elementary grades, manual training is provided through paper and wood work, followed by drawing and drafting. In the upper grades (9–11), polytechnical and specialized instruction is offered through courses in the various methods of production, ranging from industrial production to efficient organization of collective farms. An attempt is made to combine school subjects with productive activity; for example, theoretical chemistry is linked with coke and gas manufacture, agricultural fertilizers, and paints. Each student in the upper grades is expected to spend a good portion of his time (about two days a week) at a factory or farm, trying to put into practical application the theories and skills learned at school. With the possible exception of the student majoring in science and engineering, the secondary school graduate is expected to work two years in a state enterprise before continuing his studies at the university or other specialized higher institutions.

Finally, under the new curriculum, the ethnic minority groups are given more opportunity to be taught in their native language, to study local literature, and to participate in folk dances, art, and music. However, instruction in Russian is highly desired because it enhances the opportunity for social mobility. Knowledge of Russian opens new avenues for occupational and geographical placement. For this reason, even among these groups, Russian continues to be an important language of instruction. Furthermore, the aim of *Russification* of cultural minorities, persistent throughout Russian history, is still evident in educational policy and practice, despite governmental declarations and assurances to the contrary.

When Greece attained nationhood in the early part of the nineteenth century, she turned to her own past and to the West for educational inspiration and direction. The two most pervasive strands in her historical tradition were the ideals associated with ancient Hellenism and those of the Greek Orthodox faith. The foundations of the modern Greek system of education were laid through the Bavarian plan of 1834–36, which was modeled on the French elementary-education law of 1833 (Quizot Law) and the Bavarian system of secondary education. According to this plan, a two-ladder system of elementary-secondary education was established, which remained substantially unchanged until 1929. Secondary education was organized in the form of "two successive cycles" of schools, the hellenic schools and the *gymnasia*. The hellenic school was a three-year school (grades 5–7) with a twofold purpose: preparation for the *gymnasium*; and provision of a terminal education for students who wished to embark upon the "business of life." The *gymnasium* was a four-year school (grades 8–11), whose aim was preparation for the university.

107

DEVELOPING
SOCIETIES

7

In 1929, the hellenic school was abolished and a six-year *gymnasium* was established as the second "cycle" of formal education, the first being a six-year elementary school and the third the university. Although other secondary schools developed, the *gymnasium* was the most highly esteemed secondary school, as well as the one with the highest enrollment.[1] But for a short-lived change under the Metaxas government, the 1929 pattern remained unaltered until the recent measures.

In spite of the organizational changes made since 1836, there was no significant shift in the basic conception of education—what its scope, nature, and function should be or what its content should include. During the nineteenth century, elementary schools aimed at creating a literate population that would be engaged largely in agriculture and other low-level jobs in the primary sector of the economy. Secondary education denoted an intensely academic curriculum, the most important ingredient of which was classical Greek learning—justified not only on disciplinary, intellectual and moral grounds, but also on patriotic and religious grounds. Secondary schools aimed at the selection and training of civil servants, lawyers, teachers, and other professional people; a few commercial and technical schools prepared students for middle-level occupations in business and industry.

The humanistic ideal and its Hellenic-Christian basis have characterized Greek secondary education up to the present time. The curriculum has been expanded to include more of the sciences and such subjects as music and physical education, but the essential educational function of the secondary school has remained the same. For an influential segment of enlightened opinion, the *raison d'être* of the *gymnasium* since 1929 has become almost synonymous with secondary classical education.

In the twentieth century, the *gymnasium* has been the boon and at the same time the bane of Greek secondary education. Its academic emphasis has perpetuated an intellectual tradition of a color very dear to the Greeks. However, its monolithic character could not meet the demands of a changing society and serious problems were created. First of all, it stifled any significant growth in scientific, technical, or vocational education at a period when the country has been relying more and more on industry for its economic development and, hence, in need of more skilled technicians and better trained personnel.[2]

Second, it contributed to the creation of what has been called "an intellectual proletariat." Many of the graduates of the *gymnasia*, unable to secure white-collar jobs for which their education allegedly prepared them, became ready followers of doctrines considered inimical to Greek democratic beliefs. Third, the large number of drop-outs [3] before completion of the six-year course created another unemployment problem, for these people were not prepared for any kind of occupation. And, finally, the standards of secondary education suffered because of the increasing num-

---

[1] In 1932-33, there were 148 *gymnasia* with 48,617 pupils, 218 *semigymnasia* with 8,552 pupils, and 13 lyceums with 2,474 pupils. See Ph. M. Vatalas, "Ekpaideusis," *Megalē Hellēnikē Enkyklopaideia*, X (1934), 317.

[2] See K. D. Antonakaki, *Greek Education: Reorganization of the Administrative Structure* (New York: Bureau of Publications, Teachers College, Columbia University, 1955), p. 90.

[3] According to the latest statistical evidence, about 50 per cent of the students entering the *gymnasia* drop out before completion of their studies. See the memorandum by D. Pippas, in *Porismata Epitropēs Paideias*, June 24, 1957—January 10, 1958 (*Athēnai*, 1958), C. viii, 139-52.

ers of students, lacking the requisite intellectual competence, who found
hemselves in the *gymnasia*.

In 1957, this unsatisfactory state of affairs prompted the Government to
entrust to a special committee the important task of making recommendations for an educational renaissance. In 1959, a major act was passed, aimed
at the reorganization of the entire system of secondary and technical education.

ADMINISTRATION AND CONTROL

Modern Greece has maintained a highly centralized system of education,
headed by the Minister of National Education and Religions. The Minister
is a political figure appointed by the party in power, and he is legally responsible for formulating and executing educational policy at the elementary and secondary school levels. The Constitution of 1952, which is
in force today, explicitly states that education should be under ultimate
state supervision and that the goal of the schools is to develop national
consciousness based on the ideals of Greco-Christian civilization. In the
performance of his tasks, the Minister is assisted by a staff organized in
bureaus and councils. He presides over the Central Service, which is comparable to a national board of education and has jurisdiction over public
and private elementary and secondary schools. Higher educational institutions do not come directly under the Ministry; they are largely autonomous.

The functions of the Central Service include preparation of bills, directives, and regulations concerning the administration and operation of
intermediate districts and agencies; appointments and transfers of teachers
and other school personnel; management of the budget, school buildings,
and curriculum development; and selection of textbooks. Another agency
performing important functions at the national level is the Educational
Council, consisting of eleven permanent plus two temporary members (the
former are appointed by the Minister, the latter are elected by the teachers)
and having advisory, administrative, and supervisory responsibilities. The
Council advises the Minister on such matters as establishing new schools
and curricula; issuing new courses of study; and regulating methods, discipline, examinations, and evaluation of instruction in schools. The Council
has the power to certify, classify, and promote teachers and to assign
teachers to school districts throughout the country. Furthermore, the
Council performs judicial functions in that it conducts "disciplinary trials"
regarding teachers. The Council is divided into two main administrative
bodies, one having supervisory functions over secondary education and the
other over elementary education. In sum, it would be accurate to say that
the Council, originally intended to represent the profession, in reality
controls and supervises education in Greece. Although its decisions are
submitted in the form of advice to the Minister, they are almost binding
upon him and have to be carried out within fifteen days unless they are
sent back for further consideration.

Recently, there have been some changes in the central administrative
structure, which pertain more to organization than to functions. As a result
of the 1959 act, the following agencies were established: two directorates,
one for general education and the other for vocational education; a Superior
Educational Personnel Administration Board to deal with problems affecting teachers; a Superior Board for Educational Programs to deal with the
curriculum; and a National Board of Education and a Coordinating Board

for Vocational Education "to bring education more into touch with the needs of everyday life." [4]

The Ministry exercises its control over schools and teachers through intermediate administrative agencies. These agencies have very little original jurisdiction—for the most part, they carry out the policies and directives issued by the Ministry. There are about 120 educational districts at the elementary school level, which fall into nine general inspection areas, each headed by an inspector-general and a district council. There are 20 districts at the secondary level, each one administered by an inspector-general and a council.

The supervisory councils of secondary education at the district level consist of an inspector-general, a high school director, and a general inspector of elementary education or a judge. The supervisory councils of elementary education have comparable membership. The main functions of the councils are to supervise the school personnel (they assign teachers to local schools after the original appointment by the Ministry); to place and promote elementary school teachers; and to make reports to the Ministry concerning the operation of the local schools. The general inspectors, who are appointed by the Ministry, have direct jurisdiction over the schools (both private and public) in their district. They are expected to study the local problems and to report directly to the Ministry.

The principal of each school has administrative, supervisory, and instructional responsibilities. Because facilities and appropriate personnel are lacking, the school principal is the main student disciplinarian and guidance counselor; however, he has no disciplinary power over the teachers, except the power to report them to higher authorities. In addition to his administrative and other duties, the principal also has a rather heavy teaching load. The faculty of each school has several important prerogatives, such as selecting a textbook from the approved list, promoting students, preparing the class schedule, deciding on extracurricular activities, etc.

Local control of education is totally alien to the Greeks. According to a law passed in 1932, local school boards were to be created in each district to represent the local community, the parents, and the school. The members were supposed to be elected; however, in practice, because of lack of appropriate election machinery and procedures, the members of the board are appointed by the local political authority. For all practical purposes, school boards do not participate in major educational decisions at the local level; they have very little power, indeed, over school issues and policies.

The main source of income of public schools is taxation. Until recently, secondary schools charged a tuition fee, which constituted another source of income. Since tuition fees in elementary and secondary schools have been eliminated, financial support of education is the responsibility of the government. In 1951–52, the share of the Ministry of Education in the national budget was 7.4 per cent; in 1953–54 it was 6.1 per cent. It has been estimated that in recent years, from 1.3 to 1.8 per cent of the national income was spent for education, a rather low percentage when compared with countries of similar economic potential.

In sum, it may be said that the Greek educational system represents a highly centralized pattern. The main source of executive and legislative

[4] Kingdom of Greece, Athens, Ministry of National Education and Religions, *Bulletin of the Studies and Coordination Service*, V, No. 5 (1962), 9.

power is the Ministry and its advisory councils. The decisions made at the national level are implemented through the local supervisory councils, the general inspectors, the inspectors, the school principals, and the school faculties. It is interesting to note that the reorganization plan introduced in 1959 made very few changes regarding the locus of power concerning the administration and control of education.

ORGANIZATION OF THE SCHOOLS

The Committee on Education, which presented its Report in 1958, had concentrated mainly on the organization and content of secondary education. It envisaged secondary general education in terms of "two complete cycles" of *gymnasium* studies, totalling six years. These "cycles" would provide an essentially humanistic education—the first with a more "practical" bias, the second with a more "theoretical" one.

The first "cycle," called the *pregymnasium*, would be open to graduates of the elementary school who had passed a "lenient examination" in Greek and mathematics; its purpose would be the completion of the elementary general education and the provision of the necessary preparatory training for higher studies or for the various vocations. Admission to the second "cycle," however, would depend on successful completion of the *pregymnasium* course and on passing a "rigid examination." This second stage would aim at the intellectual stimulation and disciplining of the student's faculties through an introduction into the cultural values of the Hellenic-Christian tradition, and the development of self-sustained Greek Christian citizens and leaders.

The Committee then called for a thorough "revision" of the curriculum. It urged that more attention be paid to the "spirit of classical learning" rather than the *form*; that more time be spent and more material covered in the teaching of mathematics; that modern languages (French and English) be strengthened; and that students be trained to communicate their ideas with "correctness, logic, and clarity."

In its conception of the scope of secondary education, however, the Committee also stipulated that "vocational" education be provided in institutions of various kinds. It repudiated the narrow definition that vocational education denoted special technical training in the performance of certain vocational skills; instead it proposed technical preparation (theoretical and practical) as well as a broad general education as its constituent elements. Hence, the Committee recommended that no vocational training be given in the elementary schools and that in all vocational schools, religion, Greek, mathematics, and civics be required subjects.

Government steps for the implementation of the Committee's recommendations began in 1959. On June 11, the Minister of Education submitted a bill titled "Reform of Technical and Vocational Education, Organization of Secondary Education, and Administration of Education." After a stormy debate, the bill was passed and was signed by the King on September 2, 1959.

This 1959 act established three fundamental goals toward which educational policy should be directed: (1) secondary education should be organized to perform adequately its twofold function—preparation for further studies and provision of a terminal education for students who seek employment after graduation; (2) technical education should be revamped and brought within the purview of national public education; and

111

(3) the ideal of humanism should pervade all types of secondary education.[5]

Perhaps the most revolutionary element in the recent measures was the conception and reorganization of vocational and technical education. Since World War II, considerable dissatisfaction has been voiced at the neglect of technical and vocational education, and at the "nonfunctional" relationship between education and economic development.[6]

In order to remedy this generally recognized educational evil, Legislative Decree No. 3971 authorized the establishment of a three-grade system of schools: two four-year upper-technical schools for "sub-engineers"; six three- or four-year secondary technical schools for technical assistants and foremen; and lower-vocational schools (one to four years in duration) for craftsmen and agricultural workers. The upper-technical schools will admit (1) graduates of the *gymnasia* or secondary technical schools after passing an entrance examination and (2) the secondary technical students who have completed the junior section of the *gymnasiun* or who are graduates of lower-vocational schools, which in their turn will admit graduates of elementary schools. The degree of direct vocational preparation will depend on the grade of school. In the main, however, all types will provide both general education and vocational training. The law also authorized the establishment of a college for teachers of vocational and technical education and a General Directorate for Technical Education, with the necessary councils for the preparation of curricula, approval of textbooks, and supervision.

Another decree (No. 3973) provided for the coordination of the administration of technical and vocational education, which had hitherto been under seven ministries. All kinds and grades of such schools, except three special schools, were placed under the jurisdiction of the Ministry of Education. Finally, the law provided for the establishment of a Co-ordinating Council for Vocational Education within the Ministry of Education.

Another significant feature of the recent reforms, was the conception of secondary-general education in terms of two "cycles" of studies of the same duration as those recommended by the Committee on Education. The first "cycle" (grades 7-9) will be general and humanistic in nature and will lead either to the second "cycle" (grades 10-12)—diversified to include classical, scientific, and technical courses—or will lead directly to certain occupations. It is as yet difficult to assess the extent to which the reforms have been implemented. Also, the recently elected government of Premier Papandreou has been in the process of developing new plans for educational change. Accordingly, available information on the organization of schools and enrollments refers mainly to the prereform period.[7]

[5] Kingdom of Greece, *Legislative Decree (Act)*, No. 3971, "On Technical and Vocational Education, Organization of Secondary Education and Administration of Education," September 2, 1959, Chap. 1, Article 1.

[6] See, for example, *Greece on the Road to Prosperity: The Preliminary Five-Year Programme*, pp. xi-xii.

[7] As this book went to press, the Greek government introduced new legislation with some revolutionary proposals on reorganizing Greek public education. The new bill sought to extend compulsory education to nine years, organize pre-university education into three stages (six years of elementary school, three of *gymnasium,* and three of *lyceum*), introduce a system of electives, and create a Pedagogical Institute concentrating on research in child development and the socio-economic contexts of the school. Furthermore, the bill provided for automatic admission into the universities for those who were awarded an "academic diploma" upon graduation from the *lyceum*.

One of the major problems of Greek education is the diversity of elementary schools. These are classified under one of four categories, depending upon the number of rooms in the school and upon school enrollment. The four types of elementary schools are: (1) *Monotaxia*, one-room schools that have one teacher for all classes, with a minimum of 15 and a maximum of 40 pupils; (2) *Ditaxia*, two-room schools that have two teachers for all classes, with a minimum of 41 and a maximum of 80 pupils; (3) *Tritaxia*, three-room schools that employ three teachers for all classes, with a minimum of 81 and a maximum of 120 pupils; and (4) *Polytaxia*, four- to six-room schools that may have four to six teachers for all classes with a normal enrollment of from 121 to 200 pupils. The five-room school has from 161 to 200 pupils, the six-room school from 201 to 250 pupils.

A major concern of the educational reformers has been to reduce the number of the first category of schools (*Monotaxia*), which constitute about 50 per cent of the total number. In addition, however, there have been attempts to lessen the high drop-out rate in both elementary and secondary schools. According to the statistics, furnished by the Committee on Education in 1958, of the total number of students (about 180,000) entering the first grade of the elementary schools, at least one-third do not complete the six-year course. There is a progressively higher rate of attrition from the first to the sixth grade, and this in spite of the fact that education is compulsory at this stage.

Of the total number of public elementary school graduates—about 120,000 annually—50,000 or about 40 per cent enter the six-year public *gymnasium*; however, of this number, only 50 per cent attain a *gymnasium* diploma. Here, again, the attrition rate is progressively higher. This enrollment pattern is further constricted and it reaches a peak at the university level. Thus, only 24 per cent (about 6,000) of the *gymnasium* graduates enter institutions of higher learning; and of this percentage, only half graduate.

Assuming enrollments remain relatively stable over a period of time, it is interesting to observe that just over 3 per cent of those entering the first grade of the elementary school can expect to enroll in an institution of higher learning and less than 2 per cent can expect to graduate. To put the pattern of opportunity in different terms—of 100 students entering elementary school, about 66 can expect to graduate, 30 of the 66 can expect to enter a *gymnasium*, 14 of the 30 to graduate from a *gymnasium*, 3 of the *gymnasium* graduates to enter a higher institution, and 2 of the 3 to graduate. It should be noted that of those who discontinue their education at the various steps of the educational ladder, about one-third receive some form of technical or vocational training and eventually engage in middle- and low-level occupations in industry, commerce, and services. Those who drop out from the elementary schools enter the primary occupations of fishing, agriculture, forestry, and the like.

In addition to the public system of schools, there is a variety of private schools—both elementary and secondary. In 1960-61, there were 285 secondary-private schools, compared to 544 public; however, the private schools enrolled only 44,306 students compared to 233,490 in the public schools. Some of these institutions—e.g., Athens College for Boys, Peirce College for Girls, Anatolia College, and Valayianni School for Girls—are highly prestigious secondary institutions, and a relatively high percentage of their graduates continue their education at home and abroad.

Much has already been said about the reform of Greek education, attempted in order to adjust to the demands of the modern world and to matters affecting the curriculum of the schools. Under the new act of 1959, the secondary school offers four courses of study—ranging from strictly classical and humanistic programs in the *gymnasia* to practical or vocational education in the lyceums or evening schools. The act has not greatly affected the curriculum of the elementary schools.

The aim of the elementary school in Greece, as set forth by statute, is "the moral, religious, and national education of students, as well as the imparting to them of the indispensable skills and knowledge for life." At this level, the curriculum ranges from courses in the fundamentals (reading, writing, and arithmetic) to religious instruction and physical education. The content of the modern elementary curriculum was laid down in 1929; it has been modified subsequently to include the following instructional subjects: Greek orthodox religion (which is the State religion), including Bible reading, catechism, hymns, and church history; reading and writing of the Greek language, primarily modern Greek at this level; practical arithmetic; elementary geometry; history of the Greek nation; highlights of world history; geography; elements of natural history and chemistry, with particular emphasis on their application to hygiene, agriculture, and daily living; singing; penmanship; drawing; crafts, although this is not to be thought of as trade-training; and physical education. For ethnic and religious minority groups, an exemption in the law permits children to receive religious instruction in their own faith.

A student enrolled in a secondary school in Greece is expected to attend approximately 37 hours of weekly instruction (each hour is 50 minutes long). Depending on the type of school (e.g., classical *gymnasium*, practical lyceum, etc.) and the particular concentration in one field, the program prescribed by the Ministry is mandatory for all secondary-school students. Throughout the six years of secondary education, certain subjects have traditionally dominated the curriculum. According to the 1959 syllabus, ancient Greek was taught in every grade and consumed approximately one-fourth of the total weekly schedule—that is, 51 hours of classical Greek out of a total of 213 hours per week over a six-year period. If one added to these hours the time spent on religion (12 hours), Modern Greek (18 hours), Latin (12 hours), history (18 hours), philosophy (4 hours), one would find out that more than one-half of the total school program was committed to the classical-humanistic-religious tradition of Greece. Furthermore, one would indeed be amazed to discover that Greece, a country eagerly trying to attain the technological progress and level of industrialization of Western Europe, paid very little attention to scientific subjects in her schools. Instructional hours in mathematics (22 hours), and in science (19 hours) constituted less than one-fifth of the total instructional time.

The 1959 measures stipulated certain changes in the curriculum of the secondary schools, the most pertinent of which affected the study of the classics and science. But the actual changes in these subjects as revealed by the new syllabi fell short of the provisions of the act. Thus, for example, Latin was eliminated from the three-year *pregymnasium,* and the hours of mathematics and science were increased (in the case of mathematics from 10 to 12 total weekly hours over the three grades, and in that of physics, from 9 to 12). As yet syllabi for only three sections of the three-year senior-secondary cycle have been drafted—classical, foreign languages, and home economics. Curriculum changes at this level have been very minimal, except for the limited diversification into the three types of streams or schools in the first class. The program of the foreign language section in the first class includes six weekly hours of ancient Greek, three of modern Greek, three of mathematics, four of one foreign language, and five of a second foreign language. In the home economics section, only three weekly hours are devoted to a foreign language, while five hours are given to home economics. The remaining subjects are given equal emphasis in these two sections. In the classical section of the first class, eight hours are devoted to classical Greek (previously it was nine), four hours to modern Greek (previously three) and four hours to mathematics (previously three). The rest of the curriculum has remained unchanged; and in the second and third classes, students in all three sections are taught the same subjects.

Although curriculum changes were recommended in the 1959 Education Act, they were by no means revolutionary; and even those changes that were made were completely diluted in the actual plans for curriculum reorganization. The reasons for the slow pace of reform and the hesitancy to make radical changes in the school curriculum are many. First of all there is the backward pull of the deeply entrenched classical-humanistic tradition. Second, there is the potent force of powerful "pressure" groups and organizations—notably the School of Philosophy of the University of Athens, the Federation of Secondary School Teachers, the Philological Society, and the Greek Orthodox Church—that have vested interests in the preservation of the *status quo.* Third, although there is an expressed desire to strengthen other forms of education, there are no visible rewards (material, intellectual, or spiritual) that would compare with those traditionally associated with a *gymnasium* type of education. Fourth, closely related to the previous point is the fact that there has been a sharp distinction drawn between manual and nonmanual work; and a corresponding differentiating attitude has been attached to the curriculum of various types of schools. Fifth, there is a scarcity of skilled personnel in the sciences, foreign languages, mathematics, and technical subjects, and of facilities to carry out any large-scale program of curriculum reorganization. In conclusion, it should also be stated that even if there were radical changes in the curriculum, it is questionable whether the desired goal of making education more related to the needs of modern society could be attained without concomitant changes in the occupational structure, in the values attached to different occupations, and in the social, material, and other rewards of education in the society at large.

TANGANYIKA

Tanganyika is one of the latest African territories to emerge as a self-governing nation. Compared to other areas in Central and West Africa, its contact with the West, especially Britain, has been relatively brief. In

1884, it was brought under German influence and in 1920, the United Kingdom—under a mandate from the League of Nations—assumed the administration of the territory. In 1946, Tanganyika became a United Nations Trust Territory under British administration; its political status was clarified and increasing attention was given to its economic, social, and political development. Finally, in the Fall of 1960, it emerged as a self-governing territory and in December 1961 attained complete independence.

Economically, Tanganyika is predominantly agricultural, with the large majority of its population engaged in subsistence activities. Racially, its population consists of three major groups: Africans—about 8,663,000, or 98 per cent of the total population; Asians—Indians and Pakistani numbering about 72,000; and Europeans of several nationalities—about 21,000. The African population itself is culturally diverse. There are about 120 different tribes varying in size, social structure, language, and religion.[8] The majority of the people live in rural areas. Socially, there is a relatively simple stratification, which until very recently coincided with the racial divisions. The Europeans generally occupied the highest positions in the government and the private sectors of the economy; the Asians had the middle positions (retail merchants, skilled and semi-skilled positions), and the Africans occupied the lower positions (unskilled laborers and peasant farmers). With the elections of a Legislative Council, however, the majority of the seats have gone to Africans.

ADMINISTRATION AND CONTROL [9]

Since the Education (African) Ordinance as amended in 1954 and 1958, all secular education has been in the hands of a Director of Education (now Minister of Education), who has been assisted by a central Advisory Committee on African Education. In discharging his functions with respect to primary and middle schools, the Director is advised by a Native Authority Education Committee, which consists mainly of native Africans. These Committees advise the Department on issues such as registration of schools and school management, and their recommendations are normally acted upon by the Department.

The Department of Education is the main policy-making body. It drafts plans for educational development and submits them to the legislative branch of the government for approval. Laws and ordinances are executed either directly by the Department or by the Provincial Education Officers and the African School Supervisors, who operate at provincial or local levels.

The most important function of the Department and its agencies is to classify and accredit schools. The schools that meet the prescribed governmental standards are fully recognized and listed in Part I of the register. These schools are divided into two major categories: (a) maintained schools and (b) voluntary schools. The former are managed by the central or native authorities; the latter, subdivided into those which receive government assistance (aided schools) and those which do not (unaided

---

[8] Betty George, *Education for Africans in Tanganyika: A Preliminary Survey*, U.S. Department of Health, Education, and Welfare, Bulletin No. 19 (Washington, D. C.: Government Printing Office, 1960), pp. 2-3.

[9] Since independence, no major structural changes have taken place. Therefore, in describing the educational system, we shall employ the same terms used during the pre-independence period.

schools), are managed mostly by Christian missions. All types of schools have a uniform curriculum, employ licensed teachers, and are subject to government inspection. The voluntary schools have been the most numerous, equalling about 60 per cent of all schools offering the first eight years of education, and the majority have received substantial financial aid from the government.

The second major category of schools consists of subgrade or "bush" schools. These schools were brought under national supervision in 1954, and they were listed in Part II of the register. Generally, these schools have been substandard with respect to curriculum and the educational background of their teaching staff. They provide instruction that is roughly equivalent to the first two years of primary school. Many bush schools are affiliated with Christian missions, and they often offer religious instruction in conjunction with secular subjects. While Part II schools are registered and, hence, legally sanctioned by the government, they do not receive any government aid. They are supported by missions and other voluntary organizations. It is claimed that the main reason substandard schools have been tolerated by the government is the scarcity of schools that meet the standards of Part I of the register. With independence and the emphasis placed on educational development, it is expected that these schools will gradually disappear.

Another way the Department of Education exercises control over the schools is through certification of teachers. Teachers, like schools, are registered (in Part I or Part II of the register), depending on their qualifications and level of educational attainment. Part I of the register includes teachers who have completed an accredited teacher-training course and who have, in general, met all the government requirements for certification or a license. Part II includes substandard teachers who do not possess a teaching certificate, but who have met some of the prescribed Departmental requirements. These categories of teachers correspond to the school categories, i.e., Part I teachers are employed in Part I schools, and Part II teachers in Part II schools. Furthermore, inasmuch as teachers are civil servants, they come under the jurisdiction of the central government. Through its representatives, the Department of Education inspects the schools, examines their records, and supervises secular instruction. If the school conditions are not satisfactory, the Department may order it to be closed. The reasons for removing a school from the official register are inability to meet legal standards regarding facilities, curriculum, textbooks, and teachers' certification or disregard for peace and order and the moral welfare of the pupils.

A powerful device of control of education is the system of grants-in-aid. In the case of voluntary agencies, the Department allocates funds from the central government and native authorities only for schools that meet standards comparable to those of the Government schools. Thus, by controlling the purse, the government can force a school out of existence, if for one reason or another it does not conform to its prescriptions and regulations.

Until independence, the approved system of education in Tanganyika received financial support from Colonial Development and Welfare grants. Since 1961, the government has increasingly relied on its own funds and the funds collected from local native authorities, voluntary agencies, and school fees paid by parents. Funds from native authorities are earmarked for primary and middle education. The major cost of African education is underwritten by the central government. Of the total school expenditure in 1958 (£4,666,580), less than 19 per cent was met by native authorities, less than 14 per cent by voluntary organizations, and 68 per cent was contributed by the central government.[10]

Since there is no compulsory education in Tanganyika, parents are expected to contribute to the operation of the schools. The government argues that since only a portion of the total population is profiting from formal education, it is only fair that primary school fees—covering expenses for materials and equipment—be charged. The payment of fees partly accounts for the fact that in 1959, of the primary-school age-group (approximately 19 per cent of the total African population), only about 42 per cent was actually in schools. The irony was that these schools could accommodate many more children than those who actually attended.[11] It is expected, however, that gradually the central and local governments will assume complete financial responsibility for the education of all children in the primary grades and that, correspondingly, fees will either be reduced or eliminated.

ORGANIZATION OF THE SCHOOLS

Educationally, there are diversities in structure and opportunity corresponding to the various ethnic groups. Thus, in addition to the education provided wholly or in part by voluntary agencies in *catechetical* or *bush* schools, the African system is organized on a four-four-four basis. There is a four-year primary stage, a four-year middle or intermediate stage, and a four-year secondary stage. The function of primary education is to provide basic skills of literacy and citizenship. The middle and secondary schools are selective institutions, admission to which depends on competitive examinations. Middle schools generally perform a dual function. They prepare for further education in the secondary or trade schools and for paid employment. Secondary schools provide an education, primarily academic in nature, that leads to various goals. A boy who completes ten grades may enter a teaching-training course for Grade I teachers or a technical institute, or he may seek general employment. A girl may enter training courses for medical assistants, policewomen, clerks, and social development workers. A student who completes the full twelve years takes the Cambridge Overseas School Certificate and, thus, qualifies for higher studies or for direct general employment.

In addition to this type of general education, there are provisions for technical and vocational education. There are two technical schools, both of which accept students who have successfully completed the middle stage. One of them prepares students for various trades in the building and engineering industries; the other is limited to the building trades. Technical and vocational education are provided also in the Technical Institute in Dar es Salaam, in the College of Commerce at Moshi, in the

---

[10] George, *op. cit.*, p. 26.

[11] Another reason for the relatively low attendance in primary schools has been the preference of many parents to send their children to a bush school where they can be taught by teachers of their own religious denomination. See chapter on Tanganyika in Helen Kitchen, ed., *The Educated African* (New York: Frederick A. Praeger, Inc., 1962), pp. 145-59.

Natural Resources School at Tengeru, and in full-time residential courses for the training of engineering assistants and handwork teachers.

The Europeans and Indians have their own schools organized on a six-six plan, six-year primary and six-year secondary schools. Secondary schools are entirely academic in nature and aim for examinations that lead to a School Certificate and Higher School Certificate, and thereby to higher education or general white-collar employment. A large number of European children attend schools outside Tanganyika, either in Europe or in neighboring Kenya. Hardly any children from these groups go into technical or vocational schools.

Educational opportunities for Africans in Tanganyika have been found to be limited at all levels. In 1956, it was estimated that only 39.1 per cent of the primary school age population attended school. The Five-Year Plan for the years 1957-61 estimated that at its completion the percentage would increase to 45. Opportunities at the middle and secondary levels are extremely limited. Of the total number of those finishing primary school, only 13.7 per cent enter the first grade (or *standard*) of the middle schools, and only 2.1 per cent enter the first standard of the secondary schools. This represents a ratio of one to seven in the former case, and one to 48 in the latter. Of the same number, only 8.4 per cent complete a middle school course, and only .23 per cent (or one in 435) a secondary school course. The percentages, of course, decrease and the ratios increase dramatically if the first-grade population is taken as the base. Only one in 67 enters a secondary school and one in 625 completes the course.[12] There is also a considerable dropout at all levels of education, although over a twelve-year period (1947–59), there has been a vast improvement, especially in the primary schools.[13]

In addition to the high drop-out rate, education in Tanganyika is plagued by other problems. First, there is a shortage of technicians at the subprofessional or semiprofessional level—craftsmen, handymen, middle-category technicians, agricultural assistants, and engineering assistants. Second, there is a shortage of teachers, especially in the primary schools. The ratio of pupils to teachers in the primary stage is 56.6 to one. In the middle schools, there is a shortage of women teachers and in the secondary schools, of African teachers.

These problems have been discussed recently by individuals, groups, and missions; as a result, various suggestions and plans have been made. In its report of 1961, the International Bank for Reconstruction and Development recommended the expansion of educational facilities at all levels; the diversification of post-primary education; the establishment of an Institute of Education; the full utilization of space in the existing primary schools; and the reduction of wastage (drop-out), particularly in the case of girls.[14]

[12] These percentages and ratios have been computed from data in the following documents: *Tanganyika Annual Summary of the Department of Education, Statistics*, Government Printer, Dar es Salaam, 1958, hereafter cited as *Statistics*, 1958; Tanganyika, Department of Education, *Triennial Survey for the Years 1955-57*, Government Printer, Dar es Salaam, 1958; Tanganyika, *Statistical Abstract*, 1959, Government Printer, Dar es Salaam, 1959; *A Five-Year Plan for African Education 1957-61*, Government Printer, Dar es Salaam, 1958.

[13] The International Bank for Reconstruction and Development, *The Economic Development in Tanganyika* (Baltimore: The Johns Hopkins Press, 1961), p. 310.

[14] *Ibid.*

In the Spring of 1960 the Committee on the Integration of Education published a report, whose conclusions were generally accepted by the Government. This Committee addressed itself to discriminating practices in admission policies, especially in the secondary schools, and made specific recommendations for their elimination. At the same time, a new Three-Year Plan for 1961-63 was presented to the Legislative Council, aiming at extension of secondary education, so that more Africans could be trained for civil service positions. Another Three-Year Plan, prepared by the Director of Education in 1959, recommended that primary education be extended to six years; that two-year intermediate schools provide preparatory education beyond the primary stage for the secondary schools; that most of the existing middle schools be either mainly academic or have an agricultural or handicraft bias; and that the remainder of the middle schools be converted to secondary schools of various types. African political leaders themselves have expressed their views on the course that Tanganyikan education should take. The feeling has been expressed that the response to Tanganyika's challenge for the development of a "free, prosperous, and democatic" society rests on a more equalitarian, more expanded, and more functional system of education, especially in so far as it affects the preponderant African population.

CURRICULUM

The basic subjects of the primary school as outlined in a handbook issued by the Department of Education are the following: language (which includes reading, writing, language, and composition); arithmetic; nature study; and geography. Handiwork, gardening, and religious instruction are also taught in the primary grades. In 1957, English was introduced in the upper grades of the elementary school in addition to Swahili, the native language. Actually, beginning with the upper-middle level, English becomes the medium of instruction; Swahili is taught as a second language until the School Certificate Level. Although the problem created by the existence of many local dialects has not been completely resolved, the linguistic situation in Tanganyika is not as acute as in other African new states. A case in point is Nigeria, where there is no common vernacular or *lingua franca*, but a number of different languages or dialects competing with each other for dominance. In Tanganyika, on the other hand, Swahili seems to have become dominant; by and large, it has developed into the language of nationalism.

The curriculum of the middle schools as outlined in a provisional syllabus issued in 1952, had a two-fold purpose: (a) to provide a preparatory education for those who would continue into the upper school, and (b) to offer a terminal education for those who would seek employment in their respective communities. Consequently, in addition to the conventional subjects—e.g., arithmetic and practical geometry, English, Swahili, geography, history, civics, and science—the middle school provided different curriculum streams with a vocational or practical bias, corresponding to the needs of the particular community. For example, in agricultural and pastoral areas, school boys combine formal instruction in agriculture and animal husbandry with farm work according to season. In the urban schools, the program emphasizes commercial and industrial subjects and allows for time to be spent on handicraft (drawing, native craft, woodwork, brick, tile and cement-block making, tinsmithery, etc.) For girls, the practical aspects of the curriculum are represented in homecraft, which includes housewifery, laundry, and cookery. All in all, the curriculum of the middle schools, especially those in rural areas, reflects a relatively heavy practical bias in that more than half of the time is devoted to farmwork and handicraft (a total of about 39 forty-minute periods per week). Arithmetic, Swahili, English, social science, and general science comprise the other part of the curriculum (about 30 periods per week).

The majority of students in the middle schools do not continue their education beyond that stage. Those who want to enter secondary schools or teacher training and trade schools are required to take a general entrance examination. A school-leaving certificate is issued to those who have not passed the selective test.

The four-year secondary course purports to equip the individual with knowledge and skills that would enable him to make a contribution to the life and development of his community. Also, the course prepares for the external examination—the Cambridge Overseas School Certificate examination—which qualifies the individual for entrance into the university. However, regardless of the goals stated in the secondary school syllabus of 1955—e.g., meeting the needs of the community—the curriculum at this level is largely determined by the Cambridge Overseas School Certificate examination, which is academic in its emphasis.

The subjects included in the four-year course are English, Swahili, mathematics, science or domestic science, needlework, and social science. Provisions are also made for religious instruction and for art or handiwork. Considerable time is spent on the history and geography of tropical Africa and on current affairs. Although English is the language of instruction, Swahili is taught as a separate subject and it is used in connection with religious instruction.

The curriculum of the four-year secondary school is mostly academic, although recent efforts—e.g., the Five-Year Plan—sought to incorporate technical and commercial subjects. Whether in the foreseeable future the people of Tanganyika will move away from strictly academic, humanistic, and bookish education to a more "practical" orientation—i.e., education geared to local economic and social needs—remains to be seen. Many Africans have assumed that modernization and industrialization in the West occurred under the classical-humanistic curriculum and, hence, that it would be reasonable to expect similar outcomes in Africa. African political leaders believed that an academic education would be the only type that would eventually allow them to compete on an equal basis with the West and to develop a high economic and political status in the community of nations.[15] What these people failed to realize was that technological development in the West during comparable periods of economic development occurred in spite of the academic bias of the secondary schools. On the other hand, the observation that the West was modernized and industrialized at a time when the academic curriculum was predominant is correct.

The problem facing Tanganyika in its plans for educational change are bound up inextricably with social, political, economic, and cultural problems. In general terms, they may be said to obtain in other African countries, especially those that were under the influence of Britain. The West-

121

15 John Wilson, *Education and Changing West African Culture* (New York: Bureau of Publications, Teachers College, Columbia University, 1963), p. 45.

ern system of education that was transferred to Tanganyika resulted in the breakdown of traditional, indigenous, political, and social systems and in the creation of a different social stratification with a different social elite (mostly European) acting as a reference group for African aspirations. In their new setting, the Western educational institutions—especially the secondary schools—acquired a new function. They became the chief avenues for occupational and social mobility among the Africans.

Very often the curriculum in itself was not as important as just going through certain schools and passing certain examinations. For this reason, attempts to change the curriculum by including more practical studies—especially in the middle schools—have not been very successful. This probably will continue to be so, as long as there is an occupational structure that rewards differentially, in terms of prestige and income, those who graduate from academic institutions. Incidentally, this has been found to be true in England, with its modern and technical schools.

On the face of it, one could argue, as indeed many have argued in the case of underdeveloped countries, that what these countries need for their economic development is more technical education, more agricultural training in the schools, and generally more of any kind of education. They need more education to suit the needs of their people for increased production, higher per capita income, and a generally higher standard of living. But such aims cannot be viewed in isolation from the rate of general economic growth itself, the aspirations of the people, the occupational structure, and the ideological traditions of a society.

Educational change must proceed hand-in-hand with social change in general. Perhaps it may be wishful thinking or mere political propaganda to assume that educational change by itself can bring about social improvement or that it can be a panacea for all social problems. Plans for the indiscriminate expansion of technical education will be foredoomed where the economy functions at the subsistence level or where technical careers do not offer the same rewards as are offered by the civil service or the professions.

Tanganyika has not as yet reached the "take-off" stage of economic development. The secondary academic schools cannot be said to contribute to unemployment among school leavers, as is the case in Greece and Turkey. Indeed, more secondary school graduates are needed to staff the various branches of the civil service and to proceed to institutions of higher learning for training in the professions. Similarly, the expansion of technical and vocational education must take into consideration the growth of industry.

TURKEY

Prior to the movement towards "modernization" or "Westernization," which can be traced as far back as the last decades of the eighteenth century, education was almost exclusively in the hands of the religious groups in the society—the Doctors of Islamic Law known as *Ulema*—and the various other religious functionaries, from the *Ulema* down to the local *imam*—the parish priest, so to speak. The Ottomans established schools that were joined to mosques; and they organized a graded system of education, from the lowest *mekteb* (primary school) to the highest *medrese* (higher religious college). In addition to these religious schools, there were several other agencies that performed significant educational functions. For example, the famous Palace School (*Enderun Mektebi*) recruited the choicest youth from among the non-Moslem subjects of the Empire (mostly the Christian subjects); it trained them in what may be called a combination of the liberal, vocational, and physical elements of education and prepared them for high positions in the Royal Court, in the army, and in the civil bureaucracy. There were also what may be called the informal educational agencies, such as the various bureaus of the Government, the mosque, and so on.

Early educational reform in the Ottoman Empire started at the top of the social hierarchy; in particular, it began with changes in military education. Soon, however, it became evident that a total reorganization of the educational system was necessary. In spite of several plans to build a graded educational structure from primary schools to universities, major attention was focused on the upper levels of education. In Ottoman times, and indeed later, the priority given to these levels was justified on what has been called the *Tuba Ağaci* theory of education. In Turkish folklore, the *Tuba Ağaci* was a tree that had its roots in heaven, but cast its delightful shade and fruit on the earth. As *per analogiam*, reform of education should start at the top of the system—i.e., with the secondary schools and the universities. By so doing, the fruits of education would spread to the rest of the system and the society. Hence, throughout the nineteenth century, we find several attempts to set up various kinds of schools, mostly at the post-elementary level.

Another important aspect of the educational reform of this period was the attempt to place education more in the hands of the state than of purely religious and private agencies. It was also during this period that the two famous schools for the training of government officials were set up: the *Mülkiye* in the 1850's and the Imperial *Lise* of Galatasaray in 1868. Both schools were essentially secular in their orientation, they were supported by the government, and they were open to all nationalities of the Empire. The *lise*, in particular, was modeled after European academic secondary schools, especially the French *lycée*. The French influence continued to be pervasive in Turkey until very recently, when it was superseded by the American.

The introduction of foreign ideas and institutions had a corroding impact upon the intellectual fabric of the Ottoman society and upon its institutions. A new type of elite—basically secular and western in orientation—was created, which brought about conflicts with segments of the traditional religious doctors of Islam.

In 1923, Turkey was proclaimed a Republic and one year later, the Caliphate was abolished. Authority was henceforth vested in the hands of a National Assembly, with Kemal Atatürk as its first President. The story of the period since the proclamation of the Republic has been one of constant reform and reconstruction, aimed at the complete modernization of the society. It was necessary to build a new social order in the political, economic, and legal sectors; perhaps more importantly, it was necessary to create new values, new ideologies, and new ways of looking at things.

The first step in the direction of educational reform was to make the state the sole agency responsible for the education of the people. This step was consistent with the general secularization program of the Republic. The traditional *medreses*—almost invariably identified with religious conservatism and reaction—were closed, and all other religious schools were taken over by a central Ministry of Education. Even the teaching of religion was discontinued by 1935. Only recently have there been attempts to revive it. The teaching of Arabic and Persian in the *lises* was proscribed, and the Roman alphabet replaced the Arabic script. All schools (except the foreign schools) were placed under the direction and control of the Central Ministry of Education; and there was a reorganization of the system into primary schools, middle schools (*orta*), *lises*, various types of technical schools, teacher-training institutions, and universities.

ADMINISTRATION AND CONTROL

The administrative structure of Turkish education is centered in the National Ministry of Education. The Minister makes all final decisions affecting the administration of all the schools in the country. His signature must appear on all orders, even in the case of relatively minor matters such as appointment and transfer of teachers and use of textbooks in the schools. In the performance of his functions, the Minister is assisted by three advisory bodies: The Educational Council (*Maarif Şurasi*); the Committee on Instruction and Education (*Talim ve Terbiye Kurulu*); and the Committee of General Directors (*Müdürler Komisyonou*). The Educational Council—consisting of high officials in the Ministry, the rectors of the universities, the deans of the faculties, a number of school principals, inspectors, teachers, and others—discusses and advises on matters of educational policy, especially on curriculum questions and school regulations. The Committee on Teaching and Training—comprising six members—prepares courses of study for submission to the Council (*Şura*), examines textbooks, and passes judgment on proposed legislation. The Committee of General Directors—including the various department heads in the Ministry—considers matters of administration of schools; it is especially concerned with the appointment and transfer of teachers and administrators in post-elementary schools.

Under the Minister there are two permanent under-secretaries (*müsteşars*): one responsible for technical education and the other (the regular) for all other types of education. The *müsteşars* are, theoretically at least, career educators, but nonpolitical appointees. Together with the general directors, the *müsteşars* conduct all the administrative affairs of the Ministry; however, in all cases, the Minister's approval is mandatory.

Under the regular *müsteşar* there are at least nine "directorates": the General Directorates of Primary Education, Secondary Education, Higher Education, Teacher Education, Private Education, Fine Arts and Physical Education; and the Directorates of Libraries and of Museums and Antiquities. The General Director of Primary Education generally controls primary schools through provincial inspectors; he is responsible for the curriculum, the assignment of teachers to provinces, and, to some extent, for the supervision of provincial budgets. Similarly, the General Director of Secondary Education is in charge of middle schools (*orta okul*), *lises*, six recently-established colleges (*kolej*), and schools for the training of religious leaders (*Imam-Hatip*). In contrast to the primary education department, the secondary department exercises direct control over the administration and educational activities of each individual school.

At the provincial level (Turkey is divided administratively into 67 provinces), the governor of each province (who is appointed by the Central Government) acts as the representative of the Minister of Education. Theoretically, therefore, each governor is responsible for all education in his province. The governor is assisted and advised by a council, consisting of a director of education (*Maarif Müdürü*)—appointed by the Minister and responsible to the governor—and by the heads of various local political units. This provincial-administrative body is in charge of primary education, but it operates within a framework of regulations set up by the central Ministry. It appoints, assigns, disciplines, and removes teachers; it appropriates monies for the construction and operation of schools; and, through a corps of school inspectors, it sees that the directives and regulations of the Ministry are carried through.

Each province is further subdivided into subprovinces (*kazas*). An education officer (*Maarif memuru*), appointed by the Ministry, is responsible to the deputy-governor (*kaymakam*) of each subprovince and to the provincial director of education.

Although such an administrative arrangement has the semblance of a balance between central and local control of education, in the last analysis the Turkish system is another example of a highly centralized pattern where policy-making and administration of the schools are conducted and regulated at the ministerial level. This is even more apparent in the case of secondary education. The Ministry at Ankara appoints teachers and principals; it makes appropriations for buildings, repairs, and equipment, which are earmarked in the national budget; and it has its own inspectors, although the provincial governor also has the right to inspect secondary schools and to report any observed irregularities.

The tight bureaucratic control over schools is further typified in the duties and powers of the local school director or principal (*müdür*). The responsibilities of the *müdür* encompass administration of school affairs and supervision of classroom instruction; these tasks, however, are minutely prescribed by regulations issued by the central office. The director exercises control over the classroom work of the teachers; he has the authority to inspect classes; he is expected to see that each teacher provides course outlines; he has the power to report to the ministry if the outline is not followed; and he checks on homework assignments. In addition, the *müdür* must hold meetings with teachers to discuss matters of school policy; and, at the end of the school year, he must evaluate teachers' performances for purposes of promotion or transfer. According to a principal of one of the foreign schools in Turkey, "It is difficult to imagine a system in which less opportunity is given for individual schools and teachers to exercise initiative, and in which all changes and adjustments must come from a place as remote from the real-school situation." [16]

Expenditures for the public system of education are underwritten by the National Government. Since 1935, there has been a trend toward a centralized system of financing. In 1935, the National Government contributed 47 per cent of the total educational expenditure, while the provincial and village governments contributed 53 per cent. In 1948, however, the central government's financial support of education rose to 88 per cent, while that of the provinces and the local authorities decreased to 14 per cent. Since the 30's, there has also been an increase in the amount

[16] Maynard, *op. cit.*, 103.

of money spent on education. In 1932, 9.3 per cent of the National Budget was earmarked for education; in 1955, the percentage rose to 12.6; in 1963, it was 16.3 per cent.

Roughly speaking the school system, beyond a common primary stage, is twofold: the general system—consisting of middle schools, *lises*, and the universities; and the technical-vocational system—comprising trade schools, technical schools, higher-technical schools, and technical universities. There are also several overlapping features, however, so that it is actually difficult to talk of one system, rather than of several interlocking paths or tracks of education. In spite of a provision in the constitution and the substantial growth in enrollments since the proclamation of the Republic, the goal of universal free-compulsory education has not yet been realized. Only about 45 per cent of the age group in the fifth and last year of the primary stage were at school in 1961–62. The rate of attrition in the five primary grades is high, and in many villages there are children who have not received the benefits of any formal education at all.

Beyond the five-year elementary stage, there is a network of three-year schools, consisting of the middle school (*orta okul*), the normal school, the commercial middle school, boys' and girls' trade schools, and a school for the training of religious leaders (*imams*). Of these middle stage institutions, the *orta* school has occupied and continues to occupy a pivotal position in the general educational system of the country. Originally a mere adjunct to the academic college-preparatory *lise*, it has developed both as a terminal institution and as a feeder for the academic and higher-technical schools. The present function of the *orta* school is threefold: (a) to give a general education beyond the primary school with a modicum of practical knowledge; (b) to prepare for the academic and other types of *lise*; and (c) to prepare for higher-trade and professional schools. Since 1923, and especially since 1950 when the Democrat Party came to power, the growth of the middle schools has been dramatic. In 1923–24, there were only 72 such schools; in 1949–50, the number rose to 285; in 1957–58, it was 555; and according to the latest figures, in 1961–62, there were 694 *orta* schools, enrolling 317,938 students. Parallel to the *orta* schools there are various categories of vocational, technical, and professional schools— each of which provides both a terminal education and preparation for higher schools of the same type. In general, each category constitutes a separate track with variations in the type of vocational or technical training. Thus, for example, the Building Trades Middle School—a three-year vocational school—leads into a two-year Building Trades Institute, which, in turn, leads into a two-year higher-technical school. Likewise, a three-year Girls' Middle Trade School leads into a two-year Girls' Trade Institute and then into a two-year Secretariat School. This middle-stage category of schools also includes Teacher-Training Schools (Normal Schools) for primary school teachers. The three-year lower-normal school leads into a three-year higher-normal school for *orta* school teachers and, thence, into a pedagogical institute for *orta* and *lise* teachers. In general, the nomenclature applied to the vocational and technical schools is as follows: At the middle level (ages 12–14), these institutions include trades' schools, commercial middle schools, normal schools, and schools for *imams*; beyond this level (ages 14–15 or 16 or 17), there are trade institutes, commercial *lises,* higher-normal schools, and higher schools for *imams.* In 1961–62, the total enrollments in vocational and technical schools (including the higher institutes) were 72,241, and in the two types of normal schools 28,424.

Since the establishment of the Republic, the academic secondary schools —known as the *lises*—witnessed similar high increases in enrollment as the middle-level schools. In 1923–24, there was a total of 1,241 students in these schools; in 1958–59, there were 45,408; and in 1961–62, the number soared to 82,062. The *lise* is a three-year institution following the three-year *orta* school. Aside from the commercial *lises* referred to previously, there are four major types of *lise* in Turkey: public; private Turkish; minority; and foreign. The minority and foreign *lises* are operated and supported by the minority groups (Greeks, Armenians, and Jews) and by foreign nationals (English, American, Austrian, German, French, and Italian) respectively. Admission into the *lise* is contingent upon successful completion of the *orta* course and passing of an entrance examination.

Above the secondary higher cycle (*lise* and higher-technical institutes), there is a network of institutions of higher learning, ranging from the universities (Ankara, Istanbul, Ege, Erzerum, Istanbul Technical University, and Middle East Technical University) to the School for Applied and Fine Arts, the Technical Teacher Training College for Women, and the Higher Islamic Institute. After passing an examination, *lise* graduates may enter any of these institutions, except the Higher Islamic Institute, which recruits its students from the lower-religious schools. In some cases, for example, in the case of training teachers, only graduates of the *lises* and the higher-normal schools are eligible for admission into the Pedagogical Institute, the highest teacher-training institution in the country. Similarly, only graduates of the *lises* are eligible for admission into the universities.

CURRICULUM

The curriculum of the primary schools in Turkey, like that of similar schools in other countries, emphasizes the rudiments of knowledge about nature and the social sciences, the development of language and basic mathematical skills, physical training work with arts and handicrafts, and some music appreciation. A recent report on the primary school program and on proposed revisions thereon, presented in detail the objectives of primary education and the principles upon which it should be based. This rather interesting document describes the tasks assigned to primary schools and attempts to place them within a framework that is psychologically sound and in line with Turkish national aims and aspirations. Although one might commend the soundness and comprehensiveness of this suggested conceptual framework, one is also struck by the lack of a realistic approach to what primary schools can actually do. In addition to basic skills of literacy, the primary school child in Turkey is called upon to do the following things: (a) to learn habits conducive to a hygenic way of living; (b) to "attach a special value on all mortals and lifeless objects" around him; (c) to utilize the senses more efficiently; (d) to make good judgments and to learn "scientific thinking methods"; (e) to acquire the feeling and outlook for making good use of spare time; (f) "not to despair in case of failure"; (g) to grasp the basic principles of good family life, and to attach a value to the family; (h) to learn simple housework and skills needed for daily life in the family; (i) to grasp "the role of manpower and natural resources in the development of community and the whole country"; (j) to grasp "the importance of good consumers in the economy of the country"; (k) to learn the importance of scientific knowledge and technique in the advancement and development of societies; and (l) to develop feelings of patriotism and democratic living and behaving, and "to feel proud for being the son of a great nation with an honorable history." [17]

The curriculum of the *orta* school includes Turkish, modern foreign languages, civics, history, geography, natural science, mathematics, religion (Islam), drawing, music, physical education, housekeeping, child care, commerce, and agriculture. Of these subjects, the humanities (Turkish, modern foreign languages, history, religion, music) occupy by far the largest single portion in terms of weekly hours (35 per cent of the total weekly instructional hours). Sciences and mathematics come second with 21 per cent of the weekly hours, and commerce and agriculture third with 6 per cent. Three hours (one in each grade) are devoted to civics, drawing, and physical education, respectively. Within the humanities group (a total of 34 instructional hours), fourteen hours are devoted to Turkish language and reading. It should be emphasized that there are no electives in the *orta* curriculum and that if a student fails in two or three of the fourteen courses, he must remain in the same grade and repeat the whole year. It is also interesting to note that, since the establishment of the Republic, an attempt has been made to introduce a practical bias in the curriculum. Yet, the essential purpose of the *orta* school has remained unaltered; in spite of concerted efforts to channel students to practical occupations, the overriding consideration in their minds is to continue their education into the academic *lise*.

The *lise*, for its part, continues and extends the general humanistic-scientific training of the *orta* school. The curriculum of the first *lise* class is uniform and compulsory for all, except for a two-hour elective chosen from music, art, and a second foreign language. It includes Turkish language and literature, history, geography, mathematics, biology, physics, chemistry, foreign language, physical education, and military training. In the second and third classes, there are two streams—scientific and literary, with corresponding variations in emphasis. Psychology is included in the second class; sociology, philosophy, and logic are included in the third. The distribution of the humanities and the sciences is about equal in the first class. But in the second and third classes, about three-fourths of the weekly hours are allotted to the respective academic streams.

The objectives of the *lise* curriculum have been stated in several ways: (a) as the creation of cultured, cultivated men, who have acquired the highest mental, moral, and physical attributes through the study of the usual disciplines; (b) as the attainment of a humanistic culture based on the European (especially French) notion of *culture générale*, (c) more narrowly, as the training of Turks who are committed "to the Turkish lan-

[17] For the full text of these objectives, see Republic of Turkey, Ministry of Education Directorate General of Primary Education, *Report on Proposed Revisions in the Primary School Program* (Ankara: Ministry of Education Printing Plant, 1962), No. 1, pp. 3-12.

guage, the principles and policies of the Turkish revolution, and in general to Turkish ideals." [18]

The curriculum of the various types of vocational and technical schools includes basic general education courses and vocational subjects, depending on the specific technical training with which the school is associated. Thus, for example, in the schools for "master builders," 14 weekly hours are devoted to the Turkish language, history, geography, citizenship, and civics; 26 hours are given to various subjects pertaining to the building trade; and 2 hours to military studies. In general, the basic principle underlying vocational education in Turkey is to provide separate schools for a group of related needs, rather than to provide one comprehensive school for all needs. For example, there are building-trades schools, chemical schools, mining schools, etc. In each school, there is a core of general-education subjects, which are compulsory for all students, and separate technical specialties, allowing for student option.

It appears that the Turkish government is eager to expand technical and vocational education in order to meet the needs of its industrial, commercial, and agricultural enterprises. Although the government is enthusiastic about the development of technical education and contributes considerable sums of money for this purpose, such an enthusiasm does not seem to be shared by many parents and students, who continue to prefer the academic middle and secondary schools. As in most developing societies, a technical-vocational type of education does not confer the same prestige as the academic type. As a consequence, although in Turkey there is a great demand for technically-trained manpower, students flock into the *orta* and *lise* schools in the hope that they will be able to secure positions in the already crowded white-collar occupations. In addition, Turkey has recently been losing many skilled technicians to Germany, primarily because of higher pay. The Turkish authorities have allowed this migration of labor in the hope that they will return better-trained.

129

[18] For a good descriptive account of the nature and purposes of the curriculum of the Turkish *lise*, see Maynard, *op. cit.*, pp. 201 ff.

THE CONCEPT OF POLITICAL SOCIALIZATION

Political socialization has the explicit purpose of molding the behavior of the young and the immature into politically and socially relevant form. Or, to put it in another way, political socialization is the process through which a person acquires his basic political orientation from his environment.

According to recent observers, political socialization has been and continues to be a major function of all systems of education, regardless of the prevailing social ethic or political and economic practices in the given state. Political socialization, as an explicit function of the schools and as a legitimate social process, gained additional impetus in the twentieth century, mainly as a result of the two world wars and the ideological conflicts between East and West, which have vied with each other for the minds of youth and for political influence over the uncommitted states of Africa and Asia. Furthermore, the recent emergence of new states has shouldered the schools with the responsibility for the development of national consciousness and political consensus.

CIVIC EDUCATION AND POLITICAL SOCIALIZATION

8

Levine has identified at least three mechanisms through which political values are acquired: (a) imitation of adult roles in the child's immediate environment; (b) instruction in political ideologies and accepted values; and (c) motivation to learn about the political world in order to satisfy emotional needs.[1]

In this chapter, we shall focus on the second mechanism; and in this connection we shall, for the most part, limit ourselves to the formalized activities through which the schools of selected countries perform the task of "politicizing" the younger generation. Such activities are often organized in the form of courses that may be known by different names. Thus, for example, the Japanese provide "moral education," the Germans "political education," and the Americans "civics" or "problems of democracy." This purpose is also pursued through such traditional subjects as history, literature, geography, and so on. While generally the content of these courses differs from country to country, the major function is the same, namely, to induct the young into the political culture of the society.

It should be emphasized at the outset that the examination of this problem from a cross-national viewpoint poses at least two difficulties: (a) the dearth of empirical research on the effects of the various school programs; and (b) the diversity in the issues involved and the multiplicity of indices applied in what little research there is available. Here we shall analyze representative practices, when feasible assess their effectiveness, and, wherever possible, make cross-national comparisons. Our analysis of patterns of political socialization provides only a beginning; our purpose is to identify some of the dimensions of this process and to raise questions for future investigations.

131

POLITICAL EDUCATION IN COMMUNIST COUNTRIES

The major purpose of teaching history and the social sciences in the Soviet Union, as expressed in the writings of Russian scholars and in the official pronouncements of the government, is to inculcate in youth an unquestioned loyalty to the Soviet system and the Marxist-Leninist ideology. This goal is reflected in the curriculum, the methods of instruction, and the textbooks and materials used in the classroom. Several studies reveal that the Soviets have made concerted efforts to glamorize the Russian State and its past and to debunk the Western world with its "decadent capitalism and dominant bourgeois culture." Upon reviewing history textbooks used in the Soviet Union since the Revolution, one writer has found that they contain strong anti-American sentiments. For example, before the war, the Americans were considered exploiters of the proletariat, but they were regarded with much admiration and jealousy for their accomplishments. Since the destruction of Nazi Germany, however, America has been depicted as the main threat to communism. Anti-American sentiment reached its peak after World War II and around the time of the Korean War, when strong propaganda attacks were directed against the American military bases, the Truman Doctrine, and the Marshall Plan.[2] In addition,

[1] Robert Levine, "Political Socialization and Culture Change," in *Old Societies and New States*, ed. Clifford Geertz (New York: Free Press of Glencoe, Inc., 1963), 299-301.

[2] Konstantin F. Shteppa, *Russian Historians and the Soviet State* (New Brunswick, N.J.: Rutgers University Press, 1962), pp. 321-60.

distorted pictures of American life have frequently appeared in history textbooks. Although a conscious effort is made to deprecate America and the West, Russian history and culture receive preferential treatment: the heroic deeds of the Russian leaders before and after the Revolution are praised, the cultural contributions of Russians are discussed in detail, the theme of class struggle between the bourgeois and the proletariat is traced back to its historic antecedents, and it is optimistically concluded that the downfall of the capitalistic societies is imminent. Furthermore, history textbooks reflect a high degree of ethnocentrism. It has been found that 70 per cent of the content of these texts concentrates on the history of Russia in the last 450 years, while only 6 per cent deals with non-European cultures.[3]

The situation prevailing among countries within the Soviet sphere of influence—e.g., East Germany, Rumania, Hungary, Bulgaria, Communist China—is generally the same as in the Soviet Union. In Yugoslavia—a nonaligned but communist state—the aim of social education is to bring about political cohesion and to acquaint the students with a scientific, dialectic-materialistic picture of the world. In Communist China, all human activity is carefully scrutinized and directed by the state; even family and strictly personal matters can be discussed only within an officially sanctioned framework. Political subjects such as dialectical materialism and the history of the Chinese Revolution are discussed not only in formal courses in the schools, but also in youth organizations such as the Young Pioneers and the Communist Youth League. The main concern of the state, like that of the Soviet Union after the Revolution, is the ideological reconditioning of the people. Education must serve politics, it must promote production, and under the guidance of the party, it must serve the ends of proletarian society.[4]

The question that arises from such attempts at planned political socialization is the extent to which these states have actually succeeded in imparting to their youth the political values and attitudes of the regime. Unfortunately, we have very little concrete evidence on the educational outcomes of programs in political socialization in Communist countries. A study based on observations and interviews with Soviet urban youth claimed that, except for the political activists, young people seem to be much less preoccupied with their moral and political values than is the regime. When asked to define "communist morality," they would cite examples demonstrating such general attitudes as truthfulness, respect for women, and generosity toward one's fellows, rather than the more ideologically circumscribed communist attitudes. Only a small minority espouse or pay lip service to the moral code of the party. There is generally more devotion to Soviet "patriotism" than devotion to communism, i.e., there seems to be greater identification with the Soviet nation rather than with the more internationally oriented communist ideology.

It appears that the persistence of personal interests and values vis-à-vis those of communism has been a factor in conflicts among city youth, e.g., "individual career goals vs. the obligation to work for the 'common cause'

[3] William K. Medlin, "Analyses of Soviet History Textbooks, Used in the Ten-Year School," in *Teaching in the Social Sciences and the Humanities in the U.S.S.R.* (Washington, D. C.: Studies in Comparative Education, U.S. Department of Health, Education and Welfare, Office of Education, Division of International Education, December 1959), pp. 1-18.

[4] Theodore Hsi-en Chen, "Education and Indoctrination in Red China," *Current History*, XLI, No. 241 (September 1961), 157-63.

wherever the citizen is assigned and needed; creative drives and personal views of artistic or scientific truth *vs.* the party's version of truth;" and "curiosity about the outside world *vs.* the continued relative isolation of the Soviet Union . . ." [5] According to the author of this report, this state of mind among youth is due to the sterility of the ideology and to the fact that the Soviet Union has reached a period of normalcy that allows for the emergence of points of friction between youth culture and official doctrine. It would be presumptuous, however, to conclude that young people do not take pride in the achievements of their country or that they do not accept the idea that socialism is far superior to capitalism. Since Stalin and his "cult of the personality" have been discredited, there is generally more relaxation and freedom in the expression of individualistic goals and aspirations.

Another index of the effectiveness of educational programs in political socialization is the existence of certain kinds of "anomic behavior" among school-age youth. Taking juvenile delinquency as an example of such behavior, it has been observed that teen-age gangs and delinquents no longer characterize western societies; they have their counterparts among Soviet youth. The history of the average delinquent in the Soviet Union would be familiar to Americans: a broken home, dropping out of school in the sixth or seventh grade, association with older people who have criminal records, the committing of minor offenses, followed by arrest and attempted rehabilitation in an "educational colony." When the "reformed" offender is released, in spite of the efforts of different organizations like the Komsomol to help him, he has a difficult time finding gainful employment. The chances are that he will resort to similar criminal acts and will either return to the "educational colony" or be sent to prison.

Accurate statistics on acts of delinquency and other forms of socially deviant behavior in the Soviet Union and other Communist countries are not available. Similarly, there is very little documentary evidence on the effectiveness of political education regarding political conformity and loyalty to communist ideology. There is speculation that the program of ideological reconditioning in Red China has not been very effective in view of the recent mass exodus of Red Chinese to Hong Kong. In East Germany, the fact that of the 200,000 escapees in 1960 one-half were under twenty-five years of age raises questions about the efficacy of planned programs of political socialization in the schools.[6] The dominant role that young people played in the Hungarian and Polish unsuccessful revolts of the mid-fifties might be interpreted as an indication that the schools did not accomplish their task of inculcating in youth the political values of the regime. It is also possible that in these two countries, traditional institutions and values (the Roman Catholic religion, for example) have operated against the acceptance of new ideologies and political practices. The Prague antigovernment May day riots of 1964, which, according to reports, involved about 3,000 students, coupled with lesser incidents in 1962 and 1963 indicate considerable unrest among youth in Czechoslovakia. It is claimed that the

133

[5] Peter H. Juviler, "Communist Morality and Soviet Youth," *Problems of Communism*, X, No. 3 (May-June 1961), 16-24.

[6] For more details, see Kenneth V. Lottich, "Extracurricular Indoctrination in East Germany," *Comparative Education Review* VI, No. 3 (February 1963), 209-11.

regime allows very little room for originality and self-expression, and it thus contributes to dissatisfaction among youth.

VALUE CONFLICTS AMONG GERMAN AND JAPANESE YOUTH

Germany and Japan present us with some variations in patterns of political socialization. Historically and ideologically both countries represent quite different societies. Yet, many problems in the area of political socialization are shared in common primarily because they both lost the War and because they were subsequently occupied by the Allied powers. One of the major problems in both countries, especially Germany, is centered around the treatment of recent history, approximately beginning with the Treaty of Versailles and ending with the surrender of the Axis powers. The question is: What should the youth know about their past, and who should be held culpable for the killing of millions of people through gas chambers, conventional warfare, or atomic holocaust?

Studies dealing with political education in West Germany are generally not very conclusive. A review of four government-approved history textbooks used in the *Oberschule* and in the *Gymnasium* claimed a lack of objectivity in dealing with decisive episodes in history, e.g., World War I, the Treaty of Versailles, the formation of the Weimar Republic, Hitler's rise to power, the persecution of ethnic and religious minorities, and World War II. The study asserted that the causes of the war are inaccurately described and that the Nazis' persecution and extermination of six million Jews are discussed in a restrained and detached manner. The issue of collective guilt is not properly treated because the books maintain that it was Hitler and the other Nazi leaders who were responsible for genocide, while the majority of the German people knew practically nothing about it.[7] Another review revealed that the interpretations of the rise of National Socialism are rather narrow in that Hitler's rise to power is explained solely in terms of the contemporary sequence of events, with no conscious attempt to place the movement in a broader historical perspective.[8]

A more up-to-date study based on ten widely used textbooks claimed that there were not many distorted statements about the Nazi period. It was further stated that the brutal features of the Nazi regime were fully described and explicitly condemned, and that persecution of the Jews was documented in detail. The books include heartbreaking photographs of the Warsaw Ghetto, a description of the Auschwitz Concentration and Extermination Camp, and a section on the Gersten Report dealing with mass gassing.[9]

In spite of contradictory interpretations of history textbooks, which can be partly explained by the application of different evaluative criteria and the fact that publication dates of such textbooks varied, there is evidence to suggest that the leaders of West Germany have tried to deal with the

---

[7] Mark M. Krug, "The Teaching of History at the Center of the Cold War—History Textbooks in East and West Germany," *School Review*, LXIX, No. 4 (1961), 461-87.

[8] Ronald F. Bunn, "Treatment of Hitler's Rise to Power in West German School Textbooks," *Comparative Education Review*, VI, No. 1 (June 1962), 34-43.

[9] Grace Richards Conant, "German Textbooks and the Nazi Past," *Saturday Review*, XLVI, No. 29 (July 20, 1963), 52-53.

problem of Germany's recent past realistically. Since 1950, when a resolution was passed by the Permanent Conference of Ministers of Education, a course in political education has been compulsory in all *Länder* of the Republic; the course has aimed at providing accurate knowledge and generating an active interest in politics. The resolution left the concept of politics and its relation to democracy undefined, so that pupils would be given greater freedom in forming political attitudes and beliefs and would be inspired with a sense of responsibility and public spirit.

Several studies conducted in Germany since the war attempted to examine the political values of German youth. One survey, which dealt with questions on the Nazi period, indicated that the average German boy tends to associate certain incidents under Hitler's regime with relevant attitudes toward games and other familiar activities. For example, his attitude toward war is expressed in terms of support for the home team. If the team loses the contest, someone must have let it down or there was unfair play on the other side. In the war against the Allies, the home team (the Germans) were fighting against "unfair odds." Hence, the average boy would conclude with the thought that "if both sides had had the same chance, we would have inevitably won." According to some investigators, the question of war guilt—a moral question—is beyond the average boy, but not beyond the intellectually able student who moves spontaneously from the historical and the political to the moral level. The Ellwein study, conducted under the auspices of the Munich College of Political Sciences in 1955, observed that political education is effective only when all teachers accept and internalize democratic values (and there are reasons to believe that there are a few "intractable" ones who are opposed to them) and when instruction is reinforced by practice outside the school. Among those interviewed, there was a fear that political education based on democratic values would have a negative effect on the performance of what they regard to be fundamental school tasks and on the traditional authority of the teacher. The study concluded that history teaching made no contribution to the development of political values and knowledge, except when it occasionally dealt with recent events. Similar surveys revealed that knowledge about the political process was inadequate, not because of a lack of the pupils' interest or the prevalence of authoritarian traditions, but because of inadequate facilities and untrained teachers. Even when a course in civics was offered as a separate subject, as in the case of 107 Frankfurt University students, there were no significant differences between students who had received instruction in the subject and those who had not on such questions as knowledge of democratic institutions and willingness to participate actively in politics. A study of political attitudes of public high school students, conducted in the early 1960's, corroborated the foregoing findings; it concluded that a course in civics, even if taught by good teachers, does not have any penetrating influence on the political consciousness of students.

These findings would generally be supported by research conducted in the United States, e.g., the Purdue Opinion Panel Studies, but they are subject to different interpretations. For example, it is doubtful whether a mere course in civics or political education will have positive effects on the development of political consensus among students or on their understanding of the political process and their willingness to participate in political decisions. The method of instruction, the prevailing school climate, the family, and the social and cultural conditions of the given community could very well be equally important factors in political socialization. Furthermore, it is very possible that basic social institutions, such as the family or the church, might impart to the young a set of political beliefs and values that are incompatible with those taught in schools. If this clash occurs frequently and the differences are sharp, serious social and political conflicts among youth may result. Also, recent research on political socialization of American youth suggests that the pre-elementary and elementary school years (ages 3 to 13) are the formative years in the formation of basic political orientations—i.e., knowledge of and values and attitudes toward the community, the regime, and the government. When the child enters high school, very little change in political beliefs is possible; the child has already formed firmly entrenched images, some of them over-idealized, of the President, the policeman, and of other authority figures.[10] These findings, although limited, cast doubts upon the effectiveness of university and secondary school courses in shaping the political world of youth. However, we need to have more empirical data on this question in a variety of cultural settings.

In another part of this book, it was indicated that a course in moral education was reintroduced in Japan in 1958 because the ruling party felt that "the lack of a national mission and the growing tendency to question all authority seemed to point up the real void in values." [11] Not satisfied with the moral component of "social studies" introduced by the American Occupation Forces, the Japanese felt a pressing need to reintroduce studies that would not ignore the ancient myths nor slight the role of the Imperial family. Since rising juvenile delinquency and other deviant behavior and nonconformity were generally associated with the absence of a formal course in morals, it was vigorously contended that such a course would improve the conditions and would restore order and discipline among youth. It would appear, at least by implication, that the Japanese have increasingly emphasized the need for political consensus and the avoidance of social conflict and that they have placed less importance upon development of the democratic values suggested by the American advisers. It is evident that Japanese leaders have realized that a political system cannot function unless it takes some measures to transmit its political heritage and to minimize disruptive cleavages in the political orientation of its members. In the eyes of her leaders, Japan has reached a point where the state needs to become more actively involved in the preservation of the political system from irretrievable disaster. It is doubtful, however, whether a new course emphasizing Japanese mythology will operate as a catalyst of the social and psychological dislocations among youth, resulting mainly from Japan's involvement in the war, from the American occupation, and from the rapid pace of industrialization.

The value conflicts in Germany and Japan have manifested themselves in such recent events as the painting of swastikas on Jewish temples, a general anti-Semitic feeling among some young persons in Germany, mass demonstrations against the government, and the militant anti-Americanism of some youth organizations, like the *Zengakuren* in Japan. According

---

[10] David Easton and Robert D. Hess, "The Child's Political World," *Midwest Journal of Political Science*, VI, No. 3 (August 1962), 229-46.

[11] Dixon Y. Miyauchi, "Textbooks and the Search for a New National Ethics in Japan," *Social Education*, XXVIII, No. 3 (March 1964), 131-37.

to Lifton, the social-historical dislocation taking place in Japan today is due to the abrupt break with the past—the absence of a sense of connection becomes apparent.[12] The traditional emphasis placed upon beauty and aesthetics is considered irrelevant to the demands of the modern world; obligation and harmony in the family, the local group, and the nation are now regarded as sources of embarrassment, rather than of strength and pride. The life-story of a young man, as narrated by Lifton, gives a vivid illustration of the different identification symbols and styles of life (filled with psychological contradictions) one experiences in postwar Japan. At the age of twenty-five, our young man is a *Sarariman* (salaried man), who identifies with his firm and acknowledges the firm's contributions to the economic growth of the nation. At the same time, he resents his new life; to compensate for it, he engages in fantasy—stealing money and then spending it in Europe and America amusing himself. In unguarded moments, he goes into tirades against the constrained life of the "typical salaried man." Similar internal contradictions are present at various stages in his life: e.g., when he learns to hate the Americans but, later as a student, becomes a convert to many aspects of American life and is baptized as a Christian; when he joins the *Zengakuren* as an activist embracing the ideal of pure communism, and then becomes filled with disillusionment with the organization during his third year at the university.

The foregoing case indicates some of the important points of friction among Japanese youth. The conflict generally stems from attempts to become immersed in Western ideas and practices while at the same time trying to preserve a distinct national identity and value-orientation. In varying degrees, this conflict of values is observed in all of the developing countries in Africa and Asia that have come into contact with the West.

137

In comparing postwar political education in West Germany and Japan, the reader will have to admit that German leaders have demonstrated greater willingness to emphasize democratic principles in the schools than have their Japanese counterparts. There are at least two reasons that might help to explain this situation. First, Germany has historically been a member of the Western community of nations, thus some conditions for an easier acceptance of Western democratic ideas and values were present. Indeed, there was a brief democratic interlude under the Weimar Republic. On the other hand, Japan (even when she emerged from her isolation in the middle of the nineteenth century) retained her oriental authoritarian traditions, some of which could be traced to China and Confucius—Western ideas were totally alien to her. Second, the relative ease in rejecting authoritarian values and in accepting democratic values in Germany, at least at the verbal level, might be attributed to the existence of a scapegoat—Hitler and other Nazi leaders. Many people claim that the Nazi elite was responsible for the outbreak of the war and the atrocities that followed, while the majority of the German people knew very little about what was going on. Even those who did know were virtually powerless to challenge the decisions of the leaders of the Third Reich. Thus, the theory of "collective guilt" is vigorously debated by a number of people in contemporary Germany. Japan, however, presents a different, more clearcut case. There is no convenient way out through scapegoating. Beginning with the acquisition of Manchuria in 1931, the majority of the Japanese

[12] Robert Jay Lifton, "Youth and History: Individual Change in Postwar Japan," *Daedalus*, XCI, No. 1 (1962), 172-97.

people supported the policies of the government for territorial expansion in Asia and for economic hegemony in the Pacific. Although some attempts have been made to blame the militarist clique for Pearl Harbor and the war in the Pacific, many Japanese people have accepted responsibility for their share in the war. Furthermore, the image of the Emperor as a supreme and divine authority who could do no wrong remained largely intact, even after the war. While in Germany the wartime leaders were repudiated, this was not quite true of Japan.

THE CASE OF TURKEY

As in the case of the U.S.S.R., Turkey, which emerged from the 1923 Kemalist Revolution, sought to establish a new national consciousness and ideology. To this end, schools were assigned the major role of developing a new generation of men, dedicated to the political ideals of the emerging secular and Western-oriented state. Atatürk tried to make the new generation repudiate its Ottoman past by forcefully removing certain traditional institutions and practices, such as the Islamic schools (*Medreses*), Arabic script and Arabic instruction in school, the fez, the veil, and so on.

The goals of education regarding the development of political consciousness in Turkish youths are not different from those advocated in other cultures. For instance, among the objectives of national education in Turkey are respect for the national flag, knowledge and appreciation of "the great Turks whose services have made the great Turkish nation," and a desire to save the Republic by emulating the deeds of national heroes. Furthermore, respect for the family and other social institutions are stressed in the schools.[13] Reference is also made to knowledge and appreciation of democratic principles such as equality before the law and the rights and responsibilities of citizens. In view of certain political and social events that have occurred during the Republican period, one wonders whether principles like those enunciated by official bodies like the Ministry of Education have actually taken roots in the political behavior of the people. This doubt is particularly strengthened by the notorious *Varlik Vergisi* (capitation tax) that, according to some authorities, discriminated against ethnic minorities such as Armenians, Greeks, and Jews.[14] A national survey conducted in 1959 on the basic value systems of *lycée*-level students revealed that the Turkish youth is quite authoritarian, but that this authoritarianism tends to be counteracted by solidarity in values and by an increasing commitment (not necessarily expressed in behavior) to certain forms of democratic ideology. Furthermore, the findings indicated a strong political consensus among Turkish youths on such diverse topics as voting in a national election, the position of Mustafa Kemal in modern Turkish history, and the role of religion in modern life. The first two questions elicited overwhelmingly favorable responses, while the third indicated a striking rejection of religion as a subject a parent should try to teach his child. The investigation concluded that in comparison with high school youths in other countries, Turkish respondents exhibit very little cynicism and alienation. Also, in Turkey, the feeling of nationalism

138

[13] *Report on Proposed Revisions in the Primary School Program, op. cit.*
[14] See, for example, Bernard Lewis, *The Emergence of Modern Turkey* (London: Oxford University Press, 1961), pp. 291-96.

among youths is relatively high, which is another indication of strong political homogeneity.[15]

The high degree of consensus on certain political issues manifested among students in *lycée*-level institutions would lead one to hypothesize that Turkish youths develop political beliefs, values, and attitudes at the lower levels of education. The fact that political education (basic civics) is stressed in the primary and middle schools but not in the *lycées* would lend further validity to this hypothesis. As we pointed out earlier, research conducted in the United States has shown that basic political attitudes are developed and fixed between the ages of 3 and 13. This might well apply to Turkey.

With some qualifications, one could say that the schools and other relevant institutions have succeeded in "politicizing" the Turkish youths in the sense of developing certain new ideologies and minimizing conflict and social disorganization.[16] On the other hand, one might argue that a high degree of political agreement and a corresponding absence of political or ideological pluralism would tend to support the perpetuation of a monolithic state and would stifle innovation and experimentation. There is always a danger in accepting things as they are, without asking many questions.

EDUCATION FOR EFFECTIVE CITIZENSHIP IN THE UNITED STATES

The process of political socialization in the United States is not radically different from that in the countries we have examined thus far. Like the Soviet Union and Turkey, America, being a new nation, had to create and impart to a younger generation a new political mythology and new national symbols. The task of creating political consensus became a major school function; it was sought primarily through formalized activities such as "homerooms," independent courses in citizenship or history, and through strict observance of national holidays—celebrated by means of patriotic ceremonies, parades, and school plays. In addition to instilling patriotism and allegiance to the nation, the American public school made a deliberate effort to acquaint youths with democratic principles and to foster a respect for democratic institutions. In order to realize the latter goal and to supplement formal instruction in citizenship, democratic procedures in the classroom were stressed and both teachers and students were expected to participate actively in the affairs of the local community. The trend toward citizenship education culminated in the 1918 report of the N.E.A. Commission on the Reorganization of Secondary Education, which included

---

[15] Frederick W. Frey, "Education: Turkey," in *Political Modernization in Japan and Turkey*, eds., Robert E. Ward and Dankwart A. Rustow (Princeton, N.J.: Princeton University Press, 1964), pp. 205-35.

[16] The absence of disruptive conflict is not entirely warranted in view of: the 1955 incidents in Istanbul and other cities, in which Turkish mobs destroyed property belonging to various ethnic minorities and desecrated Christian churches; the successful coup d'état against the Menderes government and the subsequent military trial and execution of Menderes and two of his ministers; and the 1962 and 1963 abortive coups against the Gürsel government, primarily involving military cadets in Ankara. The extralegal ways (revolutions or coups d'état) and the supporting role of the military through which a change of government is frequently affected reinforces the doubt about actual internalization of democratic values and practices among the Turks.

the development of effective citizenship and ethical character among its cardinal principles. A special committee of the National Council for the Social Studies listed, among others, the following characteristics of a good citizen: "[a good citizen] treats all men with respect, regardless of their station in life; rejects distinctions based on race, creed, or class; exerts his influence to secure equal opportunity for all . . .; upholds the principle that all men are equal before the law . . .; believes that the right to vote should not be denied on the basis of race, sex, creed, or economic status; values, respects, and defends basic human rights and privileges guaranteed by the United States Constitution." [17] While all school subjects were to contribute to the task of developing the good democratic citizen, courses in the social studies were expected to carry the major responsibility. These courses generally centered in the traditional academic disciplines of history and political science, but the focus was expected to be on the practical needs of citizenship. Later, special subjects—commonly known as "Problems of Democracy," "Current Events," or "Civics"—were introduced into the high school curriculum. Such subjects aimed at redefining and consolidating the ideals and practices of the American democratic state, which were somewhat jolted as a result of two world wars and a great depression.

We have stated that American schools were given the tasks of developing patriotic citizens, dedicated to the American democratic institutions and ideals. One could justly claim that since independence, Americans have been successful in developing a new national consciousness and a distinct American culture. However, it is very difficult to assess the specific role of the school in this enterprise. It would be of interest, perhaps, to point out that most of the studies concerned with the relationship between formal courses in social studies and democratic attitudes were either inconclusive or their results were negative. One of the conclusions of the 1935 New York Regents' Inquiry on Citizenship Education was that "quantity of work done in the social studies is not reflected in more liberal attitudes." [18] The Syracuse and Kansas Studies of Citizenship corroborated these findings by suggesting that social studies courses did not have much effect in changing attitudes. [19] A more recent study, completed by the Purdue Opinion Panel, concluded that a separate course in U. S. Government or in Civics is not related to liberal attitudes, which were defined as agreement with the Bill of Rights, rejection of or low scores on fascist ideology and Marxism, less extreme feelings toward communism, and disagreement with "superpatriotic" statements. On the other hand, liberal attitudes were related to geographical region of the country (the Midwest and South being the least liberal), place of residence (urban pupils were more liberal than rural), amount of education of pupils' mother, absence of political-party affiliation, and low scores on religious belief. It was also found that on several criteria, American youths exhibited attitudes that could be interpreted as authoritarian and unfavorable to minority groups. [20]

[17] "Characteristics of the Good Democratic Citizen" in *Education for Democratic Citizenship*, Twenty-second Yearbook, ed. Ryland W. Crary (Washington, D. C.: National Council for the Social Studies, 1951), pp. 154-60.

[18] Franklin Patterson, et al., *The Adolescent Citizen* (New York: Free Press of Glencoe, Inc., 1960), p. 72.

[19] *Ibid.*, pp. 83-88.

[20] H. H. Remmers, ed., *Anti-Democratic Attitudes in American Schools* (Evanston, Illinois: Northwestern University Press, 1963), pp. 18-60, 103-21.

These findings lend themselves to different interpretations and observations. In view of what seems to be an absence of any relationship between formal instruction and the formulation of liberal attitudes, it would be reasonable to hypothesize that such attitudes—if developed in school—are developed through other activities. On the other hand, one could attribute the lack of effectiveness of such formal instruction to the way courses are organized and taught. It may very well be that if courses were more analytic and functional in their approach, rather than purely descriptive, they would foster a more critical attitude toward political issues. This lack of effectiveness may also be related to the unrealistic content of many courses in political education. For example, on the Lockian-Jeffersonian-Jacksonian tenet of "consent of the governed," one writer has marshaled empirical evidence that casts doubts upon the existence of this ideal. It was found that less than 20 per cent of the adult population takes an active part in the affairs of the government; no president has been elected by a popular majority of the total number of eligible voters; although urban areas constitute about 70 per cent of the population, they are under-represented in state legislatures (they elect only 20 per cent of the legislators); most policy-makers at the national level of administration are appointed rather than elected; more than half of the American industry is organized along oligopolistic lines, i.e., 50 per cent of the industry is owned by approximately two hundred corporations; and less than 1 per cent of the American people are informed, interested, analytical, and active in foreign affairs.[21]

Turning now to the existence of certain authoritarian and antidemocratic patterns among youths one could raise the following questions. Is this a recent phenomenon or has it always existed among youth? Is this related in any way to the schools and what they teach, to family patterns of authority and relation, or to the prevailing conditions in the society at large? Is it possible, for example, to entertain the hypothesis that this phenomenon is part of the general mood of World War II and the ensuing Cold War? In the late 40's and early 50's, an organized movement, championed by the late Senator McCarthy, tried to purge the government and other semipublic organizations of Communists or sympathizers. During this period of ultra-rightist-radical reaction to the alleged Communist victories in the Cold War, practically everybody was suspect of disloyalty. Immigrants had to prove that they were not bearers of contagious beliefs; world renown personalities, such as the Dean of Canterbury and Pablo Picasso, were denied entry visas because of their political views; and since then, anyone applying for a government post has had to swear that he will not advocate its overthrow. The whole movement implied lack of faith in American institutions to withstand the pressures of Communist propaganda.[22] Although the movement to combat the danger of an over-exaggerated Communist threat is not nearly as strong as in the heydays of McCarthyism, there is evidence to suggest that a revivified radical right is trying to use similar tactics and—by using various means of intimidation

[21] Fred M. Newmann, "Consent of the Governed and Citizenship Education in Modern America," *School Review*, LXXI, No. 4 (1963), pp. 404-24.

[22] William Petersen and David Matza, eds., *Social Controversy* (Belmont, California: Wadsworth Publishing Company, Inc., 1963), pp. 260-63.

and pressure—to force youths and schools to comply with their social and political values.[23]

While it is expected that many American teachers treat such controversial topics as communism in the spirit of scholarly inquiry and objectivity, it is not unrealistic to say that even countries having a democratic tradition and professing to be the champions of Western democracy inescapably engage in political indoctrination and intolerance. Katz has pointed out that despite their inherent ideological differences, both the Western and Soviet systems recognize the value of political education and its importance in maintaining the political system; and both provide, formally or informally, for political acculturation. On the whole, according to Katz and other writers, the process of political socialization seems "to be identical in both types of society." [24] The ritual of saluting the flag, the use of one language of instruction as a means of assimilating immigrants, and concern for the preservation of "the American way of life" are offered as indications of a conscious plan in America to teach nationalism and engage in political education. After surveying school programs reported in both official and unofficial documents, Bereday and Stretch concluded that the *amount* of political exposure in schools in the United States is greater than in the Soviet Union. From the statistical data they present it is obvious that confrontation with political and social ideas and issues decreases with age in both countries, but more markedly in the Soviet Union. It is possible that Soviet educators operate under the assumption that the formative years in the internalization of the political world are those spent in elementary school and that political and moral attitudes and beliefs are firmly established before children leave the eighth grade. Nevertheless, it should be understood that mere exposure, calculated on the basis of the distribution of subjects in the curriculum, does not necessarily indicate the degree of depth and intensity of treatment. It is conceivable that a short but well-planned program of political education, presented by highly qualified and enthusiastic teachers, might be more effective than a long program, taught unsystematically by incompetent and apathetic teachers. According to Bereday and Stretch, the differences in political "exposure" between the two systems (especially the fact that more time is given to political education in the United States than in the Soviet Union) are reasonable, because it takes more time to elicit allegiance to the nation in a new, pluralistic, and free society than in a more traditional, monolithic, and controlled society. In addition to this explanation, one could maintain that the Soviet system does not generally emphasize the humani-

[23] See, for example, John P. Lunstrum, "School Policy and Controversial Issues," in *Crucial Issues in the Teaching of Social Studies*, eds., Byron G. Massialas and Andreas M. Kazamias (Englewood Cliffs, N.J.: Prentice-Hall, Inc., 1964), pp. 178-86. Similar practices are reported by Lawrence E. Metcalf, "Anti-Communism in the Classroom: Education or Propaganda?" *Nation*, CXCIV, No. 1 (March 10, 1962), 215-16; and by Donald W. Robinson, "The Teachers Take a Birching," *Phi Delta Kappan*, XLIII (February 1962), 182-88. Also see Roland F. Gray, "Teaching about Communism: A Survey of Objectives," *Social Education*, XXVIII (February 1964), 71-72.

[24] Joseph Katz, "Common Ground Between Communist and Western Education," in *Communist Education*, ed., Edmund J. King (Indianapolis: Bobbs-Merrill Company, Inc., 1963), pp. 284-304. George Z. F. Bereday and Bonnie B. Stretch, "Political Education in the U.S.A. and the U.S.S.R.," *Comparative Education Review*, VII, No. 1 (June 1963), 1-16.

ties and social sciences because of its present commitment to subjects that contribute directly to industrial and scientific development.

SUMMARY

From our analysis here, it is evident that all societies engage in political socialization. The school is one among several social agents—e.g., family, church, job, youth organizations—performing this task. In its overt form, political acculturation in the schools is supposed to take place through formal courses—especially through courses in history, the social sciences, and the humanities. In many countries, political education in the classroom is supplemented by extracurricular activities and/or work in school clubs and youth organizations. Implicitly, the educational system and its subdivisions transmit certain political norms to the young. In England, for example, those who attend a modern secondary school accept the politically passive role implicit in the culture of the school. This is not true in the case of the comprehensive high school in the United States, which has more or less rejected certain a priori inequalities that are accepted and fostered by many European secondary schools.

While the process of political socialization appears to be a universal function of national systems, the content and interpretations of the political world vary from country to country. We have observed, for instance, that textbooks and other classroom materials in the Soviet Union and in the United States give different emphases and present different (often contradictory) views of historical and contemporary social problems. Each system tries to imbue the young—implicitly or explicitly—with its own particular notions of authority, legitimacy, the role of the citizen, and of the good life; at the same time, it strives to present negative interpretations of politically alien systems.

The schools, in their attempt to politicize the young, operate under the assumption that formal instruction in social or political education affects the political beliefs and values of students. While it is logical to assume that explicit instruction in politics will have an effect on the political attitudes and knowledge of the individual, most of the studies reviewed here failed to establish conclusively this relationship. Also, the success of a school program in political socialization depends not only on the competence of the teachers and the availability of facilities and materials, but also on the general conditions in society as well. A course in civics or government can never be effective in changing students' political beliefs if corresponding changes do not occur in the social milieu. This has been demonstrated in a dramatic way in certain countries, where after World War II, the schools began to impose new values that were incompatible with traditional beliefs; in some instances—as in Japan and Germany and to a lesser degree in Poland and Hungary—this value contradiction has created serious social problems.

There is no research evidence, except for limited studies conducted in the United States, to indicate the most appropriate ages during which political ideas and values are formed. The research conducted in the United States suggests that the pre-elementary and elementary school years, i.e., the years between 3 and 13, are the most crucial in internalization of the political system. The hypothesis of optimum age in the development of

143

political attitudes is a subject that should be investigated in a cross-national setting.

Twentieth century societies have witnessed various social trends—industrialization, urbanization, interdependence, world wars, etc. These conditions have either accentuated the conflict in values, or they have brought about a strong movement toward "conformity." Extreme forms of social controversy or group conformity have, in many cases, resulted in social strife, violence, and/or behavioral deviation. It appears that a stable society needs to strike a balance between social consensus and social disagreement or, to use Ralph Linton's words, to have a core of cultural uniformities while, at the same time, providing cultural alternatives. In modern monolithic states, youths accept the political and economic ideology of the ruling elite on faith; there is comparatively little conflict or civil disobedience. However, the apparent absence of conflict is often deceptive, as in the case of Turkey and some of the eastern European countries that have recently witnessed violence, mainly as a result of students' reactions to certain policies of the government.

In view of the paucity of empirical research in this crucial area, we should like to suggest that rigorous investigations be carried out, possibly using cross-nationally stable categories, which would examine (a) the political beliefs and actual behavior of children and adults in a variety of socio-economic environments; (b) the kinds of beliefs and values, in effect, imparted by different institutions such as the family, school, social club, job, peer group; and (c) the relation between patterns of socialization and outcomes such as identification with the nation, political stability, democratic pluralism, and intelligent participation in political decision-making.

One of the persistent goals of educational policy in contemporary societies has been the so-called democratization of education. Democratization can be viewed in terms of two dimensions—the quantitative and the qualitative. In its quantitative context, democratization commonly refers to expansion of educational provisions, increased educational opportunity, high rates of literacy, and so on. Qualitatively, democratization of education is the extent to which education contributes to participation in the political process, freedom of inquiry, the existence of a loyal opposition, etc. In this section, we shall examine these two dimensions separately.

GROWTH IN SCHOOL ENROLLMENTS

In dealing with questions of school enrollments, we must bear in mind that the figures provided by world organizations such as UNESCO and the international Bureau of Education have been collected from documents submitted by the respective governments. Hence, some of these figures are inflated or based on very rough estimates; many figures are presented in different units of measurement, thus creating difficulties in interpreting enrollment trends over a period of time; student enrollments classified under the categories of primary and secondary education

DEMOCRATIZATION OF EDUCATION

9

do not always reflect comparable age groups or types of schools, because school organizations vary from country to country; as a result of major reorganizations of the structure of some educational systems—e.g., England and the Soviet Union—the available figures do not accurately reflect certain changes that have taken place over the last thirty years. Nevertheless, the figures compiled by UNESCO, however crude, provide some indication of this aspect of democratization of education.

Of the nine countries in Tables 9-1 and 9-2, Tanganyika, Turkey, and to a lesser extent, the Soviet Union have shown dramatic increases in primary school enrollments (ages 5 to 14) since 1930. For example, over a period of approximately thirty years, enrollments in Turkey have increased 400 per cent; in Tanganyika, 240 per cent; and in the Soviet Union, 44 per cent. The United States registered an increase of approximately 34 per cent; Japan, 18 per cent; and France, 17 per cent. The dramatic increases in Turkey, Tanganyika, and the Soviet Union are further borne out when one looks at the enrollment ratios between the estimated mean population of five to fourteen years of age, and actual average enrollments. On the other hand, countries like the United States, France, and Japan—which have shown increases in overall enrollments—have shown slight decreases in enrollment ratios. Clearly on the basis of trends shown in Tables 9-1 and 9-2, the least-developed countries have made the greatest progress in the expansion of primary education. This, of course, may not be surprising,

TABLE 9-1   Trends in Primary School Enrollments 1930-54

Country	1930-34			1950-54		
	Estimated mean population 5-14 years (000)	Average enroll-ment (000)	Enroll-ment ratio	Estimated mean population 5-14 years (000)	Average enroll-ment (000)	Enroll-ment ratio
United Kingdom (England & Wales)	6,554	5,542	85	6,337	4,362	69
France	5,982	5,018	84	6,505	5,099	78
Germany (Federal Republic)	10,469 (1931)	7,590 (1931)	73	7,704	5,826	76
Greece					944 (1954-55)	
U.S.S.R.	38,700	20,812	54	39,400	27,806	71
United States	25,098 (1931-33)	22,682 (1931-33)	90	27,479	23,585	86
Japan	14,873	10,695	72	18,711	11,348	61
Tanganyika	1,668 (1946-49)	133 (1946-49)	8	1,816	260	14
Turkey	3,686	564	15	5,047	1,651	33

Source: Based on UNESCO, *World Survey of Education, Primary Education,* Vol. II, 1958.

because most of these countries started almost from scratch. Moreover, although there were sharp increases in numbers and enrollment ratios, the percentage of children of primary school age actually enrolled in schools is relatively small. For example, in Tanganyika, only 14 per cent of this age group was enrolled in primary schools in 1950-54; and although the figures for Turkey show a 193 per cent increase in 1930-54, only 33 per cent of the corresponding age group was in school. In this connection, it is also of interest to note that these two countries rank the lowest in rates of literacy.[1] In the United States and France, we observed that although there was an increase in absolute enrollments at this level of education, there was a relative leveling off in enrollment ratios. The substantial decreases registered in the United Kingdom are largely due to the reorganization of the system after the 1944 act. When this factor is taken into consideration, one finds that the leveling-off process applies to the United Kingdom as well.[2] It appears that in developed societies, the growth of primary school

[1] According to the 1963 figures, literacy rates (expressed in percentages) of people 15 years and over were as follows: United Kingdom, 98-99; France, 96-97; West Germany, 98-99; Greece, 75-80; U.S.S.R., 98-99; United States, 98-99; Japan, 98-99; Tanganyika, 5-10; and Turkey, 35-40. *Population Information for 127 Countries* (Washington, D. C.: Information Service, Population Reference Bureau, October, 1963).

[2] Other estimates made on enrollments in European countries over the period 1950-60 support our observation of such a leveling-off process. In Europe as a whole, there was only a 6 per cent increase (30,000,000 to 32,000,000) during this period. See Frank Bowles, "Education in the New Europe," *Daedalus*, XCIII, No. 1 (Winter 1964), p. 379.

TABLE 9-2   Changes in Primary School Enrollments 1930-60   147

Country	Average enrollment 5-14 years (000)			Per cent increase or decrease		
	1930-34	1950-54	1959-60	1930-39, 1950-54	1930-34, 1959-60	1950-54, 1959-63
United Kingdom (England & Wales)	5,542	4,362	4,355	—21	—21	—.16
France	5,018	5,099	5,900	1.6	17	16
Germany (Federal Republic)	7,590 (1931)	5,826	6,934 (West, 5,138; East, 1,796)	—	—8.6 (East & West)	—12
Greece		944	927	—	—	—1.00
U.S.S.R.	20,812	27,806	30,000 (1960-61)	34	44	8
United States	22,682 (1931-33)	23,585	30,349 (1960-61)	4	34	29
Japan	10,695	11,348	12,591 (1960-61)	6	18	11
Tanganyika	133 (1946-49)	260	451 (1960)	96	240	73
Turkey	564	1,651	2,785	193	400	69

Source: Based on UNESCO, *World Survey of Education, Primary Education,* Vol. II, 1958, and *Current School Enrollment Statistics,* September, 1962.

enrollments took place prior to 1930. In such countries, as will be shown later, the increases have taken place at the secondary and university levels rather than at the primary level. This suggests that in the less-developed societies, the problem of democratization of education encompasses all levels of education; in the developed societies, it is confined more to the upper secondary and higher levels of schooling.

A recent study estimated that over a ten-year period (1950-59), there was an increase of 57 per cent in world-primary school enrollments, which exceeded by far a 17 per cent increase in corresponding school-age population groups (ages 5 to 14).[3] According to our estimates based on our own sample only two countries (Tanganyika and Turkey) come anywhere close to the world enrollment figures. All other countries fall far short of this increase. The mean increase of enrollments in our sample countries over a comparable period of time is about 20 per cent. The difference of 37 per cent between our own data and the foregoing world data may be explained by the fact that our sample includes a disproportionate number of "developed" societies, in which an enrollment plateau had been reached earlier. It should be remembered that world estimates are perforce based on figures from a preponderant number of new states, which accounts for the overall phenomenal increase of 57 per cent. This difference between developed and developing countries is most sharply illustrated in the cases of the United Kingdom and Tanganyika, where the percentage increase was —.16 and 73, respectively.

The available figures for secondary school enrollments are not as uniform as those for primary schools. The UNESCO statistics are qualified by three types of schools: general secondary (G), vocational or technical (V), and teacher-training at secondary level (T). In some cases, only G enrollments are given; in others, G and V; and in still others, G, V, and T. Furthermore, enrollment figures for France and the Soviet Union (Table 9-4) seem to be somewhat unreliable over the thirty-year period. It is still possible, however, to make some observations about general trends at this level of education.

Tables 9-3 and 9-4 indicate that overall secondary school enrollments have increased more than 50 per cent during 1930-60 in all countries about which we have information. Japan and Turkey stand out as the two countries with the most dramatic growth (776 per cent and 736 per cent, respectively), and France registered an increase of 427 per cent. Unlike the statistics for primary education, enrollment ratios for secondary education increased during the period 1930-57 in all countries for which figures are available. Japan, France, and the United Kingdom show the highest increase in enrollment ratios during this period.

Table 9-4 indicates some other interesting trends in the expansion of secondary education. In the United Kingdom, there was virtually no increase in general education from 1930-50, but a 49 per cent increase in the ensuing decade; similarly, in the United States, there was a greater percentage growth between 1950-60 than during the preceding two decades. In Japan, on the other hand, there was phenomenal growth between 1930-50, and relatively little growth thereafter (619 per cent compared to 20 per cent). Turkey's growth has been dramatic during both periods (219 per cent

[3] Frank Bowles, *Access to Higher Education*, Vol. I (New York: Columbia University Press, 1963), pp. 96-97.

and 162 per cent, respectively). Of the eight countries for which there are data, Turkey has registered the highest percentage increase since 1950 and West Germany, the lowest (162 per cent and 5.4 per cent, respectively). Of the European countries in our sample, France has shown the most spectacular expansion of secondary education, with an increase of approximately 116 per cent. According to other estimates covering data from all European countries, Italy comes second to France in rapid enrollment growth, with a 96 per cent increase.[4] It is also noteworthy that in both France and the United Kingdom, there was a more rapid increase during the second half of the decade of the 1950's.

In our analysis of primary school enrollments, we were able to indicate that developing societies like Turkey and Tanganyika had the greatest growth in overall enrollments. This observation does not apply, however, in the case of secondary school enrollments. Over the thirty-year period (1930-60), such diverse countries as France, Japan, and Turkey have witnessed most dramatic increases; in the case of Turkey and France, a similar phenomenon occurs during the decade of the 1950's. It is significant to note that Turkey, a developing society, heads the list in terms of this criterion. However, as in the case of our estimates of primary school enrollments, such phenomenal increases in overall percentage enrollments do not in and of themselves provide a sufficient index of secondary education provision. If we look at the enrollment ratios—namely, the estimated total age group and the actual enrollment—we observe that in both France and Turkey, the number of children in secondary schools is comparatively small. On the other hand, during the period 1950-57, Japan, England, and Germany have consistently maintained the highest enrollment ratios in our sample. This indicates that in such developed societies, a plateau has been reached at the secondary as well as elementary level; thus, suggesting that the problem of democratization of secondary education is less one of quantitative expansion and more of the quality of instruction and provision for individual differences. It would also appear that the problems of quantitative expansion of previous years would henceforth apply more to the higher levels of education.

Comparing our estimates with those of world enrollments, we observe that over a ten-year period (1950-60), France and Turkey far exceed world figures. This period shows an increase of 81 per cent in world secondary school enrollments compared to an increase of 16 per cent in corresponding school-age population groups (ages 15 to 19).[5] In Turkey and France, the increases amounted to 162 and 116 per cent, respectively. All other countries in our sample registered increases of less than 50 per cent. The mean increase in secondary school enrollments for the countries we have selected (excluding Greece and Tanganyika, for which there are no available figures) is 73 per cent, which is much closer to world figures than is the primary education mean increase.

[4] Fabio Luca Cavazza, "The European School System: Problems and Trends," *Daedalus*, XCIII, No. 1 (Winter 1964), 404.
[5] Bowles, *Access to Higher Education, op. cit.*, p. 97. It would be of interest to note that substantial increases have also taken place in the higher levels of education. Over the period from 1950-59 the increase in world enrollments has been 71 per cent, compared to an increase of 13 per cent in the corresponding population age group (ages 20 to 24).

TABLE 9-3 Trends in Secondary School Enrollments 1930-57

Country	1930-34			1950-54			1955-57		
	Estimated mean population 15-19 years (000)	Average enrollment (000)	Enrollment ratio	Estimated mean population 15-19 years (000)	Average enrollment (000)	Enrollment ratio	Estimated mean population 15-19 years (000)	Average enrollment (000)	Enrollment ratio
United Kingdom (England & Wales) (G)	3,405	2,107	62	2,721	2,129	78	2,771	2,450	88
France (GVT)	2,911	391	13	2,974	902	30	2,731	1,148	42
Germany (GV)				3,809	3,160	83	4,509	3,559	79
Greece (G)					198 (1954-55)			217 (1957-58)	
U.S.S.R. (GVT)				18,283	4,892	27	19,232	6,853	36
United States (GV)	11,719	5,845	50	10,659	6,846	64	11,487	8,351	73
Japan (GVT)	6,553	1,051	16	8,667	7,564	87	8,750	8,567	98
Tanganyika (GVT)					33 (1953)			49 (1957)	
Turkey (GVT)	1,002	53	5	2,132	169	8	2,406	279	12

G = general secondary, V = vocational or technical, T = teacher training at secondary level.
Source: Based on UNESCO, World Survey of Education, Secondary Education, Vol. III, 1961.

In dealing with the question of educational expansion, one may also consider the relative distribution of female students in the total school population. Until quite recently, education—especially at the secondary and higher levels—has been limited mainly to boys. Generally speaking, this picture has changed in the twentieth century. At the primary level, the European countries and Japan have more or less attained parity in educational provision according to sex. This is not true of Tanganyika and Turkey, where in 1959-60, only 34 and 38 per cent, respectively, of the total school population were girls. In these two countries, even these figures represent a significant increase over past periods; and over a ten-year period (1950-60), especially in Tanganyika, there has been a trend toward an increase in the percentage of girls at school. Turning now to the percentage of girls enrolled in secondary schools, we notice that by 1957, France, the United Kingdom, the United States, and Japan had attained parity in educational provision according to sex; West Germany and Greece had each reached a mark of over 40 per cent of girls. The great disparities in the male-female distribution exist in Turkey and Tanganyika. In Turkey, specifically, there has not been any change in enrollment of girls in secondary school over a twenty-seven year span (1930-57); during this period, it has remained at 25 per cent.

While it would be true to say that in Europe and Japan there has been a trend toward parity of educational provision among the sexes, the most pronounced changes have taken place in access to certain types of schools and to the universities. For example, in Germany there was an increase of 11 per cent in enrollments of girls in the upper-secondary schools and of 5.6 per cent in university enrollments from 1939-55. In Italy, the proportion of female students in the professional schools increased by 16 per cent from 1938-59.[6]

The growth of school enrollments and the increased representation of girls in the various levels of education were accompanied by attempts to eliminate inequalities in the distribution of students according to social-class background. As we indicated in Part II, considerable progress has been made in the postwar decades. In all the countries we have examined, the chances of a working-class child receiving an education according to his ability and interest have, in the main, increased substantially. We have also shown, however, that vestiges of the aristocratic tradition linger on and that economic and social-class factors continue to influence access to secondary schools and institutions of higher learning. Academic secondary schools, which traditionally have carried high prestige and been the preserve of the elite groups in the society, continue to recruit a disproportionate number of students from the middle- and upper-socio-economic strata. It might be appropriate to mention, however, that even in democratic societies, it is well-nigh impossible to eliminate all factors that contribute to inequalities in education. It would appear, therefore, that democratization of education in this sense seeks to eliminate glaring inequalities, rather than to achieve absolute equalitarianism.

[6] For a more detailed analysis of the changes in female enrollments in European schools and universities, see Cavazza, *op. cit.*, pp. 405-7.

TABLE 9-4 Changes in Secondary School Enrollments 1930-60

Country	Average enrollment 15-19 years (000)				Per cent increase or decrease		
	1930-34	1950-54	1955-57	1959-60	1930-34, 1950-54	1930-34, 1959-60	1950-54, 1959-60
United Kingdom (England & Wales) (G)	2,107	2,129	2,450	3,172	1	50	49
France (GVT)	391	902	1,148 1,597 (1957-58)	2,064	130	427	116
Germany (GV)		3,160	3,559	3,330			5.4
Greece (G)		198 (1954-55)	217 (1957-58)				
U.S.S.R. (GVT)		4,892	6,853	5,459 (1960-61)			11
United States (GV)	5,845	6,846	8,351	10,249 (1960-61)	17	75	49
Japan (GVT)	1,051	7,564	8,567	9,126	619	776	20
Tanganyika (GVT)		33 (1953)	49 (1957)				
Turkey (GVT)	53	169	279	443	219	736	162

G = general education, V = vocational or technical, T = teacher training at secondary level.
Source: Based on UNESCO, *World Survey of Education, Secondary Education*, Vol. III, 1961; and UNESCO, *Current School Enrollment Statistics*, September, 1962.

The expansion of education and its corollary, the equalization of educational advantages, have raised questions as to whether the traditional institutional structure can serve the needs of the diverse school population and the demands of the modern world. The prevalent arrangement in the world patterns of education until about 1950 was the tripartite system, whereby a common primary stage led to at least three different and parallel paths: (a) preparation for the university; (b) teachers' training; and (c) technical and vocational training. Of 93 countries surveyed, 48 provided this institutional arrangement; 38 provided a secondary system, separated into two parallel lines (one leading to the university and the other to teachers' training, technical, vocational, or professional programs); and 7 provided a secondary program, common to all students, followed by technical, vocational, or college-preparatory streams. Comprehensive schools were included in the last category. In 1959, there was a significant shift in the opposite direction: twenty-seven countries provided a tripartite system; 29 a system separated into two parallel lines; and 37 a common secondary program.[7] It is apparent that viewed in a world-wide context, there has been a pronounced tendency toward a uniform pattern of secondary education and toward the postponement of choice of specialization.

The systems of education of the nine countries we have examined exhibit characteristics corresponding to all of the foregoing organizational structures. In the West European countries, although the prevailing pattern is of the tripartite or bipartite variety, there have been experiments aimed at the extension of common schooling and the postponement of selection for the different types of secondary schools. In England, there has been a growing interest in the comprehensive-school idea. In France, the most significant change in this regard has been the idea of the *cycle d'observation*. Likewise, in Germany, in addition to the *Aufbauschule*, there have been experiments to set up "alternative routes" to higher education. On the other hand, in the Soviet Union, Japan, and the United States, the idea of a common secondary program is more widespread. The United States, in particular, provides the prototype of the comprehensive-school idea. In Greece, Turkey, and Tanganyika, secondary schooling is not compulsory, and it is provided in parallel tracks.

The several experiments in the European countries and the prevailing patterns in the Soviet Union, the United States, and Japan, have been justified on the grounds that they are part of the democratization movement in education. For example, advocates of the comprehensive school in England, especially the Labour Party, claim that the tripartite system tends to discriminate against the working-class groups, children of low ability, and the so-called "late bloomers." According to them, the comprehensive school would break down social distinctions, allow for latent talent to develop, and create a framework for better communication among the citizens of a democratic society.

153

EXAMINATIONS

In the quest for a more equitable amount and type of education for all children, examinations have played an important role. Examinations have

[7] Bowles, *Access to Higher Education, op. cit.*, pp. 106-9.

performed a variety of pedagogical and social functions. For example, they have been used to gauge the intellectual capacities of students in order to allocate them to or eliminate them from schools or curriculum streams, for purposes of instruction and promotion, to tap the talent from all strata of society, and to control admission into various occupations.

One of the earliest attempts to use the examination system as a method of social selection was made by the Chinese. Between approximately 700 and 1900 A.D., the Chinese, through systematic examinations, sought to recruit talented individuals and to channel them to appropriate positions in the bureaucracy. These examinations, which tested proficiency in the Chinese classics and accomplishment in literary expression, were open to members of all social classes; for some, they served as a means of social mobility. Essentially similar functions have been performed by the English and French civil-service examinations since the nineteenth century. In these cases, until recently, emphasis was placed on the Western literary-humanistic traditions, especially the Greek and Latin classics. Theoretically, because they were open to all individuals in the society, such types of examinations would have contributed to a more equalitarian social distribution of positions in the civil service. In practice, however, certain social groups were more successful in the examinations and, consequently, were over-represented in the civil service. The reasons for this were: (a) the subject matter in which people were examined was taught in schools that were already socially exclusive; and (b) the examinations were made by people with vested interests. Nevertheless, the introduction of a system of external examinations considerably improved the existing pattern, which rested on patronage and nepotism.

These observations pertain to the use of other types of external examinations employed in connection with educational selection. We are here referring to the General Certificate of Education and the Cambridge Overseas Examination in England and the Commonwealth; the College Entrance Examination Board, the National Merit Scholarship Qualifying Test, and the Advanced Placement Examination in the United States; and the recently established university entrance examinations in Turkey. In all these cases, the avowed aim has been to set up more objective mechanisms of student selection and financial support. Because such examinations are open to all, and because they emphasize achievement and intellectual competence rather than economic and social background, they can be viewed as a democratizing element in educational selection. However, there is some evidence to show that there are disparities in the social composition of the successful candidates—i.e., a disproportionate number of students from the more privileged socio-economic groups obtain the highest scores. A recent study on the impact of the National Merit Scholarship Program on schools in the United States revealed that there was a positive correlation (correlation coefficient of .75) between success in the qualifying tests of the program and socio-economic background of the student. Schools in which children of upper and upper-middle classes predominated had higher level of success than those with children from lower and lower-middle classes.[8] As we have already mentioned in Part II, examinations, especially of the verbal variety, are never devoid of cultural

---

[8] Roald F. Campbell and Robert A. Bunnell, eds., *Nationalizing Influences on Secondary Education* (Chicago: University of Chicago, Midwest Administration Center, 1963), p. 53.

TABLE 9-5 Trends in Distribution of Successes in the G.C.E. According to Social Class Background (in Per Cent)*

Paternal Occupation	1951		1961	
	Boys	Girls	Boys	Girls
Professional and Managerial	69	69	77	70
Clerical	53	55	62	63
Skilled	48	43	56	51
Semi-skilled and Unskilled	31	28	41	34

* Percentages are based on the number of students in each occupational group.
Source: Ministry of Education, *Half our Future, A Report of the Central Advisory Council for Education* (London: Her Majesty's Stationery Office, 1963), p. 293.

biases. Moreover, most of these examinations test academic achievement or potential, which is itself socially biased in the schools.

There is another important aspect to consider when assessing the overall impact of external examinations. This relates to what may be called the unanticipated consequences of such screening devices in the schools. External examinations have been found (a) to influence the organization of the curriculum, its content and the method of instruction; (b) to segregate students and penalize the under-achievers, the late bloomers, and the slow learners; (c) to rank schools and teachers according to the number of successes in the examinations; and (d) to create elite groups of students and teachers within even one school system. For example, these consequences have been found to be true in the case of the College Entrance Examination Board (CEEB) and the National Merit Scholarship Program in the United States. A summary of research on these programs has concluded that "they have brought about changes in course content, addition of new courses, increased academic training of the teachers, addition to facilities and equipment, and introduction of special forms of preparation for the various testing programs employed."[9] Similarly, it has been found that schools participating in the National Merit program are rated according to successes in scholarship awards. This effect clearly contributes to the creation of "elite" institutions, within what has traditionally been regarded as an equalitarian public school system. While this phenomenon has created some concern among American educators, it does not come as a surprise to the student of other societies, where external examinations have been commonly used over a longer period of time. A case in point is England, where external examinations like the General Certificate of Education and its predecessors, the School and Highest School Certificates, have largely dictated the curriculum policy within the grammar schools.[10] Moreover, a breakdown of passes, shown in Table 9-5, at the Ordinary and Advanced levels in the G.C.E. over a ten-year span (1951-61)

155

[9] *Ibid.*, p. 103.
[10] For a fuller discussion of this theme, see H. Lister, "The Effects of External Examinations on the School," in *External Examinations in Secondary Schools: Their Place and Function*, ed. G. B. Jeffrey (London: George G. Harrap & Company, Limited, 1958), pp. 55-78. Also see, Ministry of Education, *Secondary School Examinations Other Than the G.C.E.*, Report of a Committee Appointed by the Secondary School Examination Council in July, 1958 (London: Her Majesty's Stationery Office, 1960), pp. 21-22.

shows that although there has been a tendency toward a more equitable social distribution, disparities based on socio-economic background do persist. Even the modern schools, which allegedly were to be free of examination encumbrances, have directed their activities toward greater successes in these examinations.

Another equally important category of examinations is what may be conveniently called "internal" examinations—i.e., selective devices used in schools for purposes of admission into various levels and types of education, of promotion from one grade to another, of diagnosis, and of programs of educational and vocational guidance. As in the case of external methods of testing, internal examinations have often been envisaged as constituting an important part of the democratization process in education. In other words, they have been used to minimize socio-economic and teachers' biases for pedagogical purposes and for admission into higher levels of education. Such internal examinations are being used universally in all contemporary societies. However, there are certain important variations in the policies adopted by different countries and in the types of examinations used. These variations, as indeed is the case of other aspects of education, reflect the ideological, social, political, and psychological factors that characterize a given society. Examinations are based on the aims of education, the kinds of capacities, skills, and knowledge deemed important and relevant, the extent to which a society places major emphasis upon the education of the few or the many, the allocation of manpower resources, and prevailing psychological theories concerning learning and intelligence.

Two of the most examination-conscious countries of the world are England and France. We have already referred to the famous eleven-plus examination, administered at the completion of the primary school course, and the controversies surrounding it. This examination has been used to assess the intellectual capacities of primary school graduates, in order to allocate them in the three types of secondary schools. Although this function has contributed to a more objective method of screening and a more equitable method of student allocation, environmental and family factors continue to play a part in a child's chances of success in such examinations and, thereby, of his entrance into certain types and levels of education. Moreover, as in the case of the external examinations, the eleven-plus has exerted an influence upon the curriculum of the primary school. In this connection, the response given by a primary school child is most revealing. When asked what he was studying, he innocently replied, "Eleven-plus!"

France does not have the comprehensive eleven-plus type of examination at the end of the primary school. But at the completion of five years in the *école primaire élémentaire*, a rigorous examination selects a small percentage of children (less than 20 per cent of the age group) for admission into the academic *lycée* or *collège*. The great majority of the rest (about 70 per cent) continue their education in the eight-year elementary school, and some (about 14 per cent) enter the *cours complémentaires* (lower secondary schools). At the end of the ninth year at school, students who do not plan to continue their education in the academic streams take the so-called *Brevet d' Etudes du Premier Cycle* (B.E.P.C.). Most of the students who pass this examination enter careers in the industrial and commercial sectors. In 1959-60, of the 178,331 who sat for the B.E.P.C., 134,679 or 75.5 per cent passed. The small number of students who are enrolled in the academic schools are subjected to rigorous examinations at the end of each grade and to the two parts of the famous *baccalauréat*: the first part is given at the end of grade eleven (about the age of 17); the second part is given at the end of grade twelve (about the age of 18 plus). The mortality rate in these examinations is very high. Of the total number of candidates who sat for Part I of the *baccalauréat* in 1960-61, only 58.9 succeeded; of those who took Part II, only 60.5 passed. The much coveted *baccalauréat* opens the way for admission into the universities. Admission into full status as a student in the university, however, depends upon successful completion of a preparatory year (*l'année propédeutique*)—a year of general or liberal education comparable in its general purpose to the beginning years of the American college. At the end of this year, students are subjected to another rigorous examination, which is passed by only about half. The stringent system of examinations continues throughout the student's university career.

As in England, examinations in France perform a multiplicity of educational and social functions. First, they provide the most important basis for educational selection or differentiation of students: the academically talented are channeled into rigorous and specialized programs, while the others enter terminal or practically-biased tracks. Second, examinations provide the means for social mobility for the underprivileged and confirm and reinforce the social status of the already privileged classes. We have already referred to the social-class character of the *lycée* and *collège*. Success in examinations is a great accomplishment and brings honor and prestige not only to the candidate, but also to the family. The *certificat d'études primaires*, the certificate earned after completion of the primary school, is framed and hung in the *salle*; those who are not able to earn it "disgrace" their parents as well as themselves.[11] Furthermore, school examinations largely determine the future occupational career of the individual. For example, the holders of the primary certificate may qualify for minor positions in the civil service—e.g., postman, clerk, and so on, while the *baccalauréat* leads to higher positions.

The system of internal examinations in France, as in England, influences the curriculum and the instructional practices in the schools. Wylie has reported that Madame Vernet, a teacher in Peyrane, drilled her students for the primary school examinations; other observers have recorded that curriculum content and classroom activities in the secondary schools are dictated by the examinations that lie ahead.[12]

The French system of examinations is enmeshed in elitist theories of government and in an intellectualist cultural tradition. Like the Platonic model, the French place heavy emphasis upon "the guiding role of the elite"; also, like Plato, they look at examinations and the schools as instruments in the selection and training of future political leaders. The type of education considered to be a basic desideratum for such training has been what is commonly known as *culture générale*, with its stress on the classi-

---

[11] For a vivid account of the psychological ordeal of parents and children regarding these examinations, see Laurence Wylie, *Village in the Vaucluse* (Cambridge, Massachusetts: Harvard University Press, 1957), pp. 91-97.

[12] *Ibid.*, p. 94; Male, *op. cit.*, p. 111.

cal humanistic heritage of the past, encyclopedic knowledge, and development of the individual's intellectual powers. Examinations like the *baccalauréat* are organized with this objective in mind, and it is assumed that the person who succeeds in them has developed the attributes associated with *culture générale*.

In recent years, there has been mounting criticism of the entire educational system (especially the examinations) and the assumptions upon which it is based. Critics contend that the present system of examinations curtails educational opportunity for many bright children, and thus causes considerable loss of talent. For example, in a survey conducted in 1955, it was reported that teachers believed that although 55 per cent of the primary school graduates had the ability for a secondary type of education, only 33 per cent chose to sit for the entrance examinations.[13] It has also been argued that the examinations, especially the *baccalauréat*, exert a standardizing influence upon school programs and stifle experimentation, initiative, and exploration. As a result, students are exposed to the same curriculum irrespective of their interests, aptitudes, and vocational goals.[14] Furthermore, it has been claimed that the content of the schools' curriculum and the subject areas measured by the tests do not include knowledge and skills concerning problems of the modern world. The concept of *culture générale* and the assumptions upon which it is based have been questioned as to their adequacy in meeting the problems of increasing specialization and technological advancement.

While criticism of curriculum inadequacies and obsolescence—a common phenomenon in many countries of the world—may be valid, one wishes that there were more empirical evidence on the actual attainments of the schools in such areas as skills, attitudes, knowledge, etc. Although we are inclined to believe so, we are not absolutely sure that the American child—who is exposed to variations in the curriculum, to experimentation, to projects designed to develop initiative and creativity—does, in fact, surpass his educational counterpart in France, England, and elsewhere in these criteria.

Turning to the United States, we do not find a system of examinations comparable to the eleven-plus in England or to the *baccalauréat* in France. The transition from the elementary to the secondary schools is automatic; admission into many institutions of higher learning, especially certain state colleges and universities, is not based on an entrance examination. The American child, however, is subjected to several types of tests and examinations throughout his school career, probably more so than his English or French counterpart. The tests being used cover a much wider sphere of the child's potential, ranging from intellectual to psychological and social criteria. If we were to compare the functions performed by such examinations in the United States with those of England and France, we would note the following: (a) in the United States, there is emphasis upon the diagnostic value of tests for purposes of educational and vocational guidance—something that has only recently been considered in European countries; (b) in American school systems, where students are allocated to different curriculum programs—e.g., college

---

[13] Olive Wykes, "Attendance at Secondary Schools in the French Fourth Republic," *School Review*, 69, No. 1 (1961), 89.

[14] See, for example, W. R. Fraser, *Education and Society in Modern France* (New York: Humanities Press, 1963), p. 54.

preparatory, commercial, vocational, and so on—examinations or tests constitute only one of the selective criteria, others being interest inventories, psychological profiles, and parental pressures; (c) school examinations in the United States do not irretrievably affect a person's future educational and vocational career; and (d) although in America, as indeed in the other countries we have examined, there is an avowed concern for social justice in education, there is also evidence that many of the standardized tests used discriminate against the culturally underprivileged groups.

In summarizing the nature and function of examinations in these three liberal democracies of the West, one could say that although they provide for social and educational selection to a degree, they nevertheless reflect certain differences in social and political thinking. To use the Weberian notion of "ideal types," we could say that the conception of education in England and France still retains vestiges of the aristocratic tradition; in the United States, it is activated by a more equalitarian spirit.

EDUCATION AND POLITICAL ELITES

The term "elite" is ordinarily used to refer to groups of people who constitute a special class, possessing certain distinctive characteristics not generally possessed by other people. These characteristics may include wealth, power, intellect, education, social graces, talents, etc. In any society, one finds what S. F. Nadel called a "plurality of elites," i.e. political, intellectual, military, business, artistic, etc.[15] Classical social thinkers, implicitly or explicitly, have employed the elite concept in their philosophies; some of them, e.g., Plato, Mosca, Pareto, and Marx, have developed intricate theories around it. In contemporary periods, there has been considerable scholarly interest in elites—particularly in the identification of elites, their patterns of recruitment, their circulation, their attributes, the means through which they maintain or exercise their power or status, and the relationship between elites and various forms of government. A full analysis of elite formation and social control is beyond the scope of this book. However, because this concept is connected with the process of modernization and democratization and because it appears that there is a functional relationship between elites and education, some attention to this topic will be given here. We will limit our analysis to the relationship between education and political leadership in selected countries. In this connection, we are going to examine the educational background of political leaders, the extent to which there is an openness in the system of recruitment, and the gap, if any, that exists between political elites and the masses.

The Ottoman Empire and Turkey provide clear examples of where education, at least theoretically, has played a distinct role in elite formation and status and has demarcated what Gaetano Mosca has called the "class that rules and the class that is ruled." This relationship may be viewed from at least three interrelated dimensions: (a) amount or level of formal education; (b) type of institution; and (c) educational or professional specialization. An examination [16] of the composition of the Turkish Grand National Assembly from its establishment in the 1920's reveals a consistently high percentage of deputies with a university educa-

159

[15] S. F. Nadel, "The Concept of Social Elites," *International Social Science Bulletin*, VIII, No. 3 (1956), 419-20.

[16] Our analysis here is based on data provided by Frey, *op. cit.*, pp. 229-33.

tion: in 1920-23, the percentage was 70; in 1954-57, it was 77. The distribution of the members of the Assembly in terms of highest educational level attained from 1920-57 was as follows: university, 73 per cent, *lise*, 12 per cent, middle school, 10 per cent, primary school, 2 per cent, and *medrese* (religious school), 1 per cent. The percentage of people with a university education was even higher among the top leaders in the political hierarchy: in 1920-23, 87 per cent of the cabinet ministers had attained a university-level education; in 1954-57, the percentage increased to 97. It is quite obvious that the higher the level of education attained, the greater the chances for membership in the chamber of deputies and the cabinet.

Historically, certain specific schools or types of institutions were known to produce a disproportionate number of political leaders. For example, the famous Palace School of the early Ottoman period was a training ground for high posts in the civil bureaucracy, and the *medreses* trained religious leaders (many of whom also performed political functions). In the nineteenth century the military academies produced many of the activist leaders of the Young Turk movement; schools like the Galatasaray *lise* and the *Mülkiye*, which later became the Political Science Faculty of Ankara University, produced many of the civil-service leaders. During the Republican period, certain *lises* have performed similar functions in the selection and training of political elites; the *Istanbul Erkek Lisesi*, in particular, may be likened to the English Eton, in that it has produced a large number of cabinet ministers and high officials. Another interesting phenomenon, which also has historic roots, is the influence of study abroad in attaining political status. In the nineteenth century, French education, in particular, was important; more recently, it was observed that of the 13 per cent of deputies who had studied abroad, 43 per cent had attended universities in France, 30 per cent in Germany, 15 per cent in Switzerland, and 6 per cent in the United States. Looking at background in terms of institutions attended, it can be inferred that certain schools play a dominant role in political recruitment.

Data regarding the third dimension, namely, educational or professional specialization, suggest that training in certain university faculties and in certain professions is an important factor in the attainment and sustenance of political power. Among the general category of civil bureaucrats, many of whom had reached positions as deputies and cabinet ministers during the First Turkish Republic (1923-60), more than half had attended the Political Science Faculty of Ankara University and 23 per cent had attended the Law Faculty. Of the cabinet ministers during the same period, from 50 to 75 per cent had come from these two faculties. It should also be noted that in Turkey, appointments to high civil-service positions—such as *valis* (governors of provinces) and *kaymakams* (sub-governors of provinces)—presuppose attendance at universities, especially at the aforementioned two faculties. It is not surprising, therefore, that 99 per cent of this branch of the civil bureaucracy are graduates of the Political Science and Law faculties of Ankara University.[17]

[17] Richard L. Chambers, "The Civil Bureaucracy: Turkey," in *Political Modernization in Japan and Turkey*, eds. Robert E. Ward and Dankwart A. Rustow (Princeton, N.J.: Princeton University Press, 1964), pp. 325-26. On the question of the relationship between parliamentary longevity or reelection rate and type of higher education, see Frey, *op. cit.*, p. 231.

If we were to generalize on the basis of the three dimensions examined, we would be justified in saying that people who have attended certain specific secondary schools, who have graduated from universities, and who have specialized in certain fields have higher chances of occupying positions of political leadership and political power. Furthermore, it would appear that amount of education is the most significant variable in entering the ranks of the political-power hierarchy. These observations would make a strong *prima facie* case for political recruitment and selection as based on universalistic criteria, which are believed to be characteristic of a democratic polity. However, certain important qualifications must be made in the case of Turkey. First, there are other variables that also appear significant. We have already stated (Part II of this book) that a disproportionate number of children in the *lises*, the only feeder schools for the universities, come from the upper-middle and upper-social classes and that certain *lises* are over-represented in their number of successful candidates for entrance to the universities and the two politically significant university faculties. It would be reasonable, therefore, to infer that social-class background is an important factor in attaining the type of education needed for political status. Second, in a society where such education is extremely limited and the literacy rate comparatively low (less than 40 per cent), the very fact that a university education is the most crucial prerequisite for political ascendancy creates major constraints in the flow and circulation of participants in the decision-making process. Moreover, this very fact widens the gap between the political elites, as well as the intellectuals and the masses. In short, education in such a society might also be viewed as an institutionalized mechanism of inequality.

A modern non-Western country that, in spite of striking differences in industrial, economic, and educational attainments, offers remarkable parallels to Turkey in the interplay of tradition and political modernization is Japan. Here, we shall confine ourselves to the relationship between recruitment and education of the political elite in terms of the three dimensions we used in the case of Turkey.[18]

Taking level of education attained as the variable, we observe that since 1937 approximately half of the opposition members of the Diet in the lower house received a university education. The overall distribution of these members in terms of our available information of education attained was as follows: in 1937, 59 per cent had gone to universities, 14 per cent to secondary and higher technical schools, and 8 per cent to elementary schools (no information was available for the remaining 19 per cent); in 1958, the distribution changed substantially in the case of members from secondary and higher technical schools (the percentage rose to 41), while the percentage of members with a university education declined to 47. On the basis of these rather limited data, we might say that in 1958 in Japan, in contradistinction to Turkey, there was a more even distribution between those with secondary and those with university training, although higher education did play a part in the recruitment of at least the members of the Japanese Socialist Party. Like Turkey, however, all higher civil servants have been drawn from graduates of the universities. As in Turkey, there has been a historic connection between attendance

---

[18] Our analysis is based on data provided by R. P. Dore, "Education: Japan," and Masamichi Inoki, "The Civil Bureaucracy: Japan," in Ward and Rustow, *op. cit.*, pp. 187-88 and 295-97.

at certain institutions and political elite membership. We have already alluded to the role played in the preparation of high government officials by the First Higher School in Tokyo and Tokyo Imperial University (now Tokyo University) since the early Meiji Government in the latter part of the nineteenth century. In 1937, of a total of 1,377 civil officials, 1,007 or 73.6 per cent were Tokyo University graduates. Looking at the educational background of the group of opposition leaders we examined before, we see that in 1937, 14 per cent had received their education at Waseda University; and in 1958, 7 per cent had attended Waseda. These percentages become significant when we consider that in 1937 there were about 47 universities; and in 1960, there were over 245 such institutions. A breakdown of this group in terms of private-state universities reveals only a slight bias in favor of national and public universities.

Looking at educational or professional specialization, we note that a sizeable proportion (about 46.5 per cent) of the higher civil servants in 1937 graduated from the Law Department of Tokyo University. It would appear that in Japan, a background in the legal profession is more advantageous than in Turkey for those aspiring toward high posts in the civil bureaucracy.

Data on the social origins of Japanese political elites are meagre. What little evidence exists suggests that the civil service draws a disproportionate number of its staff from upper-class families and from families of civil bureaucrats. As a recent writer stated: " . . . the children of government officials have 58.5 times as many chances to attain eminence as the average Japanese, their chances of becoming political leaders, cultural leaders, and business leaders being, respectively, 95, 50, and 45 times greater than the average." [19]

We now turn to an examination of the relationship between education and political leadership in a Western industrially-advanced parliamentary democracy, namely, the United Kingdom. The association between the prestigious Public Schools, the two ancient universities (Oxford and Cambridge), and a career in Parliament, the finest "club of London," or in the civil service has been proverbial. Although this continues to be the case, in the last fifty years or so, there have been certain changes in the social composition and educational background of the English political elite.[20]

Taking the time-span from 1918 to 1951, we observe the following characteristics and trends. During the period 1918-35, of a sample of 1,003 Conservative members of Parliament, about half possessed a university education; of a sample of 444 Labour M.P.'s, only about 18 per cent possessed a comparable education. In 1951, of 321 Conservatives, 202 or 63 per cent had university training; of 296 Labourites, 111 or 37 per cent had similar training. A large number of Labour M.P.'s had only an elementary education; most Conservatives had a higher education. If we turn to the category of "cabinet ministers" during the period of 1916–55, of 100 Conservative ministers, 70 per cent had a university education; of 65 Labour ministers, only 45 per cent had a similar education. It is interesting to add that since 1945 there has been a decrease in the number of Labour-

[19] *Ibid.*, p. 298.
[20] Our analysis of the English political elite (M.P.'s and Cabinet ministers) is based on statistics given by W. L. Guttsman, *The British Political Elite* (London: MacGibbon & Kee, 1963), pp. 105-7, 291, 336.

ites with only an elementary education and an increase of those with a university education; no members of the Conservative Governments in 1951 and 1960 have been listed as possessing only an elementary education.

In the case of the English pattern of elite recruitment, we have ample evidence to indicate that certain schools and universities have produced and continue to produce a disproportionate number of political leaders, especially among the Conservatives. Outstanding examples of this phenomenon are the so-called "Great Public Schools," notably Eton and Harrow, and the two universities, Oxford and Cambridge. For instance, as late as 1951, 32.5 per cent of the Conservative M.P.'s had attended Eton and Harrow, and 80.5 per cent Oxford and Cambridge. The corresponding percentages among Labourites were 2.0 and 45 per cent, respectively. The predominance of these institutions is also apparent when one looks at the type of institution attended by cabinet ministers. During the period 1916–55, 45 per cent of the Conservative ministers had gone to Eton and Harrow, and 62 per cent to Oxford and Cambridge; the corresponding percentages among Labour ministers was 8 and 28 per cent, respectively. It is important to note that over a span of thirty-three years (1918–51), there was no appreciable change in the distribution of M.P.'s who had attended the four prestigious institutions. In fact, in the post-1945 period, there was an increase from 10 to 15 per cent of members of the Parliamentary Labour Group who had attended Public schools.

When we turn to the field of specialization of political executives (cabinet members), we find that during the period 1886–1950, law, business, and journalism constituted their major occupations, the percentages being 32.4, 29.3, and 28.6, respectively. Below these categories were those with "education" as their occupation (16.5 per cent), landowners (14.6 per cent), and military men (8.7 per cent).[21] Another set of data indicates that in 1918 and 1950 the percentage of businessmen among the newly-elected Conservative M.P.'s remained consistently high (40 and 41 per cent). During the same years, the number of barristers and solicitors increased from 18.5 per cent to 22.0 per cent, and of journalists from 2.5 to 7 per cent. On the other hand, the number of landowners and military men decreased significantly from 6 to 0 per cent and from 12 to 3.5 per cent, respectively. There seem to be similar trends among Labour leaders. By the fifties, as the party became more national, the number of middle-class M.P.'s with a professional background had increased. As Guttsman has stated, "Nothing illustrates this more pointedly than the fact that the teachers had ousted the miners as the strongest occupational group on the Labour benches." [22]

Although the civil service in England is a separate category from the political groups we have discussed above, a cursory examination of the educational characteristics of some of its members sheds more light on the theme of this section. In the most comprehensive study available on this subject, it was reported in 1950 that about 63 per cent of higher civil servants (assistant secretaries and above) had attended a university. Within the total group of such officials, about 26.5 per cent had attended Oxford and 20.8 per cent Cambridge. Only 4.7 per cent had received their training in what are often known as "Redbrick" universities (excluding

163

---

[21] Harold D. Lasswell, Daniel Lerner, and C. Easton Rothwell, *The Comparative Study of Elites*, Hoover Institute Studies, Series B: Elites, No. I (Stanford: Stanford University Press, 1952), p. 30.

[22] Guttsman, *op. cit.*, pp. 242-43.

London and the Scottish universities). Although the percentages of those who had attended the ancient universities were still substantial, they actually represented significant decreases from previous periods. In the nineteenth century, these universities monopolized open-competition entrants to the higher civil service; between 1949 and 1952, there was a decrease from 89 to 74 per cent. On the other hand, there were increases in the representation of entrants from London and other universities.[23] As in the case of M.P.'s and cabinet ministers, these data suggest that attendance at a university is an important prerequisite for entrance into the higher civil service; more important than this is attendance at Oxford or Cambridge. Before commenting further on the English pattern, we shall examine some comparable data in another Western industrially-advanced democracy, the United States.

A breakdown of the members of the United States Congress of 1937 and 1951 in terms of level of education and type of specialization reveals the following trends: (a) the number of Representatives and Senators without a university or college education decreased substantially. In 1937, 31 per cent of the members of the House and nearly 21 per cent of the members of the Senate had not received such education; in 1951, the percentages were 18 and 14, respectively. (b) Of those who had attended a college or university, the majority went to private rather than state institutions. (c) In both periods, there was a very high representation of people who specialized in law, this representation having increased considerably by 1951. In that year, lawyers constituted 56 per cent of the members of Congress, the higher representation of lawyers being in the Senate. (d) Businessmen, journalists, and teachers were the next important groups represented, with percentages of about 17, 8, and 5, respectively.[24]

Turning now to the executive branch of the government, Merriam, writing in 1949, reported that of the thirty-two Presidents of the United States two-thirds had been college graduates, ten had only a common school education, and one (Andrew Johnson) had no formal education at all. It is also relevant to note that with one or two exceptions, all of the presidents up to that time had attended private colleges or universities located in the eastern part of the United States.[25]

Taking another sample of top political leaders (Presidents, Vice-Presidents, Speakers of the House, Cabinet Members, and Supreme Court Justices) from 1789 to 1953, C. Wright Mills has found that 67 per cent graduated from colleges, the majority from Ivy League and high-status eastern institutions such as Harvard, Yale, Princeton, Dartmouth, Amherst, and so on. The same writer also observed the predominance of lawyers: of the 513 top politicians included in Mills' sample, three-fourths were

[23] See R. K. Kelsall, *Higher Civil Servants in Britain* (London: Routledge & Kegan Paul, Ltd., 1955), pp. 118-45.

[24] Percentages are based on statistics given by George B. Galloway, *The Legislative Process in Congress* (New York: Thomas Y. Crowell Company, 1953), pp. 371-74. A comprehensive summary of research on American political leaders is given by Wendell Bell, R. J. Hill, and C. R. Wright, in *Public Leadership* (San Francisco: Chandler Publishing Company, 1961).

[25] Charles Edward Merriam and Harold Foote Gosnell, *The American Party System* (New York: The Macmillan Company, 1949), pp. 151-52. All four subsequent Presidents have been college graduates.

lawyers and one-fourth businessmen.[26] The legal profession has also been found to be heavily represented in state legislatures and in the executive branch of the governments of the states. Unlike the other political groups we have examined, farmers were among the three highest occupational groups represented in the state legislatures in 1949. Of 7,475 state legislators, 23 per cent were classified as businessmen, 22 per cent as lawyers, and 19 per cent as farmers.[27]

Clearly, in the United States, level and type of education seem to be important preconditions for the attainment of high political office. There also seems to be a strong relationship between socio-economic background and high posts in the political hierarchy.[28] It would appear that anybody "cannot become President of the United States;" some have distinctly more chances than others!

On the basis of the foregoing examination of education and political elites in Turkey, Japan, England, and the United States, the following general statements may be made. Perhaps the most significant observation in this elite-education nexus is that in spite of great differences in economic, political, and social development, these societies have been characterized by striking similarities in the relationship between formal education and the rise to political prominence. These similarities may be summarized as: (a) university education has become increasingly important as a qualification for elite membership; (b) background in law and related occupations has become another important qualification for high political office; and (c) attendance at certain educational institutions enhances one's chances for entrance into the ranks of the "ruling class." Although education is increasingly becoming a necessary condition in the formation of political leaders, one should not conclude that it is a sufficient condition. Social and economic factors are also relevant. Indeed, the whole process of political elite-formation is far more complicated than it appears at first sight. One should also consider such factors as native intelligence, ethnicity, religion, marriage, age, personality characteristics, charismatic qualities, club membership, and so on.

A second major observation is the high representation, especially in England, Turkey, and the United States, of what Lasswell and his collaborators have called "specialists in persuasion"—e.g., lawyers, businessmen, journalists, teachers, and civil servants. These authors have associated the prevalence of such elites with pluralistic stable societies of the Western variety and their absence with monolithic societies like the Soviet Union. The case of Turkey presents us with certain paradoxes and raises further questions. Although there is an over-representation of "specialists in persuasion," one could not classify Turkey as a pluralistic society in the Western meaning of the term, nor indeed could one call it a stable democracy.[29] In view of this phenomenon, what seem to be the differentiating characteristics between Turkey and stable societies like England and the United

165

26 C. Wright Mills, *The Power Elite* (New York: Oxford University Press, Inc., 1959), p. 402.
27 Belle Zeller, ed., *American State Legislatures* (New York: Thomas Y. Crowell Company, 1954), p. 71.
28 Mills, *op. cit.*, pp. 400-402.
29 We have already referred to the military coups as a means to gain political power. For a more detailed discussion of the authoritarian political climate under the Gürsel regime, see Richard D. Robinson, *The First Turkish Republic* (Cambridge, Massachusetts: Harvard University Press, 1963), pp. 249-79.

States? We should like to suggest the following possible explanations regarding Turkey: (a) there has been less a tradition of parliamentary government and more one of militarism and authority vested in the hands of one individual or a small group of individuals; (b) as we have stated in our chapter on political socialization, although there seems to be a commitment to democracy as a political ideal, there is little evidence to suggest that such a commitment has been translated into actual political behavior; and (c) although it has a most highly educated class of rulers, it also has the least educated class of ruled. Consequently, there is a great gap between the political leaders and the masses, particularly as this affects the channels of communication.

In conclusion, it may be said that it is not the presence or absence of political elites that differentiates monolithic from pluralistic, or unstable from stable societies. Elites of this type have existed and continue to exist in all societies, and education has been used as one of the means for the recruitment and training of such people. What seems to differentiate the one type of society from the other in so far as the political elites are concerned is the extent to which they are accountable to the popular will, they are not hereditary or self-perpetuating, and they operate within a political system whose legitimacy is beyond question.

OTHER DIMENSIONS OF DEMOCRATIZATION

There are certain other aspects of the concept of democratization, which, unlike those we have discussed thus far, are more difficult to define or to assess. Moreover, they raise questions of a different order, mostly philosophical in nature. While such questions might conceivably fall within the purview of comparative education, we feel, as we stated in the introduction, that a comprehensive and systematic examination of them would require another volume. Here, we shall merely raise some questions of this order, which we hope might prompt the reader to further inquiry.

We have seen that there has been a substantial expansion of educational facilities and that today there are more children enrolled in schools than ever before. While this may have contributed to or, in the long run, may contribute to higher income or a higher standard of living, the question remains whether it has also contributed to the development of certain other attributes often associated with education. One such attribute is the development of the individual qua individual—i.e., his intellectual potential; his understanding of himself, the society in which he lives, and the larger international community; his ability to appreciate the artistic experience of mankind, and so on. Most nations of the world, either explicitly or by implication, espouse this as an important goal of education. The problems, however, consist of the extent to which the educational system contributes to the realization of these aims, whether there are inconsistencies or restraints inherent in the social and political philosophy of a society, and whether plans at educational change run counter to such professed aims. For example, in the Soviet Union, according to DeWitt, although there is a constitutional provision guaranteeing the individual's right to an education commensurate with his abilities and talents, the individual is highly circumscribed if his educational interests and competencies do not coincide with the plans of the regime.[30] Although in the societies

---

[30] DeWitt, *op. cit.*, p. 8.

of the West the educational system provides the individual with more opportunities to develop the aforementioned qualities, the extent to which he actually develops them is still a subject requiring further research. In this connection, one could comment on the possible effects on this aspect of education of the recent attempts by many societies at educational planning or planned educational change. Educational planning seeks to establish a more rational basis for the attainment of certain social goals. Thus, as Cavazza pointed out, educational planning *per se* "is neither intrinsically democratic and 'liberal' nor intrinsically coercive and socialistic." [31] Some societies, like the Soviet Union and Turkey, have embarked upon programs of national development and planning, including educational planning, in order to attain certain goals of the post-revolutionary regime. Rather recently, other societies have in varying degrees embarked upon programs of planning for educational change. There are at least two possible consequences of national educational planning: First, it might bring about the expansion of educational provision and all that is associated with it; Second, it might result in paternalism and rigidity. We have seen that in most systems there has been a quantitative expansion of education; such an expansion, however, has not necessarily been accompanied by fundamental reforms, especially the types of reforms that would contribute to the development of the individual qualities previously mentioned. Planning somehow implies considerations regarding groups rather than individuals. This is perhaps another paradox of the modern world and of modern education: on the one hand, there is a pressing need for social efficiency; and on the other, there is an attachment to "the human condition."

Another clearly related question is whether educational expansion has created the conditions for freer individual expression, for a more active participation in the body politic, for what Pericles called "sound judges of policy," and for greater respect for human welfare and dignity. Many feel that education is its own reward—i.e., the more one is educated, the greater is his possibility of developing these qualities. Thus, they believe that the future and hope of mankind lie in educational advancement.

Finally, we have seen that in most countries education has become an important prerequisite for political leadership. We have no evidence, however, that a society characterized by a highly educated group of leaders (a meritocracy) is necessarily a better society. Together with amount and level of education, there must also be a qualitative element widely diffused among rulers and ruled for better interaction and for a cooperative partnership in the affairs of government.

[31] Cavazza, *op. cit.*, p. 409.

This book has dealt with patterns of education in selected societies, past and present. We have sought to analyze these patterns not only in terms of certain structural elements of systems of education, but also in terms of their relationship to other social institutions and practices. On the basis of our previous analysis, we shall draw certain generalizations and formulate propositions that might have a more universal application or that might be tested in other contexts.

1. Patterns of education have been influenced by the degree of interaction of at least three basic elements: contacts with other cultures, traditional beliefs and institutions, and indigenous attempts to innovate and experiment. This interaction is most clearly typified in the case of Japan. The sources of the present Japanese system encompass the age-old Confucian principles, western values and practices (especially French and American), and internal innovations such as the creation of appointed local school boards. The introduction of western liberal ideas into an authoritarian, semi-feudal society in the late nineteenth century created serious social conflicts that have persisted and, indeed, have become accentuated in

168

CONCLUSIONS
AND
GENERALIZATIONS

10

recent years. The strength of each of the two major elements (traditional and western) in shaping educational policy, has resulted in an intense and not easily resolved conflict. On the other hand, in a country like Greece, where until quite recently the forces of traditional institutions and beliefs were dominant, conflicts created by the introduction of foreign elements have not been as intense.

2.   In almost all of the societies under consideration, periods of national crises and overwhelming events have been followed by attempts at major educational reorganization. It is interesting to note, for example, that major reform of education followed World War II. In some instances, as in the case of the Education Act of 1944 in England, educational reform was directly influenced by the War. The state of war revealed several gaps in opportunities for education and in the training of people for certain technical jobs. In the Soviet Union, the postwar emphasis upon polytechnical education may be attributed partly to the losses in technological manpower and the need created to allocate a higher percentage of talent to the task of rebuilding the country. Like wars, revolutions also seem to have been accompanied by major educational reforms. In Turkey, for example, the Kemalist Revolution of 1923 was followed by attempts to establish a secular, publicly controlled system of education in place of the traditional, voluntary religious system. Likewise, internal or external events of major importance, e.g., the first Russian sputnik, the issue of civil rights in America, etc., have provided the impetus for similar educational changes.

3.   Changes in education that purportedly were "revolutionary" were not completely devoid of traditional elements. The system in Turkey—like that in Russia—which directed its efforts to secularization and democratization, has retained the elitist and centralized characteristics of the Ottoman period (or the Tsarist characteristics in the case of Russia). In addition, in Turkey, the Ottoman *Tuba Ağaci* theory of education has persisted throughout the Republican period. This suggests that although new institutional arrangements may be introduced after a revolution, and a fortiori after planned educational change, the historical social functions performed by education, as perceived by the people, tend to persist. Mere organizational or administrative change does not automatically alter basic beliefs and values about the role of education. For example, the planned attempt in England after 1944 to establish technical schools that would enjoy parity of esteem with the traditional grammar schools was not very successful because people continued to associate technical schools with inferior training, leading to low positions in the occupational hierarchy. Likewise, in Japan, regardless of the postwar legislation to establish American-style comprehensive high schools that would provide different avenues for entrance into the prestigious universities, parents continued to view the traditional upper-secondary schools, e.g., Tokyo First Higher School and Kyoto Third Higher School, as the best schools for entrance into such universities and, thereby, to the highest positions in the society. This further suggests that for educational change to be effective, there must also be concomitant changes in both primary and secondary social institutions.

4.   The degree of educational centralization or decentralization is not in and of itself an index of either the tempo or the nature of change in the educational system. In the Soviet Union, sweeping changes in the organization and content of secondary education were introduced and implemented during a relatively short period of time. In Greece, on the

other hand, where the control of education has also been vested in a central authority, educational change was both sporadic and dilatory. In the United States, which is characterized by state and local control of education, change has been uneven at both levels—i.e., innovation and curriculum change have been strongly resisted in some states and/or local communities, but fostered in others. For example, certain rural communities are known for their rigidity in the treatment of controversial issues or the hiring and dismissal of teachers. In both centralized and decentralized systems, there seem to be certain paradoxes regarding educational change. In centralized systems, while change may be accelerated, it tends to rigidify the prevailing or proposed patterns and to stifle experimentation and innovation. In the decentralized systems, although local school systems are theoretically free to innovate and experiment, in actual practice, they may be subject to local pressures as centralized systems are to national pressures.

The question of centralized and decentralized control of education is often discussed in conjunction with democratic versus totalitarian political systems. For example, it is often assumed that decentralized systems of education are democratic while centralized systems are not. Although this may be true in some cases, e.g., the Soviet Union and the United States, it is not true of France and Greece. In these two countries, there is a central authority that controls and supervises the total educational enterprise; yet, it is accountable to the popular will and subject to removal through legal procedures. One of the distinguishing features of democratic versus totalitarian systems is not the degree of centralized control, but the extent to which education is in the hands of one self-perpetuating power-group that makes all major decisions and is not accountable to public opinion.

In this connection, it might also be noted that planned educational change at the national level need be neither intrinsically liberal and democratic nor constraining and undemocratic. A great deal depends on the context in which planning takes place and the values to which it relates. For example, government stipends and forms of educational support may be used to enhance opportunities; however, they may also restrict individual initiative and establish uniformity.

5. The extent to which the educational profession participates in the formulation of overall educational policy varies from country to country. In general, however, in major decisions affecting aims, control and support of education, certification of teachers, curriculum organization, and even the selection of textbooks, the role of the educational profession is at best minimal. In the majority of cases, the power rests with political figures or legislatures functioning at state or national levels. In political democracies, decisions about education may also be largely influenced by powerful, voluntary associations that mobilize themselves and act as political pressure groups. In the United States, for example, organized groups such as the Daughters of the American Revolution, the Veterans of Foreign Wars, the American Civil Liberties Union, the American Bar Association, the National Association for the Advancement of Colored People (NAACP), and several religious organizations have from time to time taken an active part in influencing educational policy and in thinking about the place of religion in schools, the teaching of communism, the issue of racial segregation, and so on.

6. Although in the twentieth century the avowed aim has been to

establish elementary and secondary education for all, this goal has been only partially attained. In the European countries and in Japan, primary education is provided in common schools for everybody; in Turkey and Tanganyika, universal primary education has not yet been attained. At the secondary level, education is provided in different types of schools, admission to which depends upon certain selective criteria. Such schools are differentiated in terms of curriculum, length of time spent at school, vocational destinations of students, and prestige. Thus, although the complete separation of elementary and secondary education, which characterized these educational systems in the nineteenth century, has been largely eliminated, it has persisted at the secondary level. At the primary level, there are virtually no conditions regarding entrance and attendance; this is not true of secondary schools. Theoretically, admission to the secondary schools is based on the democratic notion of equal opportunity according to equal ability—i.e., on criteria of achievement rather than of ascription. In practice, however, ascriptive criteria such as family background and wealth continue to play an important part in both entrance and attendance at the various types of secondary schools.

The United States has rejected the multi-track institutional arrangement of the European countries we have examined. Instead, it has adopted the so-called comprehensive high school, which extends the idea of a school common to all beyond the primary level. Yet, even though there is no institutional differentiation in terms of types of schools, there is generally what may be called "pedagogical differentiation" within the comprehensive schools, in terms of college-preparatory, vocational-, and commercial-curriculum tracks. In addition, in recent years there has been a conspicuous trend toward specialized programs for the gifted, requiring special grouping on the basis of intellectual aptitude. What is of interest to us here is the fact that even with this type of differentiation, ascriptive criteria have by no means been eliminated. It has been found, for example, that there is a disproportionately higher representation of middle- and upper-class children in the college-preparatory curriculum and that the drop-out rate is higher among children from the lower socio-economic strata. This differentiation has recently become accentuated by the rapid growth of affluent suburban communities. The suburban school systems, although theoretically comprehensive as the urban and rural systems, in practice represent a new type of elite institution, catering to a socially and economically privileged group of children and providing better facilities, more rigorous programs, and higher quality teachers than their supposedly equivalent urban counterparts. It has been established that a very high percentage of students in these suburban schools continue their education in institutions of higher learning and that they are more successful in national programs such as the National Merit Scholarship Program and the College Entrance Examination Board.

7. In all the societies we have examined, except the American, there is a multi-track school organization. In some European countries, however, the postwar years witnessed a movement toward the establishment of comprehensive schools or the extension of the common-school stage. For example, although Conservatives in England have taken a rather lukewarm attitude, several comprehensive schools have been set up, the cause of which has been espoused by the Labour and the Liberal parties. The comprehensive schools have been justified on the ideology of democratic equali-

tarianism and, in part have represented a protest against the early selective practices of the English secondary schools. The inspiration for these educational ideas and practices has been the American comprehensive pattern. Yet, a careful look at the British arrangement reveals that within the comprehensive school, there is a tripartite differentiation, which in many respects is similar to the official secondary-school pattern. For example, because of parental and student aspirations and expectations concerning success in the General Certification of Education examinations, the comprehensive school must compete favorably with the secondary grammar school. These external conditions force the comprehensive school to provide a stream that, in rigor and substance, differs very little from the grammar school. In effect, such factors contribute to the dilution of the comprehensive-school idea as envisaged by its proponents.

As examples of the attempts to expand the common school, we might cite the *cycle d' observation* in France and the recommended *Förderstufe* in West Germany. In both instances, the aim was to add a two-year orientation stage to the primary grades. This arrangement would postpone secondary selection, it would provide a diagnostic period for better educational and vocational guidance, and it would be more democratic. This experiment has been introduced only in France; and even there, it has reached only an estimated 40–50 per cent of the elementary school students.

8. Another manifestation of the "democratization movement in education" has been the expansion of the curriculum to include modern subjects, e.g., science, foreign languages, and vocational or practical subjects. Nevertheless, the traditional Aristotelian distinction between the liberal and vocational curriculum has not been eliminated. Such academic secondary schools as the English Grammar School, the French *lycée*, and the German *Gymnasium* have incorporated science, foreign languages, and history into their erstwhile classical curriculum; however, they have remained academic in their orientation, and they provide very little, if any, training in vocational preparation. Such training is relegated to other types of educational institutions that have attained secondary-school status. Even in the Soviet Union, where since the Revolution there have been concerted efforts to break down the liberal-practical dichotomy in education and all the social accoutrements associated with it, the whole argument behind Khrushchev's attempted reorganization in 1958–59 was based on the conviction that this separation still prevailed. It would be true to say, however, that the Soviet Union has come closer to bridging this gap than any other of the countries we have examined, including the United States.

9. A professed major function of the systems of education under study has been to make the curriculum of the schools an important contributing factor to the social and economic development of the society or, to put it another way, to relate the curriculum to the needs of an expanding economy. This relationship, often referred to as "functional education," has been interpreted to mean that the school program should emphasize knowledge and skills that have direct bearing upon the national productive effort. In order to attain this goal, the tendency has been to strengthen technical education by expanding the offerings in technical and scientific subjects and by seeking to make technical-vocational courses and schools equivalent to the traditional academically-oriented ones. As described earlier, the Soviet Union represents a rather extreme case of how this aim of functional education may be implemented. On the other hand,

Greece presents us with the opposite extreme—i.e., a system that may be said to be "dysfunctional," in that it is not geared toward meeting the demands of an emerging industrial society. The need for technical knowledge and skills has become pressing in the agricultural as well as the industrial sectors of the economy. Yet, education in Greece continues to be dominated by the classical-literary tradition. Many *gymnasium* graduates seek employment in the already-crowded clerical occupations in business and government, in spite of the fact that industrial, agricultural, and mining enterprises are in dire need of technically trained personnel. As a result, there is both unemployment and under-employment among the graduates of such schools.

A similar problem is to be found in Turkey, although not in some of the developing nations of Africa. Turkey has a wide network of technical schools; however, the traditional academic *lises* produce an oversupply of students with vocational aspirations similar to those of the Greek *gymnasium* graduates, in spite of saturation in clerical positions and a dearth in technological manpower. In contrast, most African societies that have recently attained statehood are able to absorb all the graduates of the academic secondary schools. Traditionally, these schools were the sources of supply for the limited posts in the civil service. Recently, and partly as a result of independence, enrollments in these schools have increased. With the withdrawal of the colonial administrators and the expansion of the civil bureaucracy, there has been a corresponding increase in vacancies in this sector of the polity. Under these circumstances, in spite of the fact that the curriculum of the secondary schools in all such societies is academically oriented, we cannot say that education in many present-day African societies displays the imbalances of Greek and Turkish education.

The Greek case illustrates that the term "functional education" is more polymorphous than our previous definition. To most Greeks, a *gymnasium* type of education fulfills certain expectations that are not directly related to the productive sector of the society. These values and expectations, which have themselves become institutionalized because of a long-standing tradition, focus on the moral, intellectual, and spiritual development of the individual. Therefore, it is not too much of a paradox that Greek youth prefer a classical-humanistic education even though they are fully aware of the risks involved in employment opportunities. In this sense, we cannot say that a *gymnasium* education is nonfunctional or dysfunctional. What our first definition of "functional education" seems to ignore is the non-utilitarian components of education and of the broader system of values in a given culture.

Furthermore, were we to limit the concept of "functional education" to a direct relationship between the curriculum and the economic demands current at the time, we would be ignoring certain basic conditions of development in highly industrial societies such as England, the United States, the Soviet Union, and West Germany. As Peter Drucker has argued (and with good reason), in a rapidly-expanding industrial country, there is a high rate of obsolescence in both jobs and skills. Hence, an education that is oriented toward immediate practical usefulness may also be seminally dysfunctional. A strong case may be made in support of what is often referred to as a liberal education, which through certain subjects seeks to transmit knowledge about the cumulative experience of man and to develop general intellectual skills and a more flexible frame of mind.

In the long-run, these may, indeed, be the most desirable qualities of school graduates entering the labor force, a thought that brings us closer to the Aristotelian view—that intellectual development and self-cultivation are the essential purposes of education.

10. Countries with a deeply-entrenched literary-humanistic tradition have been confronted with the dilemma of reconciling their commitment to traditional values about education and to the demands of a modern technological civilization. This is patricularly true of the European countries, whose educational systems have been influenced by the Greco-Roman tradition. For example, both France and Greece have realized that in order to keep pace with technological growth, they need to pay more attention to relevant programs in the schools—e.g., technical, scientific, and vocational subjects. On the other hand, there is great attachment to the aura of "classicism" and intellectualism. The image of the educated man has been that of the literary intellectual, the classical humanist, the man with encyclopedic knowledge. This conception of the nature and value of education—in face of the perceived realities of technological advancement—has created deep pedagogical conflicts and may have been a major factor in the slow pace of educational change.

Many observers have hastily censured such systems as being conservative and culturally lagging. Although many such criticisms may be true *prima facie*, they seem to ignore the important consideration that change that seeks to undermine the basic *élan* of a society may not only be undesirable, but also quite detrimental. To tell the Greek or the Frenchman that he must abandon classicism or *culture générale* is tantamount to asking him to repudiate his "Greekness" or "Frenchness."

11. Another dimension of the development of the curriculum in recent decades has been a higher degree of specialization, which in some countries has been pushed further back in the school grades. For example, in England, a boy starts specializing in one of the curriculum streams (classical, modern, scientific, mathematical) at the age of fifteen. The results of such specialization, justified on the grounds of the need for "expertise," were caustically and humorously criticized in C. P. Snow's well-known *The Two Cultures and the Scientific Revolution*. Snow sees a deplorable split in England's intellectual life into two polar groups—the "literary intellectuals" and the "scientists"—with a total lack of communication between them. This phenomenon has been found to hold true, more or less, in other societies; our examination of programs of reform, however well-intentioned the reforms, has shown that they tend to perpetuate, rather than bridge, this polarization. Most of the proposed changes in this direction have been more palliative than curative; they have sought to ameliorate the situation by tacitly accepting the cultural dichotomy and by merely adding and juxtaposing scientific or humanistic courses, as the case may be.

It has been suggested that there is a third dimension of culture, the culture of the social sciences. This, though distinctive in the sense that it applies scientific methods and concepts in its study of man in society, occupies a position in the middle of the humanistic-scientific continuum; it attempts to synthesize the methods and knowledge of the other two cultures. The "third culture" may be viewed as a possible bridge of the historic division between the sciences and the humanities. At this stage, the social sciences have not for the most part become an integral part of the curriculum of the school; consequently, it is premature to make any judgments concerning the validity of this argument. We might hypothesize, however, that the mere addition of courses (taught separately in the traditional manner) in the social sciences would not necessarily bring about the desired effects. There must somehow be a concerted effort to integrate the various areas through curriculum reorganization, which conceivably could include interdisciplinary courses, jointly taught by members from the various curriculum departments. This type of reorganization might afford the individual a better opportunity to examine the entire gamut of man's activity and, thus, to develop a broader perspective within which he might specialize.

12. The historical development of an appropriate curriculum has raised a two-pronged question, implicit in Herbert Spencer's provocative inquiry, "What Knowledge is of Most Worth?" First, what subjects should be included in the curriculum; second, what is the relative value of such subjects? In the nineteenth century, it was almost universally assumed that classics and mathematics should constitute the staple of the curriculum, that these two subjects "disciplined the mind," and that they were the best means to create a moral and well-educated human being. Today, both the scope and rationale of subjects to be included in the curriculum have expanded and, in some cases, changed. As we mentioned earlier, subjects such as science and modern foreign languages are accepted unquestionably as essential ingredients of the general curriculum of the schools. No longer does anyone seriously advocate that the *form* of a specific area of knowledge trains specific faculties of the mind irrespective of content or that once trained or disciplined, a mental faculty as a whole is thereby strengthened and its results can be transferred to any other situation. The difference between the nineteenth century and the current conceptions of mental discipline in education is that the latter is formulated in terms of the development of such mental processes as critical thinking, scientific or "reflective thinking," or the ability to solve problems that involve the development of certain logical operations. With very few exceptions, it is no longer questioned that science disciplines the mind in the new meaning of the term. In fact, in modern discussions of the relative disciplinary value of subjects, the humanities have a hard time proving that they afford as rigorous a training as the sciences. The development of the aforementioned mental processes is regarded by almost all countries as one of the desirable aims of any scheme of general liberal education. However, no unbiased evidence has yet been established to serve as a guide in the selection of, and relative emphasis placed upon, specific subjects or courses. The lack of such evidence has partly contributed and continues to contribute to uncertainties regarding the number of subjects to be included under the rubric "general liberal education," the relative emphasis that should be given to the various areas of knowledge, and the sharp divisions between the sciences and the humanities. Areas of study are justified on the grounds that they contribute to the development of certain intellectual skills and values; yet, at different historical epochs and in different countries, different combinations of subjects have been justified for precisely the same reasons. Furthermore, subjects are included in the curriculum of many contemporary school systems on the basis of *a priori* beliefs concerning their worthiness to the individual and to the society. For example, courses in social studies and history are often justified on the grounds that they develop attributes of good citizenship—e.g., patriotism,

loyalty to the existing political institutions, and active participation in the political process—which are transferred to the individual's activities when he leaves school. Evidence of this is by no means unequivocal. Indeed, some have found that among American high school youths, there is no positive correlation between certain indices of democratic attitudes and a course in civics or government.

13. All societies engage in the "politicization" or political socialization of youth—i.e., they seek to impart the values and beliefs of the political system. This task is carried out through several agencies, among which the school has assumed an increasingly important role. Among several school activities that are perceived to bear upon political socialization, formal instruction occupies a central position. Although the goal of fostering political attitudes, values, and ways of behaving that are compatible with the dominant political ideology is a characteristic of past and present societies, the means used to attain this goal vary. Moreover, there are differences in the amount of exposure and intensity of treatment of subjects relevant to this process. In the Soviet Union, the "politicization" of youth takes place through courses in the social sciences and the humanities and through the well-known youth organizations. In the United States, there appears to be more political exposure through formal education and, compared to the Soviet Union, much less explicit activity outside the schools. In societies like ancient Sparta, where there were no schools, political socialization was done largely through youth organizations.

The very few cross-national studies in this area have focused on the goals and curriculum content of the schools. There has been very little cross-national research on school outcomes; what little does exist pertains to single countries, without attempts at comparison, and to whether there is a relationship between formal instruction and political beliefs. Furthermore, no attempts have been made to assess the role of the school vis-à-vis other institutions—e.g., the family, the church, etc.—in the political acculturation of youth. The research conducted in the United States suggests that basic political values and beliefs are formed rather early in life and that certain aspects of political authority are influenced by parents and familial relations. It would be valuable, therefore, to test such hypotheses in the context of other cultures.

14. In most Euporean societies and in those influenced by them, one of the major functions of education has been the selection and training of political elites. This had as its prototype the theoretical model described in Plato's *Republic*. The relationship between education and the attainment of high positions in the political hierarchy has been strengthened in modern times. We have observed that this has been the case with at least four societies (England, the United States, Turkey, and Japan), and one could speculate that the same observation would hold true in all societies, be they industrially advanced, developed, politically stable, or not. Therefore, it would be reasonable to infer that the composition of political elites, in terms of level of education attained, has no relationship to the extent to which educational opportunities are available in the society or to the stage of economic and political development. For instance, Turkey—which provides limited opportunities, is politically classified as "unstable" and "noncompetitive," and is at the "take-off" stage of economic development—has as highly educated a group of political elites as England and the United States. However, this similarity ends when one looks at the spread of edu-

cation among the groups from which the leaders are recruited. In Turkey, because higher education is extremely limited, the base from which the leaders are recruited is correspondingly restricted. In America, where college education is more widely diffused among the population, the chances of the individual for becoming a political leader are comparatively greater.

15. One of the mechanisms of educational selection and recruitment, particularly in modern societies, has been a system of examinations. Some types of examinations, e.g., the English eleven-plus, have been used for purposes of allocation into various educational tracks; others, like the *Baccalauréat* in France, the General School Certificate of Education in England, the College Entrance Examination Board in the United States, and several types of Civil-Service Examinations, have been used for purposes of elimination or selection of those who have the ability to pursue advanced studies or careers in the civil bureaucracy. In addition, of course, examinations have been used for pedagogical and guidance purposes.

We have seen that examinations are related to the process of democratization in education in that they seek to minimize ascriptive factors and to maximize ability and achievement. While examinatons have to a degree succeeded in accomplishing this aim, it has been shown that some social and cultural biases still persist. This is partly due to the fact that no culture-free system of examinations has been, or is likely to be, devised.

A relatively untapped area of cross-national research involving examinations is the impact (anticipated or unanticipated) that such mechanisms have upon the organization and curriculum of the schools, upon the student body, and upon the society at large. We have referred to the fact that the curriculum and teaching practices in English schools are largely influenced by the requirements of examinations. It would be valuable to look into this problem in greater detail in connection with the effects of similar types of examinations in the United States and other cultures.

16. In most of the societies we have examined, formal education has been a factor in individual advancement and upward-social mobility. It has not, however, been the only or even the most dominant factor in this respect. Assuming that it is a relevant factor and noting that in recent years there has been substantial expansion and diffusion of education at all levels, accompanied by a corresponding narrowing of the gap between the "haves" and the "have nots," to what extent will education continue to perform the same function? Suppose we have found that a university education is important for individual advancement or occupational placement; suppose further that a society has reached the stage at which practically everybody has received such an education; it would then be logical to expect that, other factors being equal, the role of a university education for the purposes stated previously would diminish considerably. Under such circumstances, advancement and placement of the individual would depend on factors other than mere attendance at a university. In America, for example, such a level of education if attained by everybody would be analogous to a high school education today. Were university education to become universal, individual advancement or upward-social mobility (in addition to depending on factors such as motivation, parental pressures, innate intelligence and so on) would probably depend upon additional years of schooling, more or different specialization, and attendance at particular institutions.

17. In our review of different educational systems, it was shown that

there were at least three patterns of educational transfer, which varied in nature and consequence. The first pattern is best typified by the attempt of the Allied Forces to superimpose American educational practices and goals on postwar Japan and Germany; the second pattern is exemplified by the British policies regarding its colonies in Africa; and Turkey presents us with a third type of transfer, in which a society voluntarily adopts foreign institutions and methods.

In Japan and Germany, the American Forces of Occupation tried to change the organization and administration of the schools, the curriculum, methods of instruction, and textbooks to conform with democratic principles. In several instances, the attempts at reorganization ran contrary to traditional beliefs and values about authority and loyalty relationships, about the country's past and its future, and about the role of education concerning the individual and the society. This situation has created serious social and personal conflicts, especially among the younger generation.

In their former colonies in Africa, the British attempted in many cases to adapt the system of the metropole to local conditions and needs. In Tanganyika, for example, they sought to use the vernacular (Swahili) in the lower grades and to introduce vocational and practical subjects in the lower schools. Nevertheless, the overall pattern of schooling, especially at the higher-secondary level, was typically English. In some cases—for example, in the Kingdom of Buganda—British institutions were introduced without any serious political and social dislocations; in others—such as the Ashanti Confederacy—the opposite was true. The reasons for this differential acceptance of British education rested on basic variations in the distribution of political power and on the indigenous systems of religious beliefs and values.

During early attempts at westernization, the Ottomans, while borrowing European (mostly French) educational institutions and practices, sought to maintain their basic Islamic culture. In some instances, foreign institutions were merely juxtaposed against the traditional *mektebs* and *medreses*; in others, attempts were made to weave the western and eastern ideas and practices into one. This type of transfer, which lasted until the Kemalist Revolution of 1923, did not drastically upset the political and social equilibrium; however, it did lay the foundations for the emergence of a revolutionary spirit that culminated in the Young Turk Revolt of 1908 and, finally, in the Atatürk Revolution.

In conclusion, we might say that in varying degrees educational change has characterized most past and present societies. At the same time, however, the forces of tradition have acted as countervailing influences. Even societies that have undergone a revolution paradoxically have not managed to "free" themselves completely from traditional institutions, beliefs, and values. In contemporary societies, modernization has been a motivating force and has brought about major changes—anticipated and unanticipated—in educational ideas and practices, as well as in the total life of a country. Education has become an integral part in the movement toward modernity, and it has always been assumed that it contributes to the creation of better human beings and better societies. Although the first part of this statement has been the overriding consideration of this book, the second could more appropriately be the subject of another study.

179

INDEX

181